A Robot Ping-Pong Player:

Experiment in
Real-Time Intelligent Control

The MIT Press Series in Artificial Intelligence
Edited by Patrick Henry Winston and Michael Brady

A Robot Ping-Pong Player:

Experiment in
Real-Time Intelligent Control

Russell L. Andersson

AT&T Bell Laboratories

The MIT Press
Cambridge, Massachusetts
London, England

PUBLISHER'S NOTE

This format is intended to reduce the cost of publishing certain works in book form and to shorten the gap between editorial preparation and final publication. Detailed editing and composition have been avoided by photographing the text of this book directly from the author's prepared copy.

This book was printed and bound in the United States of America.

Library of Congress Cataloging-in-Publication Data

Andersson, Russell L.
  A robot ping-pong player.

  (The MIT Press series in artificial intelligence)
  Bibliography: p.
  Includes index.
  1. Robotics. 2. Artificial intelligence. 3. Table tennis. 4. Real-time data processing.
I. Title. II. Series.
TJ211.A53 1987   629.8'92   87-32526
ISBN 0-262-01101-8

To Amy With Love

Contents

SERIES FOREWORD

Artificial intelligence is the study of intelligence using the ideas and methods of computation. Unfortunately, a definition of intelligence seems impossible at the moment because intelligence appears to be an amalgam of so many information-processing and information-representation abilities.

Of course psychology, philosophy, linguistics, and related disciplines offer various perspectives and methodologies for studying intelligence. For the most part, however, the theories proposed in these fields are too incomplete and too vaguely stated to be realized in computational terms. Something more is needed, even though valuable ideas, relationships, and constraints can be gleaned from traditional studies of what are, after all, impressive existence proofs that intelligence is in fact possible.

Artificial intelligence offers a new perspective and a new methodology. Its central goal is to make computers intelligent, both to make them more useful and to understand the principles that make intelligence possible. That intelligent computers will be extremely useful is obvious. The more profound point is that artificial intelligence aims to understand intelligence using the ideas and methods of computation, thus offering a radically new and different basis for theory formation. Most of the people doing artificial intelligence believe that these theories will apply to any intelligent information processor, whether biological or solid state.

There are side effects that deserve attention, too. Any program that will successfully model even a small part of intelligence will be inherently massive and complex. Consequently, artificial intelligence continually confronts the limits of computer science technology. The problems encountered have been hard enough and interesting enough to seduce artificial intelligence people into working on them with enthusiasm. It is natural, then, that there has been a steady flow of ideas from artificial intelligence to computer science, and the flow shows no sign of abating.

The purpose of this MIT Press Series in Artificial Intelligence is to provide people in many areas, both professionals and students, with timely, detailed information about what is happening on the frontiers in research centers all over the world.

Patrick Henry Winston
Michael Brady

Preface

The work described in this book is the result of a sequence of experiments that began with the idea of building an honest real-time (60 Hz) vision system. The sight of a slick, high-tech robot plodding along at a snail's pace has always rubbed me the wrong way. John Jarvis originally pointed out that moments were a simple enough, and well enough understood, computer vision operation that we really ought to be able to do them faster. They seemed well suited to making a vision system that was fast enough to serve as a sensor for a fast robot, even if the scenes had to be quite simple. I set off to make a vision system that would process simple scenes quickly, rather than process more complex scenes slowly, as did the majority of the vision and robotics community. I could then investigate tightly coupled robot/vision systems.

Two years later, I had a working vision system, and in the meantime had created a system to control a PUMA 260 robot in C. Suddenly, the need for a demonstration of the potent capabilities of the work was upon me. For reasons no longer clear, but doubtless related to the simplicity of the resulting image, I threw together a system to catch a ping-pong ball rolling in 2-D across a table. The ping-pong ball had the advantage of being very white, and the ball would break rather than allow the robot to come to harm.

After a subsequent explosion in the complexity of the code, the robot caught most of a certain class of trajectories with high reliability. It would even catch balls bounced off a piece of foam shortly before they were to be caught, amply demonstrating the true real-time nature of the system. It was clear, however, that catching the remainder of the balls would require more subtle strategies not easily captured in my program — it was likely that even trying would cause the whole thing to collapse under its own weight. Nonetheless, the demonstration was a vast success, and the volume of demonstrations prevented me from doing much additional work on the system, affording me the time for thought.

Since I could catch in two dimensions, it only stood to reason that I should be able to do it in three. About this time, I heard of the challenge/contest announced by Professor John Billingsley of Portsmouth Polytechnic (U.K.) for robot ping-pong, and since I had already thought along these lines, Professor Billingsley's proposal provided an excuse for further ruminations. (Many thanks to Professor Billingsley for his well-thought-out rules.)

Some time later, I heard a rumor that Dan Kodeschek of Yale had thought of catching objects. I put off all consideration of ping-pong, and rushed to create a 3-D catcher, since I knew it should be straightforward. The resulting system proved able to catch balls in a styrofoam coffee cup, exhibiting some spectacular behavior due to primitive error recovery code.

By this time, however, it was clear that I was going about this entirely the wrong way. Alarmingly, it appeared that if I attempted to extrapolate the system to full ping-pong, it was never going to work. There was not going to be a magic algorithm that could compute an ideal ping-pong player's response, as had been the case (at least in practice) in the previous demonstrations. Trying to address the different cases was going to result in a nonfunctional morass; the line between when to apply one strategy and when to apply another was thin, bordering on nonexistent.

What I had to do was to capture the subjective skills of a trained human. A person's skilled techniques appeared then, and now, equally applicable to a person playing ping-pong, or to a person working on an assembly line. In both cases, people make many clever motions, without seeming to expend much thought, and one can improve their performance by giving small hints such as "keep your elbow up." By contrast, a robot would need a whole new algorithm.

This book describes an experiment to try to capture this type of skilled behavior, resulting in a robot ping-pong player which can play and beat human players. Along the way to a working system, I discovered and had to solve many interesting problems. The vision system, the expert robot controller, the low-level robot controller, and the overall system design were significantly affected by the need to make the system respond accurately in a dynamic environment. By working only with static problems, the vision and robotics communities have not yet had to understand dynamic environments.

Accordingly, this book begins to pave the way. At least one chapter is devoted to each of the four major subsystems above; each chapter describes what the subsystem must accomplish, how it does so and why, and quantitatively documents its performance. Although the book has the technical content of a work oriented at robotics professionals; computer scientists, physicists, hobbyists, and the technically curious should be able to read the book and gain insight into how the system works and is put together — and an appreciation of how good the human machine really is.

The management of AT&T Bell Laboratories, and especially John Jarvis, deserve immense credit for seeing the technical merit behind a project of little instantaneous gain. I think this characteristic reflects extremely well on the quality of the institution.

I am indebted to many people for their aid in the successful completion of this work. Many thanks to Professor Richard Paul (University of Pennsylvania), for his support, encouragement, immense practical experience, and especially, wise judgement. To Professor Ruzena Bajcsy (Penn) I owe the emphasis of carrying through ideas to working results, thus eliminating the need and possibility of trying to justify ideas by hand-waving. Professor Rodney Brooks and Professor Tomás Lozano-Pérez (both of MIT) have my thanks for their suggestions on how to improve the book's readability.

Thanks to George Whyte and Richard Seide, the able mechanical and electronic construction crew. Thanks to Ray "Plot" Soneira and his indomitable ray_plot, which supported the computer graphics in this book. I am indebted to the creators of the MEGLOS multiprocessor system and the MULGA VLSI design system: Bob Gaglianello, Howard Katseff, Krish Ramakrishnan, Beth Robinson, Brian Ackland, Jay O'Neill, and Neil Weste. Thanks are also due my other colleagues at the Labs who were always ready with ideas of strategies and effects the system ought to deal with, and put up with the sound of ball against table, paddle, and wall, and the screams from man and machine as the latter attempted autorobocide at spectacular speeds. Thanks for hanging in there, King Pong.

Finally, many, many thanks to my wife, Amy, who provided marathon-level encouragement, and mental, moral, physical, and logistical support.

Holmdel, New Jersey   R.L.A.
November, 1987

A Robot Ping-Pong Player:

Experiment in
Real-Time Intelligent Control

Chapter 1

Introduction

"A Robot Ping-Pong Player: Experiment in Real-Time Intelligent Control" analyzes the construction of the first robot to play ping-pong* against humans and machines (Figure 1). What are the limitations of present robots? What makes ping-pong hard? Why investigate ping-pong? What are the applications of the technology we developed? The following introductory chapter will address these issues, then provide an overview of the book's organization.

1.1 Introduction to Robots and Their Limitations

The general public thinks of R2D2 and C3PO when someone mentions robots, but today's robots are far from that stage, mechanically or intellectually. When confronted with a real robot, the mechanism makes the biggest impression. However, in our (admittedly biased) view, it is not the mechanism that is of greatest interest, but the computer system and its programming that controls the mechanism. Figure 2 divides the robot control system into three levels. Each level maintains a specific duration of foresight, with a corresponding constraint on the time available for planning.

The robot mechanism occupies the hierarchy's lowest level: motors, encoders, and their projections into the electronic domain. Specialized joint servo processors interact with the interfaces of each joint, implementing control algorithms that cause the robot to attain specified positions, velocities, or torques. The actuator bandwidths restrict the available processing time to a millisecond per iteration. The joint servos

---

* Ping-Pong is a trademark of Parker Brothers.

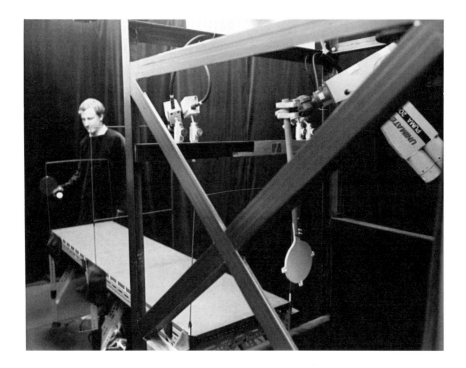

Figure 1. Robot and Environment. The robot ping-pong player takes on a human
opponent, the author, at robot ping-pong. Two of four video cameras and
the robot arm lurk in the supporting framework.

present a clean electronic interface to the middle control level, which can
specify desired robot trajectories.

At the hierarchy's summit, a high-level planner generates objectives for
the robot and monitors its performance. The planner manipulates an
abstract view of the robot system, even though it may supply details such
as the sizes of parts from a CAD/CAM database. The planner is slower
than and desynchronized from robot operation, but must be able to monitor
and modify the robot system to improve its performance. Either a program
or a human may implement the high-level planner.

The intermediating controller translates the planner's demands to the
servo controller's realities. The controller must plan a sequence of
trajectories for the servos which satisfy both the abstract requirements of

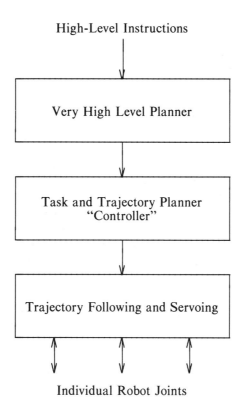

High-Level Instructions

Very High Level Planner

Task and Trajectory Planner
"Controller"

Trajectory Following and Servoing

Individual Robot Joints

Figure 2. High-Level Robot Diagram. The planner is an artificial or natural intelligence system. We will be concerned with the controller, which must integrate the task and robot constraints.

the task and the complex and concrete limitations of the physical apparatus. In the face of ignorance, the controller has no choice but to adopt very conservative estimates of the manipulator's abilities. Note that the generic term "robot controller" refers to both the task and trajectory planner, and the lower-level servoing functions.

Consider a conventional robot feeding a punch. The high-level planner might produce this plan:

```
move_to input_bin
wait_for part_present
withdraw part
move_to punch
activate punch
wait_for punch_done
withdraw part
wait_for output_empty
move_to output_bin
release part
```

The robot operates in a world that changes in very discrete steps, in response to clearly defined causes. Robot actions interlock with binary status lines and control signals to the outside world, such as "part_present" or "activate punch." Sensors such as vision can be brought into this framework by restricting their output to discrete events (though their function is also limited to start with), for example, take a picture now, the part is missing, the part is bad, or a good part is at (10 cm, 15 cm, 45°).

The robot moves from one state to another in indivisible steps: the time variable is effectively suppressed. In this "discrete-time" scenario, the physics of the environment and robot motion are considered to take place in series, because the robot assumes the world is static while it moves. The high-level planner need not consider how long any operation might take. A simple robot controller might take as long as it wants to execute the task, in the absence of temporal constraints. It need not know exactly how fast the arm can move, but can move deliberately, though it sacrifices cost-effectiveness to do so. Although we can solve many useful tasks this way, the approach begins to break down as the robot, task, and environment become more sophisticated.

Consider retrieving an object from a conveyor belt. To save time and fixturing, we wish to do so without stopping the conveyor. The manipulator must be at the right place at the right time at the right velocity to make a smooth pickup. In contrast to the discrete-time punch feeder, a continuous-time approach is required. The continuous-time robot must model the physics of the environment as it evolves during robot operation. Continuous-time systems require high sensor bandwidth — many sensor data points per second, and low latency — the time from the acquisition of data until it is applied to the control output. The lack of adequate sensor systems has hampered previous investigation of this area.

The conventional approach to the conveyor problem is to find the object's position from a single snapshot, then update the position using an encoder mechanically mounted on the conveyor belt [49]. Servo equations cause the robot to track the object. Pragmatically, this is fine for low-accuracy, low-speed applications.

To increase the robot's object-retrieval rate, the system must pick a distance by which to lead the object, such that the robot can arrive at that position at the same time as the object. To lead by as little as possible, we must know how fast the arm can move. If we have a good sensor system, we can continue to watch the object while the arm moves, fine-tuning the arm's trajectory.

In this book we will investigate the construction of a sophisticated continuous-time system, the robot ping-pong player. We will see that new problems are encountered, and new techniques must be applied, to create a robust, functioning system.

We claim that robot controllers already limit robots' performance. We can increase the robot system's speed and functionality by increasing the controller's knowledge of the manipulator's physical capabilities, and by providing effective ways to use this information.

To accomplish the robot ping-pong task, we have created an "expert controller" able to operate in the symbolic domain of the high-level planner, and the numeric domain of the low-level system. The expert controller integrates a specialized expert system and robot controller. The robot controller still exists to perform low-level functions, but the expert controller replaces and extends the robot controller's upper levels. The expert controller must exploit its knowledge of the task and robot characteristics to generate a working plan that satisfies the constraints of both task and robot. The system design is drastically affected by the need for rapid response and the need to compensate for, and be robust to, new sensor data.

Of course, we can't investigate a particular robot subsystem in isolation — we need to have working sensor, low-level control, and actuator components as well. The expert controller places its own requirements on their design. Each component poses its own problems which must be solved to create a working system.

1.2 Introduction to Robot Ping-Pong

Let us briefly overview the ping-pong system and outline the function of its components. We use the robot ping-pong rules proposed by Billingsley [8] as an international challenge and competition. The most important differences from human ping-pong are that the table is narrower than the human table, and that wire frames have been added at each end and the middle through which the ball must pass (Figure 3). The geometry places a premium on accurate placement, rather than raw speed, because the net's height limits the ball's maximum speed. The game can be played by a small stationary robot, but is challenging for both man and machine.

The computer implementation can be divided into four stages, each residing on one or more computers: a 3-D vision system, which locates the ball each sixtieth of a second; a trajectory analyzer, which determines and extrapolates the ball's trajectory; an expert controller, by far the most complex component, which implements the ping-pong strategy to produce the robot's desired trajectory; and a servo system, which causes the robot to follow the trajectory.

To understand what a robot ping-pong system must do, let us consider the decisions which must be made in the course of the return of a single ball, starting from the point at which it is hit by the opponent.

We visually track the ball, finding the (x,y,z,t) position of the ball at the end of each camera frame. After several frames, we fit some trajectory to the data, including the effect of air drag and spin. The observed trajectory is used to predict the future trajectory of the ball after it bounces on the table. We continually monitor the ball trajectory to detect infringements of the rules, and award points as necessary.

The robot must pick the position along the post-bounce trajectory at which the ball will be hit, establishing the hit position and time. A trajectory to return the ball to the opponent must be computed, considering the incoming trajectory, knowledge of the rules, and some strategy. The paddle orientation and velocity that transfers the ball from one trajectory to the other must be computed from knowledge of the paddle's characteristics.

Although ping-pong requires only five degrees of freedom (three of position, two of orientation), the robot has six. The extra dimension corresponds to rotating the paddle's handle in the plane normal to the paddle's orientation vector. Having chosen a value for this degree of freedom, the robot's joint angles may be computed.

Robot motions are then planned so that the motions complete (moving joints stabilize at constant velocity) slightly before the hit instant, taking into account the acceleration capabilities of the manipulator. Heavily stressed joints may have no setup time at all. Once the motion has been planned, the robot may be started towards the ball.

In the meantime, the ball continues moving towards the robot. We must continue to watch the ball until it is hit, refining our motion to make it as likely as possible that the ball will be returned as planned.

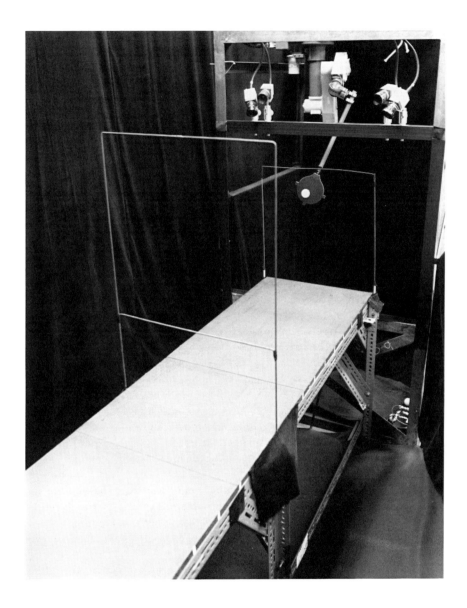

Figure 3. Table and Robot. The frames at the center and end of the table may be seen, with the robot and video cameras at back.

1.3 Why Ping-Pong is a Good Problem

As implied by the title of this book, we use robot ping-pong as an experimental task for investigating more intelligent robot control methods. Ping-pong has many advantages as an experimental task; our reasons for choosing it are both technical and nontechnical.

Starting first with the less technical reasons, we can tell whether or not we are succeeding — it is possible to visually observe improvements in the machine's performance. Observers can readily understand the problem. Ping-pong is also a stable problem: unlike many industrial problems, technological advances won't make the entire problem obsolete overnight.

Ping-pong's breadth means that we can use ping-pong as a strong common focus in describing work across many subfields of robotics, from sensing to processing to actuation to system design. The reaction time allowed to the entire robot system: sensors, processors, and actuators, is quite short. Each system component must be efficacious, fast, and have a low latency. Although many might regard the requirement for high performance in all facets as a liability, we regard it as a strength because it forces us to consider the real problems.

The sensor system must provide estimates of the ball trajectory as early as possible so that the robot may begin moving to approximately the correct place as early as possible. High accuracy must be obtained when the ball is far away, not just close up, so that the best possible spin estimates can be computed when they are most helpful — before the spin has had much of a chance to perturb the trajectory, and maximum reaction time is available. The trajectory analyzer must use a complex flight dynamics model.

The low-level robot controller must be able to operate the actuator as close as possible to its physical and electrical capabilities, unlike conventional controllers, which sacrifice performance for simplicity. The robot must be able to be made to arrive not only at a specific place, but accurately at a specific time and velocity as well.

The robot system must act long before accurate data is available. The initial data is guaranteed to be incorrect because of the long integration time required to compute spin data, and because physically the bounce does not occur until very late, yet it can have major effects on the trajectory. If the robot waits or is indecisive, there will be no time for motion. The robot must be prepared to start moving in the right direction and to continue to update the planned return as more data becomes available.

Robot ping-pong has no best solution: best can only be defined in terms of some arbitrary evaluator. We know only one true evaluator: "Who won the point?" The expert controller must pick a suitable return from those feasible for a given incoming trajectory. Despite the extra degrees of freedom, the planned return must satisfy the constraints of the robot and the rules of ping-pong. As additional data arrives, we must correct beleaguered constraints at the expense of unstressed ones.

It is this complexity that makes robot ping-pong a good experimental task. By focusing on producing a working ping-pong system, we ensure that we find the "real" problems, which aren't always obvious, and that our solutions are feasible, rather than being paper tigers.

1.4 A Preview of the Work

A primary contribution of this book is the expert controller used to do task planning and control. Conventional AI (artificial intelligence) programs manipulate symbols, whereas conventional robot controllers perform numeric calculations: to play ping-pong, the expert controller must fuse the two approaches. For example, symbolic data may represent what data is available, what alternative action has been selected, or might categorize the state of the environment.

To support numeric processing, the entire system is written in "C," but the program is structured to support symbol manipulation as well. To facilitate the combined symbolic and numeric approach, a specialized data structure, the "model," was developed which can simultaneously generate both types of information.

A crucial element of the ping-pong task is that new sensor data arrives all the time, forcing the plan to be continually modified. We will describe a task planning architecture able to cope with, and indeed exploit, the necessity of continuously updating its plan as the input data changes. The plan must satisfy the constraints of both the ping-pong task and the robot manipulator. Initially, the system intelligently "guesses" at a plan, without precise knowledge of these complex, interrelated constraints. Models encode much of the guessing strategy.

As new sensor data arrives, the expert controller modifies the plan not only to account for the changing sensor data, but to avoid problems, such as an impossible kinematic configuration, an impending degeneracy, or an overloaded joint motor. We encapsulate the expertise to modify the plan in modules called "tuners," which evaluate and incrementally improve the quality of the plan.

Of course, when a problem does occur, the system must correct it and continue operating. An exception handling system rapidly selects a low-level agent (a tuner) capable of solving a problem. The mechanism uses a hierarchical delegation of authority so that conditional responses may be made when exceptions occur in the course of correcting a previous exception.

To track the ball, we have created a 60 Hz, low-latency, four-dimensional vision system, the four dimensions being x, y, z, and additionally, t. Moments provide accurate ball centroids in the camera image plane; we describe how we compute them in real time. Our stereo vision algorithms concentrate not on the usual correspondence problem (there is only one object to correspond), but instead on high numeric accuracy: we compensate for the camera placements, lens distortion, and the ball's light intensity distribution. Unlike prior motion interpretation work, a complex model is fitted to the ball's trajectory, and used to predict its future motion.

A robot controller has been developed which provides features necessary for operation in a very dynamic environment. Several types of trajectory generators have been compared; we will justify and describe our trajectory generator. The controller generates smooth motions using quintic polynomials, which have specified initiation and completion times, positions, velocities, and accelerations. The polynomials may be respecified while the arm moves. To facilitate planning, the controller estimates the arm's capabilities based on motor torques, inertia as a function of configuration, and gravity loading. Predictive algorithms for back electro-motive-force (EMF) limiting on quintic trajectories will also be presented. Extensive feed-forward techniques ensure that the arm performs according to the estimates.

A robot consisting of sensors, processing, and actuators distributed across multiple processors must achieve accurate performance in the temporal domain, as well as the physical domain. A clock synchronization system and appropriately designed peripherals make this possible.

A complex system such as the robot ping-pong player can not be turned on suddenly one day to meet its first opponent. Instead, the system was gradually created, debugged, and analyzed to suggest further improvements. Debugging a real-time system is harder than usual, because the debugger must not alter the system's temporal behavior. A fast data logging system and a domain-independent debugger reveal the system's performance to the designer. The same logging system can be used in real time by the robot to analyze its own behavior, without adverse impact on performance, to report faults, and to provide support for learning algorithms.

1.5 Implications and Application Areas

Let us consider the application areas of the techniques we will discuss in this book.

A robot's speed is always critically important, as it determines the robot's effective cost. By making a robot system operate in continuous time, we can almost certainly increase its speed, as the robot's actions can overlap activity in the environment. The precise knowledge of time, and temporal control over motions and sensing, allow the system to be constructed so that everything happens "on schedule," rather than having to leave significant dead times. Similarly, we can plan robot motions to use all available arm capability. By understanding motion in the environment, we may not have to stop objects to operate on them, for example, we can operate on objects as they move on a conveyor belt, saving both the time and machinery necessary to stop the object.

We have developed techniques to control systems with redundant degrees of freedom. One simple example of such a system is an arm with seven or more degrees of freedom, such as the human arm. The extra degrees of freedom can be used to avoid degeneracies [63], or to maneuver past obstacles in the environment [46]. A hand is a particularly extreme example of redundancy, as hands have 12 or more degrees of freedom. Our work might be used to decide how to position objects within the hand, and how to change grasps when manipulating an object. At an intermediate level of complexity, which is perhaps of greatest interest, we can consider the control of an arm mounted on a movable base. Humans reposition their arms by moving both their legs and torso. A robot arm might be mounted on a wheeled mobile robot or a sliding track. In any case, our techniques may be used to allocate desired motions between the sluggish but long-range mobile element, and the faster but limited-reach arm. The same argument may be made for mounting limited-view sensors on a mobile platform.

The two areas described above, namely continuous-time systems and redundant systems, are outside of most current robot application areas. Continuous-time and redundant systems are more complex than current applications, but offer important advantages such as faster operation and increased reach.

There is an additional synergistic advantage to be had by building systems that are both continuous-time and redundant: robustness. When a system runs continuously, and has redundant degrees of freedom to adjust, it can be much more robust than otherwise, because the system may avoid problems by adjusting the redundant degrees of freedom. The increased robustness alone may well justify the increased complexity of making systems continuous-time and redundant.

1.6 Organization of This Book

This book contains several different classes of details which may appeal to different readers, ranging from ping-pong physics to computer system implementations. We have noted each such especially detailed section, so that readers may readily establish if they wish to skip a section.

Chapter 2 details the characteristics of the robot ping-pong task, especially areas of difficulty, and includes a comparison to the human game. The physics of the sport — aerodynamics and impact dynamics — are discussed in detail.

Chapter 3 outlines the entire system and its decomposition into subtasks. System-wide issues, such as the computing network, task partitioning, clock synchronization, data logging, and debugging are also examined.

Chapter 4 highlights the real-time vision system, which measures and then predicts the ball's position as a function of time. A variety of compensations provide maximal accuracy for objects following complex trajectories.

Chapter 5 illuminates the lower levels of robot control system, focusing primarily on generic task-independent software. The robot controller estimates the manipulator's capabilities, and ensures that the robot acts accordingly.

The expert controller requires two chapters for an adequate description. Chapter 6 sets the stage for the expert controller by presenting two principal components: the program flow architecture, and a data structure for symbolic and numeric data. In Chapter 7, we build upon these components to form modules for initial planning, temporal updating, and exception handling.

Chapter 8 ties together all the previous chapters, detailing the expert controller's utilization in the robot ping-pong system, including case studies of program components and an analysis of program performance.

Finally, the book is summarized in Chapter 9, and some long-term possibilities are explored. Will machines triumph over man?

Chapter 2

Robot Ping-Pong

The purpose of this chapter is to describe the robot ping-pong task in greater detail, to give the reader physical intuition for the later chapters. We will describe the rules, then describe some strategic differences between the robot game and the human game. Finally, we will analyze the physics of ping-pong, deriving the equations necessary to play the game.

2.1 Robot Ping-Pong Rules

The robot plays ping-pong according to international standard robot ping-pong rules proposed by John Billingsley ([8] and Appendix 1). The game has been modified to be playable by moderate-sized immobile robots, by scaling down and restricting the area that must be covered by the robots. To compensate for this, the paddle is restricted to be only 12.5 cm in diameter, whereas people use 15−17 cm paddles presenting 60% more area. A ping-pong ball is 4 cm in diameter.

The robot table is shown in Figure 4. The table's width is 0.5 meters, versus approximately 1.5 meters for the human-sized table [35]. A wire frame 0.5 meters on a side delimits each end of the table, and unlike human ping-pong, the ball must travel through this frame after having bounced exactly once. The robot must cover only this 0.5 by 0.5 meter area. Shots off the side of the table, or balls which bounce twice before going through the frame, count against the robot that hit the ball.

The net is 0.25 meters high (0.16 for humans). The height of the net and the upper bound on the height of the ball at the near side of the table limits the maximum ball speed to approximately 10 meters per second (10 m/sec); for anything but an ideal player, the limit is about 8 m/sec (20 miles per hour, mph). The minimum ball speed is 3.5 to 4 m/sec. The table is 2 meters long (2.74 for humans), resulting in maximum available reaction times of 0.4 to 0.8 seconds. Approximately 0.1 second is

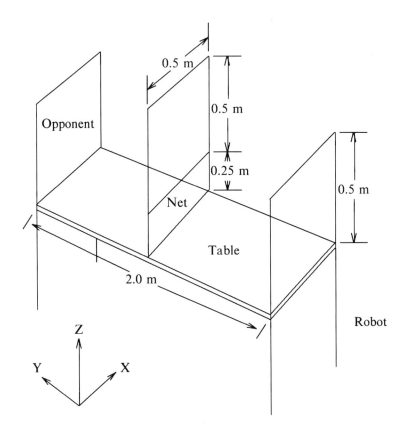

0.5 m

0.5 m

Opponent

0.25 m

0.5 m

Net

Table

2.0 m

Robot

Z

Y   X

Figure 4. Robot Ping-Pong Table. The players, background, and table are black. The ball must travel sequentially through the square frame at one end, through the center frame, then bounce once and travel through the frame at the table's other end.

lost to camera latency and accumulating enough frames (5) to get a rudimentary estimate of the ball trajectory.

Robot motion time can thus range under 0.3 seconds, or more typically 0.5 seconds, even with infinitely fast computers — robot ping-pong does require fast robots. The robot controller must be able to use the maximum capabilities of the robot if it is to be able to play the game.

Some simple robot ping-pong players have been attempted. Knight and Lowery describe a system ("Charlie") which resembles a 2-D computer plotter placed on its side, with the pen replaced by a paddle [39]. The spring-loaded paddle is released by a solenoid, and thus lacks any degrees of freedom. A mechanically scanned photo-diode system tracks the ball with analog and digital servos. According to the authors, it "was found to be capable on most occasions of successfully tracking and hitting a ping-pong ball served towards it," though there is no mention of the balls' subsequent flight. It has not played against machines or humans, only balls rolled out of a tube.

It is more a clever mechanism than a machine that truly knows and plays ping-pong. Skinner demonstrated that pigeons can play a game that resembles ping-pong [62], but it was simply a conditioned response. Both the sensors and actuators severely limit Charlie's best theoretically achievable level of play; a slightly difficult placement or spin should make it nonfunctional.

2.2 Comparison to Human Ping-Pong

The human ping-pong game has a number of advantages lacking from the robot ping-pong game which ought to be described. We also include some subtle human capabilities the robot lacks.

2.2.1 Return trajectory. The kinematics of the robot ping-pong table are much more constrained than the human one. On a human table it is nearly always possible to hit the ball a bit harder with more top-spin, or hit the ball a bit softer with a higher arc, and still have a valid shot.

Returns on a robot table must be tightly constrained in velocity. Simple ball placement strategies such as "aim for the middle of the far frame" just do not work. If the incoming shot is high, there is no choice but to generate a high-speed return to get under the wire on your own side; quickly moving balls are not able to bounce very high before they cross the other end of the table. Balls just clearing the near end of the table must be returned along high-arc lob trajectories. Normally, one would like to aim horizontally straight across from the incoming shot, displaced somewhat towards the center of the far frame, to maximize the probability of a good shot, while minimizing the ball's velocity perpendicular to the face of the paddle. (This strategy reduces the range the robot must cover, and makes the hit less dependent on the paddle surface.) If the incoming shot is wide and near a side frame marker, there is no choice but to aim for the opposing corner, because otherwise the return will strike the side marker on the robot's end of the table.

The ball's return velocity must be well planned and carefully executed. An error of 100 millimeters per second can result in 4—8 cm of error in the ball's lateral placement, and large errors in the depth of the bounce, depending on the trajectory.

2.2.2 Ball speed. Ball speeds of 20 mph (8 m/sec) do not sound very fast when one is accustomed to 100 mph fastballs. Contrary to popular lore [7][48] which claims ping-pong balls fly at 70−120 mph or approximately 50 m/sec (and thus are acted on by 25 G drag!), real maximum human ball speeds are probably 20−30 m/sec, or about 50 mph. This author has not gotten over 15−20 m/sec even on wildly uncontrolled smashes. The accepted scientific study [48] (cited as such by [25]) erred in the other direction, "measuring" ball speeds with high-speed motion picture photography of only 4.3 m/sec from the smashes of state champion players.

2.2.3 Choice of contact point. Eight meters per second does seem pretty fast when you have to stand up and face it without retreating. Unlike a person, the robot can not back away from the table to give itself more time to react.

The robot must wait for the ball to come to it, whereas people can always hit the ball at the top of the arc, or more likely at the point where the ball has a specific descent angle. At the top of the arc the ball is moving slowest and traveling roughly along the same path in space as the paddle will follow, so this strategy minimizes errors due to incoming ball position, velocity, and timing. The robot must deal with balls of widely varying ascent and descent rates, although it has some flexibility.

2.2.4 Spin estimation. Humans often point out that they watch the opponent's paddle at contact to estimate the generated spin. Vision system limitations prevent the robot from using the same strategy. Since the deflection is quadratic with respect to the distance (and time) traveled, the spin is hardest to detect just when you need the information most: when the ball is starting to fly towards you and the deflection is the least. An eventual lateral deflection of 16 cm at the near end of the table has deflected only 1 cm by the time the ball is halfway to the net. The utility of a human's early spin estimate, based on the paddle velocity, is clearly apparent.

The robot must estimate the spin solely by its effect on the trajectory. Only two components of the spin vector are visible at a time, both perpendicular to the ball's velocity vector. Consequently, spin about the velocity vector is observable only after the velocity has changed. In practice, this means that the ball's spin about the Y axis (the long direction of the table) is detectable only after the ball has risen and fallen again, and then only after considerable analysis and with marginal accuracy. When the ball bounces, the Y spin component is converted into an angular displacement between the incoming and outgoing velocity vectors in the plane of the table. At low speeds and high spins, the angular displacement can approach 90°.

2.2.5 Paddle trajectory. Humans may generate motion trajectories with linear segments and with constant paddle orientation. People are coached to do this to minimize the effect of timing error. Because of the robot's limited reach and physical geometry, this strategy is not an option for the robot, consequently, its timing requirements are more severe.

With post-bounce ball speeds of 2–3 m/sec, the ball moves at 3 millimeters per millisecond. The paddle moves at similar speeds and rotates at several hundred degrees per second. A few tens of milliseconds error can result in a clean miss; less error results in a bad shot.

2.3 Ping-Pong Physics

The following sections describe the aerodynamics of a ping-pong ball, what happens when it bounces, and how to hit it where we want. Each section is comprised of an initial qualitative discussion, followed by a quantitative analysis which may not be of interest to all readers. It is largely intended for those who may build their own ping-pong robots.

2.3.1 Aerodynamics. While in flight, the ping-pong ball is acted on by three significant forces: gravity, air drag, and the Magnus (spin) Effect. Clearly, gravity is the most predictable of the three at 9.86 m/sec^2 (referred to as 1 G). The aerodynamic forces acting upon a smooth rotating sphere are surprisingly still a matter of debate among physicists.

Air drag is a function of speed and can cause surprising effects [25], but is usually claimed to exhibit a quadratic speed dependence. Two adjacent papers, [31] and [70], respectively propose a quintic polynomial (but mainly linear) and a quadratic dependence of drag on velocity. We have adopted the quadratic assumption, which appears better supported and has at least some support from our experimental data. At nominal speeds, drag exerts 0.3 G, though the value is quite speed sensitive.

Spin affects the flight of the ball according to the Magnus Effect, named after its inventor (according to Lord Rayleigh [53] in the late 1800's). Even now, the Magnus Effect appears poorly understood, as even the sign of the force can change with speed [13]. According to Watts and Ferrer [67], the Magnus force is linearly proportional to the forward velocity. An approximation is experimentally developed in [55], which states that the Magnus force is proportional to spin and the square of the velocity, similar to the drag. Once again, we use the quadratic proportionality. A moderate-speed ball with a 50 Hz top-spin, or an intentionally side-spun shot, is subject to 0.3 G due to the Magnus Effect.

We can now formulate the ball's equations of motion. Given the velocity vector $\vec{v}$, and the spin vector $\vec{w}$, the ball accelerates at $\vec{a}$:

$$\vec{a} = -C_d |\vec{v}| \vec{v} + C_m |\vec{v}| \vec{w} \times \vec{v} - \vec{g} \qquad (1)$$

The vector $\vec{g}$ is the acceleration of gravity. The drag coefficient, C_d, is such that the terminal velocity (where $C_d |\vec{v}|^2 = |\vec{g}|$) comes out to 9.5 m/sec, as reported by [12]. Based on experiment, we use $C_m = $ 4E-07 sec/mm for the Magnus Effect. The term involving C_m has a vector cross product, so the force due to the Magnus Effect acts at right angles to the spin vector and at right angles to the velocity vector. The $\vec{w}$ vector remains essentially unchanged during flight because the only torque acting on the ball is a negligible drag antiparallel to $\vec{w}$, which slowly reduces the spin rate.

Note that Equation 1 is a system of nonlinear coupled differential equations, and that it is generally intractable. Given initial values for the parameters, we must numerically integrate to find the future values.

2.3.2 Bouncing on the table. To be able to predict the ultimate trajectory of the ball as early as possible, the system must be able to predict the bounce off the table. The result of a bounce is determined by the incoming velocity and spin vectors, and the properties of the ball and surface: quite a few things to know accurately. The analysis of the bounce on a table serves as a basis for the subsequent discussion of how to hit the ball (Section 2.3.3).

In the direction normal to the surface, the rebound is determined by the coefficient of restitution (the retained fraction of the original velocity). For a bounce on a table, the coefficient of restitution must be between 0.86 and 0.91 [35]. Unfortunately, it is not necessarily uniform over the entire table surface. Additionally, the ball is made from two halves which are pressed together, leaving a seam. The outcome of the bounce depends on the relative position of the contact area (about 5 mm diameter) and the seam.

In the horizontal plane, the post-bounce ball speed is determined by the ball's spin and the table's coefficient of friction [14]. Normally, an initially spinless ball will continue after a bounce with approximately 60% of its initial horizontal velocity. A ball hit with a significant 60 Hz top-spin can acquire up to 40% more velocity than before the bounce. The resulting velocity is affected by the local coefficient of friction, local table orientation (all tables are warped to some extent), and by the presence of the seam.

As should be apparent, it is difficult to predict the ball's exact velocity after a bounce, even with completely accurate trajectory information. We originally thought that spin could be regarded as a second-order effect, instead, the spin critically affects the bounce off the table (and paddle).

We will now derive the physics of a ball's bounce off of a table, generalizing the results of Brody [14] from 2-D to 3-D. The derivation requires first-year college physics. A ball's bounce contains two primary elements: the vertical component, with lossy deformation-driven rebound; and the horizontal component, where energy is dissipated in the frictional slip between ball and table. We will begin by considering the vertical direction.

When a ball bounces vertically on a table, its kinetic energy is converted into potential energy, stored as the deformation of the ball from its nominal spherical shape, then the process reverses so that the ball ultimately travels upwards without deformation. The process is not perfect: some of the original kinetic energy heats the ball and induces vibrations in the ball, table, and atmosphere. Consequently, the final velocity is less than the original.

Empirically, it has been found that the ratio of the final and initial velocities is some specific fraction, determined by the characteristics of the ball and table. This gives us:

$$v_{fz} = -\epsilon v_{iz} \qquad (2)$$

where ϵ is conventionally known as the coefficient of restitution.

At a detailed level, what this says is that a force, $N(t)$, has acted for such a duration as to cause Equation 2 to be true. We can write this as:

$$m(v_{fz}-v_{iz}) = \int N dt \qquad (3)$$

where the integral is taken over the short contact time of the bounce (1 msec). Of course, the actual shape versus time of the function N may be very complex. Combining Equation 3 and 2, we can obtain:

$$\int N dt = -mv_{iz}(1+\epsilon) \qquad (4)$$

which says that even if we don't know the shape of N, we at least know what its integral is. We will use this result next to predict the horizontal portion of the bounce.

The next component we must consider results from the frictional force between table and ball. The magnitude of the force is μN, where μ is the coefficient of friction, and N is still the force, normal to the table surface, exerted by the deformed ball. We must know the direction of this force as well. The force acts along the relative direction of motion of the ball on the table. This direction is dependent not only on the ball's velocity, but its spin vector.

If we consider a vertically dropped spinning ball, it is clear that each small surface patch on the ball is moving relative to the table; empirically we know that this will cause the ball to jump off to the side. The velocity of a surface patch (namely, the one that hits the table) is:

$$\vec{v}_{rel} = \vec{v}_{ball} + r\,\hat{k} \times \vec{w} \tag{5}$$

Note that we assume that $\hat{k}$ is the table normal. If we select only the portion of the patch's velocity in the plane of the table, we have:

$$\vec{v}_{rel} = (v_x - w_y r,\; v_y + w_x r,\; 0) \tag{6}$$

We are mostly interested in the direction of $\vec{v}_{rel}$, $\hat{v}_r$:

$$\hat{v}_r = \|\vec{v}_{rel}\| = \frac{\vec{v}_{rel}}{|\vec{v}_{rel}|} \tag{7}$$

The force acting on the ball during a collision is:

$$F = -\mu N \hat{v}_r + N\hat{k} \tag{8}$$

We can now start assembling the final result. We have to compute two things: the ball's final velocity and its final spin vector. We can use the impulse relation $\int F dt = m\Delta v$ to find the final velocity, and the analogous relation $\int T dt = I\Delta w$ to find the final spin. We have:

$$\int F dt = -\int \mu N \hat{v}_r dt + \int N\hat{k} dt \tag{9}$$

$$m(\vec{v}_f - \vec{v}_i) = -\mu \hat{v}_r \int N dt + \hat{k} \int N dt \tag{10}$$

$$m(\vec{v}_f - \vec{v}_i) = (\mu \hat{v}_r - \hat{k}) m v_{iz} (1+\epsilon) \tag{11}$$

and finally,

$$\vec{v}_f = \vec{v}_i + (\mu \hat{v}_r - \hat{k}) v_{iz} (1+\epsilon) \tag{12}$$

Similarly, we can find the spin, starting from the torque equation:

$$T = I\Delta w = \vec{F} \times \vec{r} \tag{13}$$

The radius vector is the radius of the ball along the table normal $\hat{k}$ and the force vector F is the same frictional force, so we compute:

$$\frac{2}{3}mr^2\Delta w = -\mu N r\,(\hat{v}_{ry},\; -\hat{v}_{rx},\; 0) \tag{14}$$

A bit of algebra resembling the final velocity calculation (Equation 12) produces:

$$\vec{w}_f = \vec{w}_i + \frac{3\mu}{2r}(\hat{v}_{ry}, -\hat{v}_{rx}, 0)v_{iz}(1+\epsilon) \qquad (15)$$

Equation 15 may be seen to leave the Z component of $\vec{w}$ unchanged (the zero in Equation 15 corresponds to the Z component of that vector). We have neglected the possibility of frictional torques acting along the table normal, which would change w_z. This simplification is empirically justified.

As we have seen, even though we don't know the detailed profile of the impact force N, we can still find its effect on the ball's velocity and spin because we do know its effect on the vertical component of the ball's velocity. It is this trick that is due to Brody, though we have generalized it here to the full three-dimensional case.

The derivation above does make one subtle assumption, namely, that the vector $\hat{v}_r$ remains unchanged during the collision. We will show that this is true, except that $\hat{v}_r$ may go to zero. In this case, there is no further frictional force, since ball and table are synchronized: the ball rolls.

The onset of rolling may occur at any time during the collision. Since our knowledge of the collision dynamics is determined by $\int N dt$, let us parameterize the collision with a fraction β to describe what portion of $\int N dt$ has been inflicted. We need not consider any particular time within the collision, as that would require knowledge of the shape of N, only the fraction of the impulse which has been delivered.

If we replace $\int N dt$ with $\beta \int N dt$ in Equation 10, it is clear we would obtain a modified form for Equation 12:

$$\vec{v}(\beta) = \vec{v}_i + (\mu \hat{v}_r - \hat{k})\beta v_{iz}(1+\epsilon) \qquad (16)$$

and similarly for the spin:

$$\vec{w}(\beta) = \vec{w}_i + \frac{3\mu}{2r}(\hat{v}_{ry}, -\hat{v}_{rx}, 0)\beta v_{iz}(1+\epsilon) \qquad (17)$$

From Equations 6, 16, and 17, we can find the velocity of the ball's surface relative to the table as a function of β. After some algebra (Equation 7 is helpful), we claim that:

$$v_{rel,x}(\beta) = \hat{v}_{rx}\left[|\vec{v}_{rel}| + \frac{5}{2}\beta \mu v_{iz}(1+\epsilon)\right] \qquad (18)$$

$$v_{rel,y}(\beta) = \hat{v}_{ry}\left[|\vec{v}_{rel}| + \frac{5}{2}\beta \mu v_{iz}(1+\epsilon)\right] \qquad (19)$$

which shows that $\hat{v}_r = \|\vec{v}_{rel}\|$ remains unchanged during the collision, as originally claimed. Furthermore, we observe that $\vec{v}_{rel}$ will go to zero when:

$$\beta = \frac{-2|\vec{v}_{rel}|}{5\mu v_{iz}(1+\epsilon)} \tag{20}$$

The onset of rolling must occur before the impulse is completed, that is, while $\beta < 1$, so rolling occurs if (note that $v_{iz} < 0$):

$$|\vec{v}_{rel}| < -\frac{5}{2}\mu v_{iz}(1+\epsilon) \tag{21}$$

Once rolling has begun, no further frictional forces act on the ball. We can find the resulting final conditions by substituting Equation 20 into Equations 16 and 17, while leaving the component of the velocity along the table normal $\hat{k}$ unchanged. After the usual work, we obtain:

$$\vec{v}_f = (\frac{3}{5}v_{ix}+\frac{2}{5}rw_{iy}, \frac{3}{5}v_{iy}-\frac{2}{5}rw_{ix}, -\epsilon v_{iz}) \tag{22}$$

$$\vec{w}_f = (\frac{2}{5}w_{ix}-\frac{3v_{iy}}{5r}, \frac{2}{5}w_{iy}+\frac{3v_{ix}}{5r}, w_{iz}) \tag{23}$$

To briefly describe this section's equations use in practice, we first determine if the ball will roll or slide, using Equation 21, then use either Equations 22 and 23, or Equations 12 and 15, respectively, to compute the resulting velocity and spin.

2.3.3 Hitting the ball. A ping-pong player must know how to hit the ball to cause it to fly in a specific direction. The multilayered rubber paddle surface dramatically affects the bounce, ranging from surfaces designed to be insensitive to the incoming spin without creating spin, to very sensitive surfaces that put high spin on the ball [57]. Depending on the spin and the surface, the ball can shoot off in quite different directions. The physics are not at all understood; professional players rate the surfaces qualitatively [56], though they assign numeric ratings. On the positive side, only the properties of a localized area of the paddle must be known — hopefully only the very center. The rubber surface results in a longer contact time and larger contact area than a table bounce, ameliorating the seam's effect. The lower coefficient of restitution reduces sensitivity to the incoming velocity.

Assuming that we have the ball's incoming velocity vector, spin vector, and a desired outgoing velocity vector, we need an algorithm to compute the paddle's orientation and velocity at the moment of contact that will cause the ball to fly off along the desired trajectory. Let $\vec{I}$ be the incoming ball velocity vector, $\vec{w}$ be the spin vector, $\vec{O}$ be the outgoing velocity, $\vec{v}$ be the paddle velocity, and $\hat{o}$ be the paddle orientation (i.e., the paddle's normal vector).

To obtain a system of equations we can solve, we must first simplify the problem. The ball's spin contributes an additive term to the ball's final velocity $\vec{O}$ which is in the plane of the paddle, perpendicular to the ball's spin vector $\vec{w}$:

$$\Delta\vec{O} = P_{sivo}\, r\, \vec{w} \times \hat{o} \tag{24}$$

where $\Delta\vec{O}$ is the increment in velocity due to the spin, P_{sivo} is a paddle-dependent constant, and r is the radius of the ball.

We estimate the paddle normal $\hat{o}$, then compute $\Delta\vec{O}$ and subtract it from the ball's desired final velocity $\vec{O}$:

$$\vec{O}' = \vec{O} - \Delta\vec{O} \tag{25}$$

If we then plan the hit for this adjusted final velocity $\vec{O}'$, assuming that the ball has no spin, it will wind up going in the desired direction. By this trick, we have eliminated one variable ($\vec{w}$) from the impact planning algorithm. However, accuracy depends on a good paddle orientation estimate for the initial correction process. We perform the planning process twice so that the orientation estimate $\hat{o}$ during the second iteration (the computed orientation during the first iteration) is quite accurate.

The moment of impact may be modeled in the (moving) coordinate system of the paddle, where the impact may be resolved into normal and tangential components. The bounce off the paddle resembles the bounce on the flat tabletop, but we assume (with justification) the paddle is very sticky: the ball always rolls, never slides. The required algorithm must find the correct frame of reference in which the impact produces the desired outgoing trajectory. For the special case of a spinless ball with the paddle normal parallel to the paddle velocity ($\hat{o} = \|\vec{v}\|$), the system may be solved in closed form using vector algebra.

We begin by finding a convenient coordinate system in which to express the physics of the impact:

$$\vec{a} = (\vec{I}-\vec{v}) \times (\vec{O}-\vec{v}) \tag{26}$$

and

$$\vec{n} = \vec{v} \times \vec{a} \tag{27}$$

so that $\vec{a}$ and $\vec{n}$ are vectors in the plane of the paddle (Figure 5). The vectors $\vec{a}$, $\vec{n}$, and $\vec{v}$ are orthogonal.

We use the same linear bounce model as for the table. If P_{vivo} is the velocity efficiency of the bounce along the paddle, and P_{perp} is the velocity efficiency normal to it, we must find $\vec{v}$ such that:

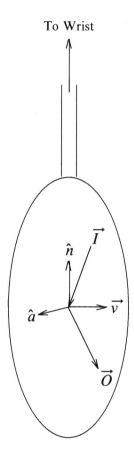

Figure 5. Paddle Impact. The $\hat{n}$ and $\hat{a}$ vectors are in the plane of the paddle; $\vec{v}$ is perpendicular to it. The $\hat{n}, \vec{I}, \vec{v},$ and $\vec{O}$ vectors are in the same plane.

$$P_{vivo} \, (\vec{I}-\vec{v}) \cdot \vec{n} = (\vec{O}-\vec{v}) \cdot \vec{n} \tag{28}$$

and

$$-P_{perp} \, (\vec{I}-\vec{v}) \cdot \vec{v} = (\vec{O}-\vec{v}) \cdot \vec{v} \tag{29}$$

are satisfied. We observe that the paddle velocity $\vec{v}$ must be in the plane of the incoming and outgoing velocities, $\vec{I}$ and $\vec{O}$, so we can write:

$$\vec{v} = m\vec{I} + n\vec{O} \tag{30}$$

Note that we find the $\hat{o}$ estimate as $\|\vec{O}-0.6\,\vec{I}\|$ based on this relation.

After some vector algebra, we can find that:

$$m = -P_{vivo}\, n \qquad (31)$$

and then that

$$n = \frac{-P_{vivo}\, P_{perp}\, \vec{I}\cdot\vec{I} + (P_{perp}-P_{vivo})\, \vec{I}\cdot\vec{O} + \vec{O}\cdot\vec{O}}{(1+P_{perp})\,(P_{vivo}^2\, \vec{I}\cdot\vec{I} - 2P_{vivo}\, \vec{I}\cdot\vec{O} + \vec{O}\cdot\vec{O})} \qquad (32)$$

Once we have m and n, we can find $\vec{v}$ by Equation 30, completing the solution.

The final spin $\vec{w}_f$ on the ball enables us to predict where it will go during the return flight. We can compute it from the initial spin and the ball's velocity parallel to the paddle:

$$\vec{w}_f = P_{siso}\, \vec{w} + \frac{P_{viso}}{r}\, (\hat{o} \times \vec{I}) \qquad (33)$$

where P_{siso} and P_{viso} are paddle-dependent constants.

From this derivation we can see that any hit consequentially puts spin on the ball, but that we can not independently control it. To achieve specific spins, we must relax the constraint that $\hat{o} = \|\vec{v}\|$, allowing slicing motions. Without loss of generality, we can have:

$$\vec{v} = v\hat{o} + \vec{v}_{trans} \qquad (34)$$

where $\vec{v}_{trans}$ is perpendicular to $\hat{o}$. If we are given $\vec{v}_{trans}$, we can subtract it from $\vec{I}$ and $\vec{O}$ to obtain these vectors in the slicing coordinate frame. We can then solve for the usual $\vec{v}$. An intelligent control system can alter $\vec{v}_{trans}$ to produce the spin it wants, as long as it can generate the appropriate transverse motion. Our machine can produce transverse velocities only in a certain direction (perpendicular to the paddle's handle, i.e., along $\vec{a}$ in Figure 5), restricting the obtainable spins. In any case, we do not presently implement spin control.

To conclude this presentation, we have modeled the paddle by five numbers: P_{vivo}, P_{viso}, P_{sivo}, P_{siso}, and P_{perp}. The exact characteristics of the multi-layer rubber surfaces used by human and robot players are doubtless very complex. It is difficult to perform experiments under gamelike conditions, so our model and coefficients represent approximations at best.

The ball's aerodynamics also present room for uncertainty. As we'll see later in the book, at least now we have the tools to begin investigating these problems.

Chapter 3

System Design

In this chapter, we will describe the system design requirements and approaches. The chapter will give the reader an overview of how the system is partitioned and describe the high-level system design. The most important developments are a global clock system that allows the system to generate accurately timed motions, and a data logging and analysis system we use to debug the robot ping-pong player. The reader should be forewarned that the latter part of this chapter contains a significant amount of low-level detail about the system's implementation.

3.1 Task Partitioning

The robot ping-pong system demands many CPU cycles for implementation. Rather than using a mainframe, which would pose many problems of its own, we have chosen to implement the system on a distributed network of microprocessors, each comparable in performance to a VAX 11/785.

The task must be partitioned into pieces that run on each processor. Unlike large monolithic parallel processing tasks, the robot ping-pong system contains a number of different activities, inducing a natural division of labor. The high bandwidth required between a peripheral and its task constrains the task to the same processor as the peripheral.

A block diagram of our hardware and software structure for playing robot ping-pong is shown in Figure 6. Later chapters will describe each of these blocks in detail; for now we will define their functions and requirements.

The flow of data through the system begins at the twin vision processors, eye0 and eye1. Each processor contains two real-time vision systems constituting a stereo pair. The vision systems impose a stringent requirement that they be serviced during a 1.3 msec vertical retrace interval, requiring the operating system to respond rapidly. Both

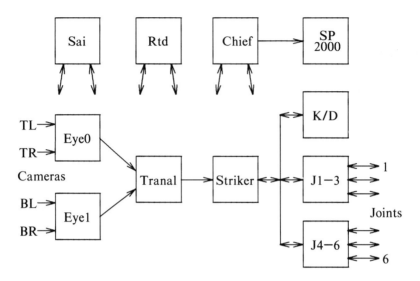

Figure 6. System Block Diagram. The cameras (bottom left, top right, *etc.*) feed the vision processors, `eye0` and `eye1`. XYZT data is sent to the trajectory analyzer, `tranal`, which produces predictions of the ball's path for the expert controller processor, `striker`. A kinematics and dynamics slave processor (K/D) and two joint servo processors drive the robot. `Rtd` is the real-time debugger, `chief` is a sequencer, `sai` is the strategy analyzer, and `sp2000` drives a video-tape system.

processors operate synchronously with the 60 Hz TV scan, putting an upper bound on the amount of processing they may do. After the vision system and its software driver have accurately located the ball's image in each frame, a stereo algorithm combines this information with camera calibration data to produce the three-dimensional location of the ball.

The position information is sent to the trajectory analyzer, `tranal`, which fits the data to trajectories, with appropriate segmentation at bounce and hit points. The abstracted trajectory is used to predict the motion of the ball, and is sent to the strategic analyzer, `sai`, which will analyze the opponent's strategy. The `sai` program currently performs only score-keeping and voice response functions. `Sai` randomly selects a saying such as "What's the matter? You got a two bit brain?" or "Hey! Stop blowing on that ball!" from a context-dependent list.

`Tranal` sends the position, velocity, and time at which the ball will cross the robot's end of the table to the real-time expert controller, striker. Striker contains both the expert controller and the low-level robot controller. After a robot motion is planned, it is sent to slave servo processors which cause the motion to occur. The main processor and slaves are tightly coupled, because they require high bandwidth, low latency, and unstructured access.

The rtd program contains the user interface, allowing the user to control and debug the system. Real-time sequencing is performed by the chief program. The sp2000 program is a protocol driver that allows a Kodak SP-2000 [10] motion analysis system to be driven under computer control to visually record and replay the system's performance, usually at 500 frames per second (though the SP-2000 can go higher).

The rtd program will be the subject of Section 3.5. The chief program will be discussed briefly in Section 3.5.2. The sp2000 and sai programs will not be discussed in this work.

3.2 Processors and Network

We use Motorola 68020 and 68000-based processors following the Sun (Stanford University) memory management architecture. Only chief and sp2000 run on a 68000 (both on the same one). The 68020-based machines contain a Motorola 68881 floating point coprocessor on-board, while the 68000 machine uses a SKY Computers FFP 5100 floating point processor board. As a rough rule of thumb, floating point operations take 5 μsec, with another 5 μsec for each operand fetch or store, though the 68020 machines are substantially faster than the 68000 machines.

The processors are connected by the S/Net [2], a high-bandwidth, low-latency inter-processor connect. Star connections fan out from a backplane bus to the individual processors. The network design minimizes the amount of high-level protocol, error checking, and flow control. Rough performance is one millisecond to transmit a 0–100 byte packet, including all software overhead (which is the major part of the execution time).

A multiprocessing and multitasking operating system called MEGLOS runs on the S/Net processors, supporting real-time programming [27]. A variety of UNIX® (AT&T) functions are provided, including a multiprocessor version of a UNIX® pipe for communication.

A micro-VAX II host acts as a file server and software development machine. The debugging system, rtd, runs on the micro-VAX during system operation. The debugging system is loosely coupled to the run-time system, so there is no need for single user operation of the micro-VAX.

3.3 Achieving Accurate Timing

To get to the right place at the right time, the robot system must be able to know and compensate for system latencies [6]. This section describes the techniques used to find, stabilize, and compensate system latencies across a distributed network of processors.

The statement (sensor output) "the ball is 0.5 meters above the table" is useless, because it is inaccurate soon after it is generated. Any sensor reading of a time-varying signal must be stamped with the time at which it was taken, as this defines the only time it has any validity. Sensor data may be extrapolated forward in time to yield predicted sensor data. The processor may plan its action based on this predicted sensor data; taking into account the processor and actuator latencies, it can start the actuator so that the actuator position will match the predicted sensor data at the same instant.

Implementing this strategy requires that we be able to precisely measure an event's time of occurrence. Microprocessor systems have timers that are readable by software (with substantial overhead). However, an approach which includes software in the measurement path is guaranteed to be inaccurate, because the processor may execute an arbitrary sequence of instructions between the event's time of occurrence and the time the software reads the timer, because cache misses, refresh, scheduling, and I/O interrupts may occur.

3.3.1 Peripheral characteristics. The imprecision of software controlled events requires that we build peripheral devices such that sensor readings are latched, or control signals output, by hardware clocks rather than by software.

The design of the sensor must be compatible with rapidly varying inputs, and able to define a precise timestamp for a given sensor reading. For example, sample and hold circuits prevent analog to digital converters from generating incorrect results; the sample/hold's control input defines the sampling time very precisely. Rather than having an interrupt request the program to read a value, the interrupt can latch the value into a register, which can then be read by the program.

Likewise, outputs should be latched by the peripheral devices under software control, but not applied to the actuators until the next hardware servo clock. The additional level of latching isolates the actuator timing from data dependencies in the control algorithm (we may even use different algorithms at different times), and from multi-tasking in the processor. The slight additional cost of a register to implement this pipelining is compensated by the gain in repeatability of timing. Our robot controller is pipelined both at the major kinematic cycle rate and at the minor servo rate.

3.3.2 Data processing. The processing system also has significant latencies which must be taken into account. The planning software must commit to generating a control signal at a specific (later) time. Consider changing the target of a robot motion while the arm is moving. To obtain a smooth trajectory, the position, velocity, and acceleration must be continuous at the transition from the old to the new trajectory. The program must commit to a specific transition time to be able to plan the new trajectory; the transition time must not be too soon or the preparations will not be completed, ultimately resulting in a discontinuity.

3.3.3 Distributed wall clock. Our sensors and actuators are distributed across multiple processors. Humans have trouble getting to meetings at the same time because we all have wristwatches with a different time (though this is not the only factor at work). Likewise, in a distributed microprocessor system, each processor has its own time. We need a "wall clock" accessible to all processors at once to maintain a consistent view of time across the system.

We implement the wall clock with a specialized `clox` board that resides in each processor; a specialized clock bus connects the `clox` boards. A wall clock must have the same value at each instant to each processor on a network. At first glance, this may seem to require that the `clox` boards be connected by a large number of wires, one for each bit. Since a clock has only two degrees of freedom, only two signals are required: one to specify the rate, and one to specify the offset. The simplest implementation uses one wire to carry a 1 MHz square wave, and another to carry pulses one clock long to effect synchronization. We select one board to generate the clock signal for all of the boards, then calibrate its clock frequency to 4 parts per million to ensure that the absolute accuracy is commensurate with the resolution. We have implemented the wall clock by a network of synchronized wristwatches.

Each processor must have a way of determining when events occur in devices attached to it. In general, this would require that a wire be attached to a signal in the device and to the `clox` board, but this is not convenient. As an implementation technique, we monitor activity on the processor's interrupt lines, which are driven from the same hardware signals we need to monitor, eliminating the wires between boards. An interrupt line must be dedicated to each signal the clock board is to be used to monitor. When the processor handles the interrupt, it reads the interrupt's time of occurrence from an event register; the timing of the read is non-critical.

The `clox` board contains a software-readable clock register which may be used by programs for time-varying decision making. In addition, it is useful to be able to obtain software execution times for diagnostic purposes: how long does this routine take on average? At most? Because of the simplicity of the access protocol, we need not access the clock via an operating system trap. The low cost of access means that we may routinely track execution times.

3.4 Data Logging System

In order to obtain a working system, we must have a way to debug it. Typical debugging techniques that add print statements or set breakpoints are impossible to use in real-time systems, as they either slow it down too much or bring it to a complete halt, in either case making the system nonfunctional.

Accordingly, our approach is to provide an efficient and easy to use means of storing data during execution. The data can then be analyzed by humans, off-line programs, or even by on-line programs (Section 3.4.3). A following section will describe the debugging tools; in this section we will concentrate on the logging system.

3.4.1 Approach. The only fundamentally fast way of logging data from a program is to store it in main memory. Even a networking system as fast as the S/Net requires too much overhead for use in logging, where several data points per millisecond may be generated. Fortunately, main memory sizes have been increasing rapidly, so we can afford to dedicate several hundred kilobytes to this function.

The log may be written to disk for permanent storage and analysis whenever it is convenient. The end of each volley is a natural time to write to disk in the robot ping-pong system. Systems which must remain in continuous operation for extended periods of time must write the log in pieces, when time is available. The structure of the log is a segmented ring buffer which allows simultaneous reading and writing. The important point is that by doing this, we decouple the storage of the data from its generation, so that time-critical code that happens to generate much log data is not forced to wait for the slower writing of the data.

3.4.2 Log entry creation. The log system's most programmer-visible part is the routine which causes data to be stored. Secondary functions initialize the log structure and cause it to be written to disk.

The objectives of the log's design were to be fast, easy to use, robust, and memory efficient. By easy to use, we mean primarily that only minimal effort should be required to add a new log entry, so we can do it easily and repeatedly during program debugging.

The obvious interface to emulate is that of `printf`, the UNIX® formatted print function. `Printf` allows arbitrary combinations of data to be printed with explanatory material. We must provide a version that can do this in real time.

Our interface routine is `printlog`:

```
printlog (LOGID, arg1, arg2, ... );
```

where the usual format has been replaced by a global variable. The *LOGID* is used as an index into a table containing the formats.

It is not desirable to convert the data to ASCII at log time — it would be neither time nor space efficient. Converting even a single floating point number takes a millisecond or more. In addition, we would be storing a lot of redundant information intended for the human reader.

Instead, the number of argument bytes is looked up in a table at log time, and the arguments themselves written to memory. A short header contains the *LOGID* value and a time stamp obtained from the clock synchronization system. The time stamp is invaluable in understanding the sequence of events in a complex system, as they may be compared across processors. Each log entry is appended with a length word that allows the log to be read in reverse if needed, improving robustness.

The resulting execution times for `printlog` are in the range of 50–100 μsec, depending on the amount of data stored. On average, we generate 90 Kb of data in a several second volley.

The data logging system does not fully format the data (using `_doprnt` from `printf`, `fprintf`, and `sprintf`) until it is presented to the human reader. Time is not critical at that time, as the human limits the bandwidth.

A small program, `buildlog`, reads a log descriptor file before a log-using program is compiled. The file contains the association between the global *LOGID* names and the format strings. `Buildlog` produces a C source file defining a table of the format strings and the number of argument bytes, plus a series of definitions for the global *LOGID* variables that initialize them to values corresponding to their position in the table.

As far as the user is concerned, once the log entry is named and a format string created, the system does the rest. Because the *LOGID*s are defined in the C file produced by buildlog (and declared as externals elsewhere), we need not recompile the entire program after adding log entries, as would be necessary if the C-macro preprocessor #define mechanism was used. The only caution is that new log entries must be added at the end of the file, and old entries allowed to remain, to avoid invalidating data that was logged previously and is currently stored on disk.

The log facility easily meets the original objectives. It has proven remarkably successful and invaluable in practice.

3.4.3 Facilities for log analysis by programs. The logged data is an important resource for programs that must analyze their own behavior. Because the raw binary data is stored, it may be efficiently retrieved. In particular, the log is the input to the demons, semi-autonomous programs that implement learning (Section 7.5.3). We have several objectives for the demons' own implementation.

The demons should process the log soon after it is generated, so that the machine can put newly learned data to work. We certainly don't want to have to run an entirely off-line program for learning. On the other hand, the demons can not be driven exactly as the data is logged, because this would slow down the main program too much, at the most critical times. Instead, the demons should run as the main program idles.

If the demons and main program share address space, the demons' implementation is simplified because the demons can access existing software in the main program. This existing software can help reconstruct a full view of events from the sketchy data that can be stored at run-time.

Our demon implementation treats the log as a FIFO (first in, first out) buffer, storing the logged data until the main program encounters an idle period; it does not use any cycles during critical periods. The demon interface acts independently of the log's transfer to disk.

The main program may prespecify the time period available to the demons; the demon driver attempts not to exceed that time. Any data that is not processed during a particular segment will be processed next time. This approach reduces the latency between event and learning to the frequency of the demons being run, on the order of once a second in our application. The demons can be run frequently if needed, as limited by the task's demands.

Each demon is implemented by a collection of subroutines which process a subset of the log entries. The demon is not an independent task since there is no saved program counter across log entries. Each demon's subroutines communicate via shared variables. The subroutines can simulate multiple demon instances using arrays of saved state, but this should be necessary only in exceptional cases.

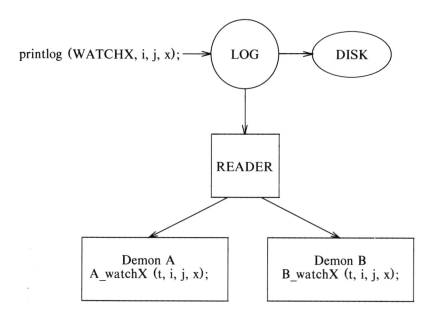

Figure 7. Log and Demon Scanner. Each demon contains a subroutine for each log entry it wishes to monitor. That subroutine is called with the same arguments as the `printlog` that generated the log entry, plus the time at which the data was logged.

The demon interface calls each subroutine with the logged data as arguments, in the same order as the `printlog` that created the log entry (Figure 7). Also, it records the time at which the `printlog` was executed. The format string does not have to be parsed to determine the argument types, instead, the logged data is dumped onto the stack (by a C routine) with the same byte packing the compiler generated for the `printlog` call that received the data.

Because of this, the demon log reader is very fast. Performance is limited by the speed of the demon subroutines and a maximum scan rate of about 750 integers/millisecond, which has proven more than adequate.

We also present a simpler, obvious interface to the log for occasional test programs — the analog of `scanf`:

`scanlog` (*LOGID*, &*arg1*, &*arg2*, ...);

`Scanlog` searches the log for the next entry of the specified *LOGID*, then returns the data. The format string must be parsed to determine the argument types so that the right number of bytes may be sent to each pointer. One pass over the log is required for each module that wishes to read the log.

3.5 Real-Time Debugger

The `rtd` (real-time debugger) program serves as the interface between the real-time system and the human controller. `Rtd` provides ways for the user to change program control inputs, initiate real-time operation, and analyze the logged data off-line.

`Rtd` operates on programs distributed across multiple processors. To distinguish between the entire program and the programs that run on the individual processors, we will call the individual programs "implementors." `Rtd` is not dependent on the implementors. At startup, `rtd` reads a list of implementors from a file. `Rtd` reads the directory of each implementor to self-configure itself.

`Rtd` has a relatively simple command parsing module. Commands are listed in a table containing the character string name of the command, and a corresponding function to call. Unique abbreviations of command names are allowed, for example, if `quit` is the only command that starts with a "q," then `quit`, `qui`, `qu`, and `q` would all be acceptable abbreviations. Batched command files, "for" loops, repeat-last-command, and a single parameter-less macro are implemented.

3.5.1 Remote procedure calls. To provide control over arbitrary functions residing in the implementors, `rtd` has a remote procedure call (RPC) facility [9] which is driven by user input. If a command name is not found in the normal list, `rtd` searches for it in data (read during the configuration procedure) associated with each implementor.

For example, the `Safe` and `Live` RPCs disable and enable robot motion (which is useful when testing new code); the `Effsp` RPC specifies a new value for the paddle's coefficient of restitution.

Each RPC is designated by an entry in a configuration file in the implementor's source directory. The entry consists of an command name, a procedure name, and a format string.

`Rtd` uses the RPC entry's format to determine what arguments are required, reads them from the command line, then sends a block of data to the implementor. The data is read by an RPC server running in the implementor (the server is a subtask within the implementor program), which calls the target subroutine with the arguments. When the implementor is compiled, a specialized program processes the RPC configuration file to produce a C source module used by the RPC server to determine what subroutine to call.

The RPC mechanism provides a clean and efficient mechanism for the user to control a collection of distributed programs that do not share address space. The configuration file decouples the `rtd` program from any knowledge of the details of the implementors.

3.5.2 Controlling real-time operation. The `rtd` program supports an access channel to the `chief` program, which sequences the multi-processor system's operation (we will describe `chief` shortly). When the user requests the initiation of real-time operation, `rtd` sends an appropriate message to `chief`, then waits for a response signaling the run's completion. At completion, `rtd` performs user-specified analysis of the just-completed run, which is why there is a "go" command instead of a "go" RPC.

The user may also request a free-running mode where `chief` will continuously cycle the system into operation. In this case, `rtd` is completely asynchronous to `chief`. The user may do any arbitrary operations while the system is in free-run mode, but there is no automatic analysis of runs, because `rtd` is oblivious to them. An RPC terminates this mode.

The `chief` program ensures that all implementors synchronously enter and exit real-time operation, allowing each implementor the chance to perform its own preparatory activities. `Chief` broadcasts state change commands to each implementor and waits for an acknowledge from each before proceeding to the next state. Any implementor may abort a run in progress via a descriptive message directed at `chief`.

The states in `chief`'s protocol are as follows:

1. Get-set — implementors begin preparing for execution, by calibrating, and by synchronizing clocks and communications.

2. Go — initiates real-time operation, which will continue until `chief` receives an abort request.

3. Stop — implementors shut down operations, purge communications; the robot is stopped.

4. Dump — causes an implementor to dump its log to disk. Sent to one implementor at a time to avoid overloading the host micro-VAX.

5. Idle — used between runs. RPCs most often arrive in this state; some are ignored unless the implementor is idle.

The chief program is implemented on a 68000 to gain access to some operating system primitives which are not available on the micro-VAX, and so that the protocol is executed promptly, especially when the system must be shut down.

3.5.3 Data analysis facilities. The rtd program is able to read the log files produced by the 680x0 processors and render them to a human-readable form. It reads the log entry description files from the implementors to obtain the contents of each entry. It corrects for the data size and byte ordering differences between the processor types.

The user may request log entries from any and all of the implementors to be displayed; rtd will produce them in their order of logging, using the timestamp written by printlog. Rtd can also produce a plot from two specified values in a log entry. For example, if the desired point of contact of the ball on the paddle is logged, rtd can produce the plot of X paddle contact point versus Y paddle contact point, which is a graphic view of the contact point wandering across the surface of the paddle.

Rtd contains built-in plotting programs designed to plot specific items in the log, for example, the cartesian command plots the arm position in various formats by reading the arm's logged encoder counts. These routines are invaluable in understanding what has happened without having to do time-consuming off-line analysis. Even though they are compiled into rtd, they are only marginally part of it. The list of commands is the only part of rtd that must be modified to add or subtract these tools, so rtd really is target independent.

3.6 Summary

The system design has been heavily driven by the requirements of real-time operation. There have been two main points. First, there must be a way of keeping accurate timing over the entire system, or the robot system would never be able to interact accurately with a dynamic environment. Second, we must have a way of recording and analyzing the system's operation off-line, if we expect to be able to get it to work. We described systems that meet both of these needs. Because of their application-independent nature, these approaches should find increasing use as more robot systems become truly real-time.

Chapter 4

Real-Time Vision System

The vision system is charged with the task of predicting the exact future trajectory of the ball through four-dimensional space-time. Given a time, it must be possible to compute the position, velocity, and spin axis of the ball. After a brief review of some current vision techniques, we will consider the environment, requirements, and basic low-level processing for the vision system. Subsequent sections will consider stereo, techniques for processing images with rapidly moving objects, the extraction of trajectories, and analyze the system's performance.

4.1 Current Vision Techniques

In this section, we will describe some existing areas of vision system research, primarily to show why they are not applicable, thus pointing out our criteria. In Section 4.2, our vision system will evolve naturally; here we wish to illustrate alternative strategies. Note that no matter what approach we choose, the vision system must "see" in real time — 60 Hz.

4.1.1 Image processing. Image processing algorithms take an image as input and produce an image as output, in some cases at the same time or with a very short delay. Such algorithms visibly run in real time, generating special effects for television shows. The processing is often a convolution operator to smooth the data or find edges. Special-purpose pipelined hardware processes the video stream [26].

Such algorithms are not directly useful for robotics applications, as they do not reduce the amount of information which needs to be processed, although they may simplify subsequent feature extraction operations. Reducing the amount of data to be processed without eliminating essential image content is fundamental to processing images in real time.

4.1.2 Binary feature extractors. Commercial vision systems process binary images to extract a variety of low bit count but useful features. Special-purpose hardware thresholds the image, run-length-compresses it to reduce the amount of data, then stores it in a conventional processor. Once stored, the data is processed for some tenths of a second to extract the features, to which statistical pattern-matching techniques are applied to make some decision. The canonical basis for these schemes is [29]; there are many current commercial imitators.

The thresholding that produces the binary image simplifies the separation of the object from the background. Binary images are only a short term aid to object/background separation, as future systems will be forced to process more complicated scenes where objects may obscure one another, causing a complex intensity distribution.

Binary images introduce a significant amount of aliasing, limiting the vision system's accuracy. In short, each pixel around the object's boundary may randomly be included or excluded from the object, depending on the pixel's exact intensity. Since there are relatively few pixels in the object, each such random decision induces substantial noise in the object's apparent position.

4.1.3 Image understanding. Advanced research-oriented systems read a gray-scale image into a frame buffer before processing it for several seconds, minutes, or even hours. Although these systems are slowly and steadily advancing in capability, their formidable processing requirements preclude their application to real-time robotics applications such as ours.

4.1.4 Motion interpretation. A considerable amount of research has been devoted to extracting the parameters of motion from a series of scenes of moving objects [59]. The two fundamental approaches are either to track the motion of individual features from one frame to the next, solving a correspondence problem resembling that of stereo vision, or to attempt to analyze the "optical flow" of the image due to the motion [33][52].

The analysis takes place off-line, and demands substantial processing time. Even still, simplifying assumptions about the motion must be made, in particular that it is slow and uniform, much unlike a ping-pong ball.

The recent work of Shariat [59] is entitled "The Motion Problem: How to Use More than Two Frames," meaning 3, 4, or 5 frames. By contrast, we will be using 20−30 frames. Bolles and Baker [11] considered dense sequences of 128 frames, but they assumed the camera center was translating linearly, without any motion in the scene.

The issue of what happens to the image due to the effect of the object in motion and the camera characteristics appears to be neglected. We will see in Section 4.5 that these effects may not be ignored.

4.2 Basic Approach to the Vision System

The vision system must not only operate quickly, but synchronously with the 60 Hz camera scan. The speed requirement imposes significant constraints on the algorithms which might be considered. We must be able to extract the ball's location from the image while looking at each pixel only once.

We must locate the ball to millimeter-scale resolution over a 1 to 2 m workspace, requiring one part in a thousand resolution. Since cameras provide only 1:250 to 1:500 resolution, sub-pixel resolution is required. We use four cameras to achieve a large field of view; they are organized as a close and a far stereo pair, respectively, the lower and upper camera pairs.

The accuracy can degrade at longer ball ranges, as long as the resolution remains high. At the long range, we still need good resolution to be able to compute the spin on the ball. When the ball gets closer, the spatial resolution and accuracy improve automatically. We need absolute accuracy better than 1 cm at the robot's end of the table.

The light on the ball is bright and diffuse: two 800 watt quartz incandescent lights with diffusers (Mole-Richardson Baby Soft-Lites). Because the lights are incandescent, there are no beat frequency problems between the cameras and the lights. We will have to correct for the lighting-dependent intensity distribution on the surface of the ball.

We must be able to separate the ball from the background image, which consists of the playing frame and the opponent. The table, background, and opponent are specified to be relatively dark (recall Figure 1). The stringent timing requirement eliminates structural analyses of the image at once.

The image differencing technique can not be applied for several reasons. First, the background image of the opponent changes constantly. Second, the shot noise in the video cameras, amplifiers, and digitizers requires that the digital image be low-pass filtered, or that we perform region finding.

Thresholding is the remaining logical alternative. The threshold is picked so that it is always brighter than the background. Thresholding requires careful attention to the environment design: we must eliminate all specular highlights. We use black velvet backdrops; the velvet has a "right way up" determined by the direction of the fibers.

If we produce a binary image by thresholding, aliasing around the ball's edges will degrade accuracy. The aliasing can be especially severe when motion blurs the image towards the background level.

Instead, we clip subthreshold pixels to zero, and translate pixels above the threshold downwards:

$$pixel_{out} = \max(pixel_{in} - threshold, 0) \tag{35}$$

The resulting system uses thresholding to suppress the background, but gray-scale processing to maximize accuracy.

The problem is thus reduced to locating the gray-scale centroid of the ball as accurately as possible against an entirely black surround. We process four images, one from each camera, 60 times a second. We base our approach on moments because we know how to compute them rapidly and they give the maximum possible accuracy.

We have ignored the problems due to the very dynamic nature of the images for the time being; we will discuss them in detail in Section 4.5.

4.3 Moment Generator

Moments have been in use in computer vision for some time [34][54], and their use in physics and statistics goes back much further. The equation defining the moments $M^{m,n}$ $(m,n \geqslant 0)$ of an intensity array $a_{i,j}$ is:

$$M^{m,n} = \sum_{i,j} a_{i,j} i^m j^n \tag{36}$$

where i is the column, j is the row, and $m+n$ is the *order* of the moment.

The zero through second-order moments are sufficient to find the area, center of gravity, angle to the major axis, and standard deviation along the major and minor axes of an object, approximating the object as an ellipse. These quantities may be used directly to pick up an object or to guide further visual processing. Second and higher-order moments may be combined to form invariants which are used to characterize an object; the invariants can discriminate among members of a set of objects.

The time required to compute gray-scale moments has hindered their use. On a VAX 11/780 with floating point accelerator, a direct calculation of the zero through second-order moments of a 256 by 256 pixel image takes 6.5 seconds. Straightforward hardware implementations of moment calculations require large numbers of multipliers, accumulators, registers, and supporting logic. Hybrid electro-optical approaches are possible [17], but suffer the same accuracy, stability, and dynamic range problems typical of analog computers.

The moment computation has been integrated onto a VLSI chip capable of computing a single zero through second-order moment of a 256 by 240 gray-scale image in real time (60 Hz). Since there are six such moments, the moment processor module contains six chips. We will discuss below a number of techniques that make the chip possible.

4.3.1 Power vector generation. We consider moment generation as a vector dot product:

$$M^{m,n} = \sum_t a_t p_t^{m,n} = (\bar{a}, \bar{p}^{m,n}) \tag{37}$$

where the elements of the vectors are in the same order as a normal TV scan: $t = i + 256j$. The element $p_{i,j}$ of $\bar{p}$ will be referred to interchangeably with p_{i+256j}.

The equation defining $\bar{p}^{m,n}$ is:

$$p_{i,j}^{m,n} = i^m j^n \tag{38}$$

The element $p_t^{0,0}$ is one for all t. The first-order moments require a counter for either X or Y, depending on the moment. Apparently, a second-order $\bar{p}$ requires two counters and a multiplier. We can write the next value of each second-order $\bar{p}$ as a function of the previous one:

$$p_{i+1,j}^{2,0} = p_{i,j}^{2,0} + 2i + 1 \tag{39}$$

$$p_{i+1,j}^{1,1} = p_{i,j}^{1,1} + j \tag{40}$$

$$p_{i,j+1}^{0,2} = p_{i,j}^{0,2} + 2j + 1 \tag{41}$$

with special cases for top of screen and left margin. We can build an iterative $\bar{p}$ generator composed of a single counter, a shifter, an adder, some AND gates, and a small control programmable logic array (PLA).

4.3.2 Bit decomposition. We can decompose $\bar{a}$ as:

$$\bar{a} = 2^7 \bar{a}_7 + 2^6 \bar{a}_6 + \cdots + \bar{a}_0 \tag{42}$$

If we substitute equation (42) into (37) and distribute, we obtain:

$$M^{m,n} = 2^7 (\bar{a}_7, \bar{p}^{m,n}) + 2^6 (\bar{a}_6, \bar{p}^{m,n}) + \cdots + (\bar{a}_0, \bar{p}^{m,n}) \tag{43}$$

Computing the dot products in Equation (43) requires only 1 by n bit multiplication, which may be implemented by n AND gates, where n is the number of bits in $\bar{p}$.

At the end of each frame, we must compute:

$$M^{m,n} = 2^7 F_7 + 2^6 F_6 + \cdots + F_0 \tag{44}$$

where

$$F_k = (\bar{a}_k, \bar{p}^{m,n}) \tag{45}$$

Equation (44) can be evaluated once per frame (60 times per second)

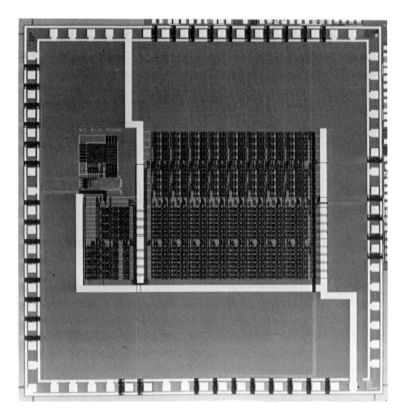

Figure 8. Moment Generator Chip. The F_k accumulators are in the center; the
   PLA and $\bar{p}$ generator are to the left.

using Horner's Method of polynomial evaluation [1]. The calculation is
performed by the processor which controls the moment generator system.

The F_k accumulators are identical, simplifying the layout of the chip.
The decomposition we used to obtain fast operation will be seen to provide
significant flexibility.

4.3.3 VLSI implementation. The techniques described above allow a
moment generating IC to be constructed [4][5]. Internally, the chip
(Figure 8) contains the control PLA and the $\bar{p}$ generator on the left side,
and a row of eight F_k accumulators across the middle and to the right. On

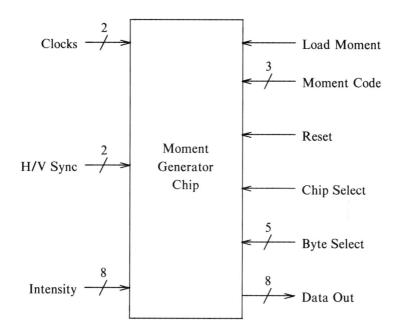

Figure 9. Moment Generator Chip Inputs and Outputs. The camera interface is on the left; the processor interface on the right.

the far right is an output multiplexor. The chip was designed using the MULGA symbolic layout system [68]. The moment generator chip is fabricated in a TTL-compatible 5 volt 2.5 micron CMOS process, contains 10,214 transistors, and is packaged in a 40 pin ceramic DIP.

A high-level view of the chips is shown in Figure 9. On one side, the chip connects to a digitized video source. An eight bit gray-scale value and a two bit sync code constitute the video input. Data input is synchronized to a two phase non-overlapping clock. The sync code represents the pixel type as follows: 00 — image pixel, 01 — horizontal sync, 10 — vertical sync, and 11 — non-image blanking pixel. The vertical and horizontal sync signals last only a single clock pulse.

On the other side, the chip connects to a processor. Five address lines and one enable line are used to select one of 32 bytes on the chip (4 bytes per F_k times eight F_k accumulators) for presentation on an "open collector" output bus. The processor may also reset the entire F_k accumulator array, or load a three bit moment select code into a latch on the chip. The processor interface is asynchronous to the video clock.

4.3.4 Image preprocessor. Taking the moments of an entire picture is not generally useful, since the moments of multiple objects are smeared together. Moments must be taken of each object individually.

Because the F_k accumulators are identical and independent, we can use the same chip to compute the moments of more than one region at a time, assigning each F_k accumulator to a single region (possibly more than one per region, however). Since the number of F_k accumulators is the same as the number of bits in the picture intensity, we must sacrifice bits of precision per region to accommodate additional regions.

Suppose we would like to compute the moments of three regions simultaneously: one region to one bit of intensity resolution, another region to five bits of intensity, and the last region to two bits of intensity resolution. Equation 44 would then be performed three times:

$$M_1^{m,n} = F_7 \tag{46}$$

$$M_2^{m,n} = 2^4F_6 + 2^3F_5 + 2^2F_4 + 2F_3 + F_2 \tag{47}$$

$$M_3^{m,n} = 2F_1 + F_0 \tag{48}$$

The intensity data applied to the chips must be specially formatted by a preprocessor that works independently on each bit of the intensity.

4.3.5 Board-level hardware. The moment generator chips reside on a Multi-Bus® (Intel) board along with the preprocessor. Figure 10 shows a block diagram of the moment generator board, including the preprocessor. A separate board digitizes (but does not store) the analog camera data, extracts the camera timing, and provides an overlay plane which overlays the image being processed with computer-generated graphics.

The intensity map converts intensity values to the desired precision and alignment. The map may perform binary thresholding, intensity windowing, nonlinear response correction, or any combination of the above. The intensity map may be used to correct for scene illumination problems or changes.

The location map defines the region of activity of each F_k; a bit is on if that F_k is to be activated at that position on the screen. To reduce the size of the location map, and simplify the host's job, regions are quantized into 8 by 8 pixel blocks. There are two sets of maps; one map of each type is accessible to the processor for updates, while the other set is being used in the current computation.

For robot ping-pong, the intensity map is configured to implement Equation 35, clipping subthreshold values to zero, and translating suprathreshold pixels down. The location map is constructed to be uniformly receptive across the entire camera image.

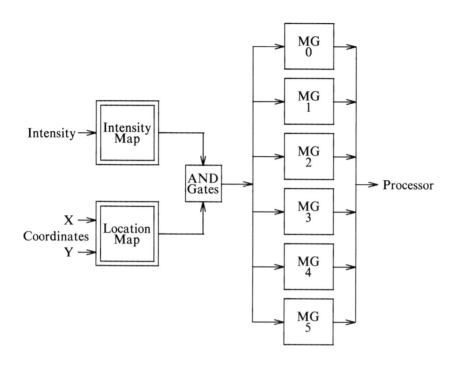

Figure 10. Moment Generator Board. The processor controls the contents of the intensity and location maps to specify what it will see.

We have to go through an entire sequence of operations to compute the moments of an image with the system: 1) set up the intensity and location maps, 2) tell the chips which moments to compute, 3) wait for the start of a frame, 4) clear the moment accumulators, 5) wait for the end of the frame, 6) read out the moments from the chips, and 7) do something with the moments. Operations 4) and 6) must be done during the vertical retrace interval, about 700 μsec.

For maximal utilization of the system, the operations sequence 1) to 7) is pipelined such that both operations 6) and 4) (in that order) occur during each and every retrace interval. While the processor uses one set of moments, the moment generators accumulate the next.

4.3.6 Summary of the moment generator. The approach described here trades flexibility for real-time operation. Conventional systems look at an image with pixel examination as their primitive operation. Because there are so many pixels, processing takes a long time. We should change our idea of what our primitive should be: rather than examining individual pixels, we can take a more holistic, gestalt view and examine whole areas of the picture. It may well be better to overkill with moments than use the gross underkill of pixel examination.

We were able to exploit the power of VLSI technology to implement a real-time feature extractor specific to a particular feature. We hope that a catalog of high-performance vision processing chips will evolve, adapting image understanding algorithms to real-time processing. Very powerful vision processors might then be built as a handful of chips.

The need to operate in three dimensions should govern the creation and selection of primitives for next generation systems. By using powerful image examination primitives, we should eventually be able to process images of complex three-dimensional scenes in real time.

4.4 Stereo and Calibration Techniques

Once the moments of the images have been computed by the moment generator boards, we can trivially compute the ball's centroid. The centroids are subject to certain corrections that we will discuss, but after correction, they are used to drive the stereo calculation, which results in the three-dimensional location of the ball.

In this section, we will describe the stereo calculation and our calibration techniques. We will then discuss lens distortion correction, which uses the residual errors from stereo calibration as its input data. Finally, we will derive compensations for the intensity distribution on the ball's surface.

4.4.1 Stereo calculation. The primary difficulty in current stereo research is obtaining the correspondence between the features in two images. Many elaborate schemes have been developed, the best known of which is that of Marr, Poggio, and Grimson [30]. In this approach, the search for corresponding features is constrained by matches in a lower resolution image, and by the requirement that the cameras be aligned such that the disparity can lie only along the horizontal axis. In this work, we do not have to worry about correspondence, since we track only one object, but we are not willing to excessively constrain the location of the camera. Since good depth information is essential, the cameras are separated by approximately a half meter. It is impossible to maintain good enough alignment to keep the disparity solely along one axis.

Accordingly, our stereo algorithm must be able to deal with arbitrary camera locations. We must know the object's location in task, not camera, coordinates. Both goals may be achieved by representing the camera position and orientation as a 4 by 3 transformation matrix:

$$\begin{bmatrix} u' \\ v' \\ w \end{bmatrix} = \begin{bmatrix} a & b & c & d \\ e & f & g & h \\ i & j & k & 1 \end{bmatrix} \begin{bmatrix} x \\ y \\ z \\ 1 \end{bmatrix} \tag{49}$$

where x, y, and z are the three-dimensional coordinates of the object and u and v are the image coordinates of the object such that:

$$u = \frac{u'}{w} \tag{50}$$

$$v = \frac{v'}{w}$$

Given two camera transformation matrices and two corresponding pairs of image coordinates, it is possible to formulate four simultaneous linear equations on the (x,y,z) location of the object, each equation corresponding to a plane in 3-space. These equations may be solved in closed form using least squares and Cramer's Rule [64].

This method is relatively efficient, especially when common subexpressions in Cramer's rule are merged. It does not give a truly "optimal" result, since this would require considering the joint probability distributions of the coordinates due to the imaging system.

4.4.2 Calibration. The cameras were calibrated by placing a computer-controlled lamp fixture in measured positions in the task workspace, then obtaining the image coordinates. A laser beam generates an accurate straight line along the long axis of the table. It turns out to be beneficial to use large calibration sources, rather than small LEDs, so that sub-pixel resolution may be obtained. We average over several hundred frames (processed in real time) to attain very precise results. We then formulate a system of linear simultaneous equations which yields the elements of the transformation matrices.

4.4.3 Interlacing. As was mentioned without explanation in Section 4.3, the vision system processes 256 by 240 pixel images at 60 Hz. The standard RS-170 camera scanning pattern specifies only 30 frames per second; each frame is composed of two fields. The fields interlace such that one field contains the odd video lines of the frame, and the other field contains the even lines. Since we wish to maximize bandwidth and minimize latency, we treat each field as a frame in its own right, resulting in 60 frames per second. As we will see in Section 4.5, there is an additional reason, related to processing rapidly changing images, which also suggests this approach.

By treating each frame individually, we have not sacrificed any accuracy, as the reader may observe that we are processing all of the information without throwing any away. We must compensate for the different location of each field's sensor array. Without a correction, the position data exhibits a distinct zig-zag pattern of several millimeters amplitude.

We achieve the correction by generating two distinct camera calibration matrices, one for the odd frames and one for the even frames. The hardware design allows us to determine the parity of the frames, so the implementation requires only bookkeeping.

4.4.4 Lens calibration. The lenses we are using exhibit considerable radial distortion. The lenses' focal lengths are 6.8 mm for the long range, upper camera pair, and 12.5 mm for the short range, lower camera pair. We have developed a simple calibration technique that does not require that any additional data be taken, require that the cameras be moved, or require specially placed patterns to be displayed before the cameras, any of which severely impede calibration. Instead, the lens calibration analyzes the residual errors after the basic camera calibration.

Lens and camera calibration are discussed at great length in [65]; it served as the resource for the basic distortion equations:

$$u_u - u_d = (k_1 r^2 + k_2 r^4) u_d \tag{51}$$

$$v_u - v_d = (k_1 r^2 + k_2 r^4) v_d \tag{52}$$

$$r = \sqrt{u_d^2 + v_d^2} \tag{53}$$

though what we will do with the equations is different. In Equations 51–53, u_d and v_d are the distorted (observed) camera coordinates of the object, u_u and v_u are the ideal undistorted coordinates, and k_1 and k_2 are the lens parameters we wish to find.

The inputs to the calibration process, u_d and v_d, are the observed coordinates of the lamps during the camera calibration. We obtain the corresponding ideal coordinates by applying Equation 49, using the measured physical lamp coordinates that served as input to camera calibration, and the camera transformation matrices that result from camera calibration. Figure 11 shows the difference vectors between observed and ideal positions of the calibration lamps, as viewed by the bottom left camera. The length of each vector has been multiplied by four to make it visible.

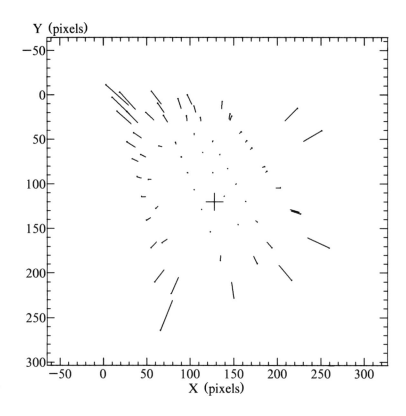

Figure 11. Lens Distortion Error Field. Lens distortion for the bottom left camera. Each vector points from the correct to the distorted position, but each vector's length has been multiplied by four.

Of course, the camera transformation matrix has been affected by the lens distortion, making the ideal coordinates less ideal. We apply the lens distortion calibration iteratively to eliminate this effect. We add an additional temporary distortion factor k_0 to the right-hand sides of Equations 51 and 52; k_0 is multiplied by r^0, that is, one. Once the lenses are calibrated, k_0 is zero and may be ignored.

The coordinates in Equation 51–53 must be relative to the camera optic axis, and must have a 1:1 aspect ratio. We use the techniques of Ganapathy [28] to extract the aspect ratio and camera coordinates of the center of the optic axis from the camera transformation matrices, then displace and scale the coordinates for lens calibration appropriately.

Let us now consider separating the lens calibration constants from Equations 51 and 52. We can write both equations as a single equation if we choose:

$$(u_u - u_d)\hat{i} + (v_u - v_d)\hat{j} = (k_0 + k_1 r^2 + k_2 r^4)(u_d\hat{i} + v_d\hat{j}) \qquad (54)$$

We are only concerned with radial distortion, so we take the dot product of Equation 54 with the normalized radius vector (from the camera optic axis to the undistorted position). By sensing only errors in the radial direction, we reduce the effect of other errors:

$$\frac{(u_u - u_d)u_d + (v_u - v_d)v_d}{r} = (k_0 + k_1 r^2 + k_2 r^4)\left[\frac{u_d u_d}{r} + \frac{v_d v_d}{r}\right] \qquad (55)$$

We have normalized the radius vector. The portion of Equation 55 inside square brackets simplifies to r, so our final equation is:

$$k_0 + k_1 r^2 + k_2 r^4 = \frac{u_u u_d + v_u v_d}{r^2} - 1 \qquad (56)$$

which is quadratic in $r^2 = u_d^2 + v_d^2$.

Figure 12 shows a plot of the error, from the right-hand side of Equation 56, versus the radius r^2. The curve resulting from fitting a quadratic to the data is overlaid. If the lens is relatively undistorted, for example our 12.5 mm lenses, the quadratic term k_2 just senses noise, and degrades performance. In this case, we fit a straight line: k_2 is zero.

The nonzero intercept of Figure 12 defines k_0. Once we apply the lens calibration to the input data taken during camera calibration, and repeat the camera and lens calibration, k_0 becomes quite close to zero.

At run time, camera coordinates are transformed to normalized coordinates, the lens distortion corrected, and the coordinates transformed back to camera coordinates, requiring 17 operations.

By formulating lens calibration so that we may use existing data, we have made it easy to apply. The lens correction is fast, simple, and accurate. Statistics on the errors remaining after camera calibration are shown in Table 1. Lens correction reduces the root-mean-square (RMS) and maximum error in the lower cameras' calibration (with 6.8 mm lenses) by a factor of seven. The upper cameras' improvement is less pronounced because there is less distortion to begin with, but lens calibration is still beneficial. After lens correction, both camera pairs have about the same RMS error, suggesting that we have eliminated lens-related effects. The lower pair is somewhat better since the ratio of viewing range to stereo pair baseline is more favorable. The remaining error is due to calibration fixture placement errors and vision system noise.

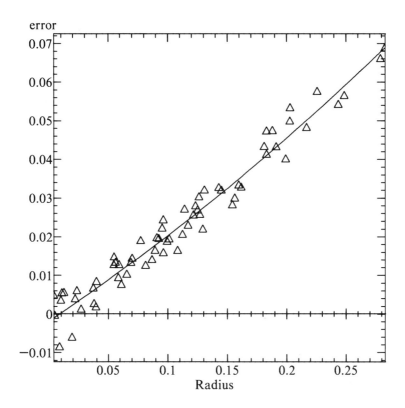

Figure 12. Normalized Radius Squared versus Lens Distortion. The plot shows the length of the error vector versus the distance squared from the optic axis. A fitted parabola is overlaid.

Camera	Uncorrected (mm)		Corrected (mm)	
	RMS	MAX	RMS	MAX
Even, Upper	1.58	3.96	1.12	2.53
Odd, Upper	1.58	4.01	1.14	2.56
Even, Lower	6.32	15.48	0.89	2.29
Odd, Lower	6.30	15.97	0.89	2.07

Table 1. Errors in Camera Calibration. The errors remaining between the computed and measured positions of the calibration points are summarized.

4.4.5 Lighting compensation. The vision system computes the centroid of the ball's intensity distribution. We need to know the ball's center of mass. The mass and intensity centroids do not coincide because the lighting is not isotropic, but strongly oriented towards the two overhead flood lights. The distance between centroids varies between zero and the radius of the ball, 18.9 mm; they are normally about 10 mm apart. This error is substantial compared to the system's other errors; we must compensate for it.

Our basic approach is to compute an initial uncompensated estimate of the ball's position, compute the location of the intensity centroid relative the mass centroid, then subtract the relative position from the ball's initial position estimate. The lighting calculations are done in 3-space, but the actual compensations take place on the camera image plane. After we have computed the corrections, we must perform the stereo triangulation a second time to find the final XYZ position.

We will first show how to compute the location of the intensity centroid, then how to map the problem into the image plane to make the corrections. We must use calculus for the derivation.

4.4.5.1 Parameterization of the problem. The sphere is illuminated by multiple lights that are distributed arbitrarily, but we assume we know their locations. Because moments are a linear operator, we can compute the offset due to each lamp individually. The weighted average of the offsets forms the centroid's total offset, where each weight is the intensity of the reflection of that light. We assume that the radius of the ball is small compared to the distance between the ball and the camera or light.

The amount of light reflected by a small surface patch may be computed from the cosine law [51], assuming that the surface is a diffuse reflector (which is visually evident):

$$I = L\, C_r \cos i \qquad (57)$$

where L is the incident lighting, C_r is the coefficient of reflection for the object, and i is the angle between the incident illumination and the local surface normal.

The incident light L does not affect the centroid offset for an individual light, so we will not consider it until later. The individual and total centroid offset is invariant with respect to the coefficient of reflection, so we can assume it is one.

We also notice that an individual light produces an error only along the vector from the ball to the light, never perpendicular to it. The offset is between zero and the radius, so we can use the radius as a normalizing quantity. We can compute a one-dimensional centroid offset between

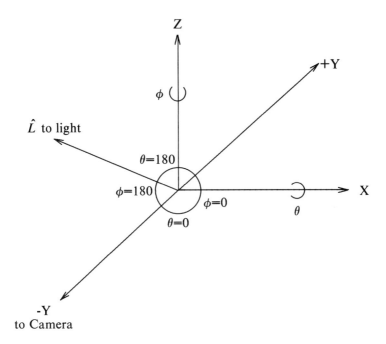

Figure 13. Coordinates for Lighting Compensation. The angle θ rotates about X, starting at $-Z$. The angle ϕ rotates about Z, starting at X. The light is in the YZ plane.

0 and 1 along the vector towards the light; then combine the offsets and relative intensities subsequently.

4.4.5.2 1-D centroid of intensity distribution on a sphere. We have reduced the problem to computing the one-dimensional moments of the ball's intensity distribution. We integrate Equation 57 over the surface of a sphere. The moments may be written:

$$M^m = \int_S I \, z^m \, dA \qquad (58)$$

where the coordinate system may be seen in Figure 13. The variable dA is the area of the patch. We have transformed the problem so that the camera is always at $-\infty$ on the Y axis, the ball is at the origin, and the light is in the YZ plane. The centroid offset then occurs along the Z axis as reflected by Equation 58.

The integral may be evaluated in the spherical coordinates (θ,ϕ) shown. The surface normal and area element are:

$$N_x = \cos\phi \tag{59}$$

$$N_y = -\sin\phi\sin\theta$$

$$N_z = -\sin\phi\cos\theta$$

$$dA = R^2\sin\phi\,d\theta\,d\phi$$

where R is the radius of the ball.

The incident illumination travels along the normalized vector between the ball position and the light, which is:

$$\hat{L} = (0, -\cos\lambda, \sin\lambda) \tag{60}$$

where λ is the angle in the YZ plane between the Y axis and the light. We assume without loss of generality that $\lambda \geqslant 0$.

We must also compute angle i in Equation 57, where i is the angle between the incident illumination and the surface normal; by Equations 59 and 60 it is:

$$\cos i = \hat{L}\cdot\hat{N} = \cos\lambda\sin\phi\sin\theta - \sin\lambda\sin\phi\cos\theta \tag{61}$$

The light illuminates only half of the sphere, so we must be careful to integrate over just the intersection of that half and the hemisphere seen by the camera. The choice of the coordinate system was essential to enabling us to evaluate the integral.

The hemisphere visible to the camera corresponds to θ between 0 and π. To find the hemisphere illuminated by the light, we find the points where the incident light is tangent to the surface by setting $\cos i = 0$ in Equation 61. The result shows the light to extend from $\theta = \lambda$ to $\theta = \lambda + \pi$. The angle ϕ does not affect the visibility decision.

We can assemble the integral from Equations 57, 58, 59, and 61:

$$M^m = \int_{\phi=0}^{\pi} \int_{\theta=\lambda}^{\pi} (\cos\lambda\sin\phi\sin\theta - \sin\lambda\sin\phi\cos\theta) \tag{62}$$

$$\times(-\sin\phi\cos\theta)^m R^2\sin\phi\,d\theta\,d\phi$$

The integral may be evaluated by MACSYMA [74] to yield:

$$M^0 = \frac{\pi R^2}{2}(1+\cos\lambda) \tag{63}$$

$$M^1 = \frac{2}{3}R^2(\pi-\lambda)\sin\lambda \tag{64}$$

The ratio M^1/M^0 is the scaled centroid offset we desire — the fraction of the ball's radius at which the intensity centroid occurs:

$$E_c = \frac{4(\pi-\lambda)\sin\lambda}{3\pi(1+\cos\lambda)} \tag{65}$$

4.4.5.3 Assembling the camera space correction. We will compute the correction in the coordinate frame of the camera. By [28], the camera calibration matrix (Equation 49) may be represented as:

$$\mathbf{T} = \begin{bmatrix} k_1 & 0 & u_0 \\ 0 & k_2 & v_0 \\ 0 & 0 & 1 \end{bmatrix} \begin{bmatrix} a & b & c & p \\ d & e & f & q \\ g & h & i & r \end{bmatrix} \tag{66}$$

where k_1 and k_2 are parameters reflecting the scaling between the world coordinates and the camera's pixel space, u_0 and v_0 are the position of the camera's optic axis in pixel space, and a through i and p through r define a homogeneous transformation matrix $\mathbf{T}_{ext}$ (Section 5.4.1). The matrix $\mathbf{T}_{ext}$ defines the relationship between the task coordinates and the camera coordinate frame.

First, we find the direction of the correction in camera coordinates:

$$\vec{l} = \mathbf{T}_{ext}(\vec{L}-\vec{B}) \tag{67}$$

where $\vec{L}$ is the position of the light in three-space, and $\vec{B}$ is the position of the ball. The camera coordinates are two-dimensional, so we set $l_z=0$, then normalize the vector to form $\hat{l}$.

The radius of the ball in this coordinate system is:

$$R = \frac{R_{ext}}{gB_x+hB_y+iB_z+r} \tag{68}$$

where g, h, i, and r are components of T_{ext}, and R_{ext} is the radius of the ball, 18.9 mm. The denominator (the distance from the camera center) shows the ball shrinking as it recedes from the camera.

The correction attributable to the light is then:

$$c_x = -k_1 E_c R \hat{l}_x \tag{69}$$

$$c_y = -k_2 E_c R \hat{l}_y$$

We adjust each camera's centroid (in camera coordinates) by the weighted average of c_x and c_y.

The weight of each light is proportional to the brightness of the image it generates, as determined by the ball's distance from the light, the portion of the ball the light illuminates (Equation 63), and the light's brightness. Other factors, such as the ball's reflectance, affect all lights equally and are unnecessary. The weight is:

$$inten = \frac{0.5\,I_L\,(1+\cos\lambda)}{|\vec{L}-\vec{B}|^2} \qquad (70)$$

where I_L is the brightness of the light.

4.4.5.4 Background light. We can also model isotropic background light that has reflected from the environment. Since the light is isotropic, the corrections c_x and c_y are zero. The intensity is a constant, most conveniently expressed as I_B, which is divided by the square of a nominal distance (as in Equation 70) to form the weight. This defines the constant I_B as the relative brightness of the background at the nominal distance from a light. In our environment, the background level is negligible.

4.4.5.5 Limitations. The intensity compensation assumes that the imaging system is linear, and to the extent to which it is not, the compensation will be inaccurate. The lens distortion, background threshold, and camera saturation all contribute nonlinearities, though saturation is only a problem for very bright objects. The camera must not perform gamma correction.

It might be possible to include the specular reflection terms in Phong's shading model [51] if it proved necessary, but it has not. Our high-quality ping-pong balls are excellent diffuse reflectors. Cheap ping-pong balls are noticeably specular reflectors.

4.4.5.6 Summary. The effect of the uneven illumination was surprisingly significant. We were able to compensate for it solely because of the simplicity of the sphere and because of the regularity of the moment computation. When trying to estimate a parameter (ball mass centroid, in our case), we would rather accurately know a slightly different parameter (a gray-scale intensity centroid), than inaccurately know a better estimate of the parameter we want. Fundamentally accurate data gives us the opportunity to apply a correction, as we have done here.

4.5 Imaging Dynamic Scenes

The images viewed by the TV cameras vary rapidly with time. Unlike our past experience in computer vision, a model of the camera's dynamic characteristics must be used to obtain accurate data.

In Section 3.3.1 we described the requirements for sensors to generate accurately timed data. Vision systems are no exception. We need to understand what the TV camera will output as a function of the scene, so that we can define a self-consistent object position and time.

4.5.1 Camera types. TV cameras are designed for relatively slowly changing scenes. The electrical output of a camera is a complex function of the time-varying light input over the time interval $(-\infty, now)$ that depends on the camera's design.

For example, vidicons have a decay function such that the output at any time might be affected by a bright image many frames ago; the effect resembles the persistence of CRT displays. Each point of the image is sampled at a different time as the beam sweeps over it, so a vertical bar moving horizontally results in a picture of a diagonal bar. This clearly makes the image interpretation process more complex.

On the other hand, CCD cameras operate as pipelined devices, integrating one image while reading out the previous one. There is no coupling from one image to the next, and no time-varying response characteristics. Every pixel is integrated over the same time interval, so the bar stays vertical.

Unfortunately, we use a third type of camera, MOS (Hitachi KP-231A), which has less well behaved timing characteristics. MOS cameras resemble dynamic RAM chips with sequential address generators. Each pixel is reset as it is being read out, therefore, the sampling interval is different for each pixel. The cameras change a horizontally moving vertical bar into a diagonal one just as a vidicon does.

Other camera types, such as CPD and CID, behave equivalently to the MOS cameras. We will begin by considering how to handle the ideal CCD device, and then how to treat MOS cameras.

4.5.2 Motion blur and integration time. A CCD camera's electrical output is proportional to the integral of the number of photons received during the sampling interval. In a static image, the photon count is proportional to the surface brightness of the scene in that direction. When the scene is dynamic, the photon arrival rate varies with time. The arrival rate must be convolved with the camera's sensitivity versus time, which is rectangular for CCD cameras.

Instead of trying to analyze the brightness versus time curve of each pixel, we shall instead consider what happens to the light emitted by each surface patch on the object. Each surface patch of a moving object will illuminate a whole region of pixels.

The brightness of each pixel watching a moving object decreases as the speed of the object increases, because each surface patch illuminates more pixels with the same number of photons per unit time. From the pixel's point of view, the object appears in its field of view for a smaller and smaller proportion of the integration interval.

In robot ping-pong, if the ball moves extremely fast (20 m/sec), the ball fades entirely below the clipping threshold and becomes invisible. This does not occur in normal play, however, pixels along the edge of the image doubtless do go below the threshold, causing the ball to appear to shrink.

If we take the moments of the smear left on the camera by a single moving surface patch, we get the average position of the patch during the interval of observation. If the velocity of the patch remains constant during the sampling interval, the computed centroid corresponds to the temporal center of the frame's sampling interval.

Since moments are a linear operator, the moment of two images' sum equals the sum of the images' moments. The moments of two patches tell us the position of the centroid of the two patches at the center of the sampling interval. The entire image is nothing but the sum of the effects of many such patches, to which the same result applies.

Consequently, the moments of an object moving at constant velocity tell us the position of the object at the center of the sampling interval. This important result is independent of the shape of the illumination versus time curve at any individual pixel.

We compute the centroid of the object from the moments, then assert that the effective sampling time, at which the ball occupied that point, is:

$$t_{sample} = t_{EOF} - \frac{t_I}{2} \qquad (71)$$

where t_{EOF} is the time at which the sampling interval ended, as determined by the `clox` board, and t_I is the duration of the sampling interval. For standard interlaced cameras, MOS or CCD, t_I is $2t_f$ or 1/30 second where t_f is the field time, 1/60 second, which we use as the frame rate.

Notice that we are computing only the object's intensity centroid. In Section 4.4.5 we saw how to find the ball's (mass) center of gravity.

4.5.3 Effect of acceleration. The ping-pong ball in our application is not traveling at constant velocity, but accelerated by gravity, air drag, and the Magnus Effect. In addition, the constant velocity assumption must be met not only in the three-dimensional world, but in the camera plane, which is even less likely in practice.

As a check, we have computed the error due to the acceleration. If the surface patch is following the trajectory:

$$p(t) = p_0 + v_0 t + \frac{1}{2} a t^2 \tag{72}$$

then the average position of the patch during the interval $[0, t_I]$ is:

$$p_{avg} = \frac{\int_0^{t_I} p(t) \, dt}{t_I} = p_0 + \frac{v_0 t_I}{2} + \frac{a t_I^2}{6} \tag{73}$$

The error induced by acceleration is the difference between p_{avg} and the actual ball position at the center of the sampling interval, $p\left(\frac{t_I}{2}\right)$:

$$e_{acc} = \frac{a t_I^2}{24} \tag{74}$$

An observed ball acceleration in the image plane from one typical trajectory was 5128 pixels/sec^2. Using Equation 74, we obtain an error of 0.24 pixels. At the center of the net, this would correspond to an error of approximately 0.5 mm. This error is acceptable, though we would rather it were smaller. If necessary, the image plane acceleration could be computed and Equation 74 used to compensate the observed centroid.

A final point is that when impulsive forces act on an object being tracked, such as when the ball bounces, no quantitative interpretation may be made of the image. It is best to delete such data points.

4.5.4 MOS cameras. As described earlier, MOS cameras reset each pixel as it is being read, thus causing the sampling interval to be different for each pixel. We must explicitly compensate for this effect. At 3.0 m/sec, the 16 msec difference in the sampling interval between the top and bottom of the image causes an apparent 5 cm shift in the position of the ball. The effect is especially noticeable when the ball jumps from the bottom of the far stereo pair to the top of the closeup pair, though it subtly distorts the data all of the time. We will ignore the minor effect due to X (65 μsec or 0.2 mm maximum), and consider the problem in one dimension only.

4.5.4.1 Scan rate effect correction. We will derive the correction by considering two surface patches, A and B, moving together at a constant velocity v. The video camera scans vertically at a rate s. Though we will derive the results only for two patches, the derivation applies recursively to describe the entire image, because moments are linear operators.

The positions of the patches, p_A and p_B, and the scanning beam p_S are:

$$p_A(t) = d_A + vt \qquad (75)$$

$$p_B(t) = d_B + vt$$

$$p_S(t) = st$$

where d_A and d_B are the positions of the patches at the start of the scan, where $t = 0$.

By setting $p_A(t) = p_S(t)$ and similarly for B, we can compute the times t_A and t_B when the scanning process intercepts the two patches. Note that the real scanning is the destructive readout mechanism; we are really talking about the center of the sampling interval, which occurred t_f earlier than the readout.

If the intensity of patch A (B) is w_A (w_B), we can compute the results of the gray-scale moment calculation observed by the vision system:

$$COG_{visual} = \frac{w_A p_A(t_A) + w_B p_B(t_B)}{(w_A + w_B)} = s\left[\frac{w_A d_A + w_B d_B}{(s-v)(w_A + w_B)} \right] \qquad (76)$$

Since the two patches are observed at different times, we have a problem in deciding upon the time to use. On general principle, a good guess would be a weighted average:

$$t_{stamp} = \frac{w_A t_A + w_B t_B}{w_A + w_B} = \frac{w_A d_A + w_B d_B}{(s-v)(w_A + w_B)} \qquad (77)$$

Now we will compute the actual centroid of the two patches at t_{stamp}:

$$COG_{actual} = \frac{w_A p_A(t_{stamp}) + w_B p_B(t_{stamp})}{w_A + w_B} = s\left[\frac{w_A d_A + w_B d_B}{(s-v)(w_A + w_B)} \right] \qquad (78)$$

A comparison of Equation 76 and Equation 78 shows that they are identical. Consequently, we have the position and time we need: at time t_{stamp}, the object was at the location specified by the observed moments of the image.

Obviously our choice of t_{stamp} was not accidental. To compute it, we observe that:

$$t_{stamp} = \frac{COG_{visual}}{s} \tag{79}$$

It is interesting that although COG_{visual} and t_{stamp} both depend on the object's velocity, as well as its relative position, we do not have to explicitly compute the image plane velocity.

When Equation 79 is applied to the entire image, COG_{visual} becomes the observed Y coordinate. Analogous to Equation 71 for CCD cameras, the sampling time for MOS cameras is:

$$t_{sample} = t_{EOF} - t_f \left(2 - \frac{y}{262.5}\right) \tag{80}$$

where $s = 262.5$ $(= 525/2)$ has been substituted, as this is the number of lines scanned per frame.

4.5.4.2 Scan-induced vertical image distortion. Although it is not a problem in our application, the skew in each line's integration interval causes the image of a moving object to be distorted vertically. This may be seen by computing the distance between the two surface patches:

$$p_B(t_B) - p_A(t_A) = \left(\frac{s}{v-s}\right)(d_B - d_A) \tag{81}$$

The image is compressed or expanded vertically by a factor of $\frac{s}{s-v}$. Even a moderate velocity of 10 pixels per frame causes $\pm 4\%$ distortion which would have to be taken into account by a program doing structural analysis of moving objects.

4.5.4.3 Application to stereo. When we apply stereo vision, we have two possible Y values, one from the left camera and one from the right, but we must have only a single t_{sample}. This illustrates a fundamental problem. The concept of stereo is predicated upon the assumption that we have two observations of the same body at the same position. Because the two cameras' effective sampling times differ, we have violated this assumption.

In practice, both Y values are similar since we have the cameras oriented predominantly in the same plane. We use the average of the two Y values to drive the t_{sample} calculation. It is also possible to use the observed camera-plane velocities and the difference in Y values to correct the Y values.

4.5.4.4 Camera interlacing. The complexity of processing dynamically changing images is a good argument against waiting for both interlaced fields and then processing them together as a single frame. Each field has a different integrating interval; by combining them together, we make it hard to extract accurate temporal information.

The first frame of video after the ball first appears is thrown away, because the ball was out of the field of view for at least part of the sampling interval. We must throw away the first two frames: the first for the odd field, and the first for the even camera field. We should similarly throw away the last two frames, though at present we do not. A frame should be thrown away only if it fails to be followed by another valid frame of the same parity (odd or even field). We can not wait two frames to see if the ball goes out of sight, but must plow ahead immediately, assuming that each frame is not the last. When we do find the last frame, we must cancel the earlier data at the last instant.

A camera without interlacing, i.e., only 240 lines of vertical resolution and an integrating interval of 1/60 second, would improve (reduce) latency, since only one frame would have to be thrown away. The reduced sampling interval would reduce the error due to an object's acceleration. We would not have to calibrate the odd and even video fields separately. The illumination required for a given output level remains the same despite the reduced sampling time, because each pixel may be twice as large.

4.5.4.5 Sensor droop. We have made the assumption that the camera sensing buckets do not exhibit leakage during the 33 msec sampling interval. This seems unlikely: dynamic RAM cells guarantee a storage time of only milliseconds, yet we expect accurate analog storage.

Leakage causes the latest photons to have a higher weight than earlier ones, manifested as a velocity dependent error. A rough compensation is to subtract an empirically determined fraction of the image plane velocity from the new centroid.

In practice, there does not appear to be a detectable amount of droop in our cameras, so we will not present the derivation. The derivation predicts the correction fraction as a simple function of the droop exhibited by the earliest photons that arrive in the sampling interval.

4.5.5 Summary. Tracking moving objects has been shown to introduce significantly more complexity than encountered in conventional static image processing. Interpreting a dynamic image sequence is certainly not just a matter of examining enough static images.

CCD cameras are seen to be highly desirable not only because of their geometric accuracy (which MOS cameras possess as well), but because only the CCD cameras enforce a common sampling interval. To reduce the sampling interval's length, we recommend non-interlaced cameras. When MOS or vidicon cameras are used in stereo pairs, align the cameras to keep the difference in sampling times as small as possible.

4.6 Three-Dimensional Trajectory Analysis

Once the position of the ball is being continuously generated at 60 Hz, the next visual processing stage is to fit a trajectory to the data, and predict the future path. The trajectory analysis process, performed by the `tranal` program, must take place each time a new data point is generated, rather than at the end of a trajectory, so that the robot plan may be continually updated. Accordingly, the analysis must be time efficient, precluding iterative searches.

The need for prediction imposes a great demand upon the trajectory fitting process. It is not enough to fit some high-order polynomial to the data; it will track the noise, and generate grossly unstable predictions. We must perform a noise-reducing fit, and use knowledge of the trajectories to perform the extrapolation.

The requirement for accurate treatment of the motion model is a distinct difference from prior work in motion interpretation, which typically makes a constant velocity assumption. The trajectory of a ping-pong ball violates this assumption immediately: the acceleration may be detected from three adjacent frames. The path of the ball deviates from a quadratic trajectory in 5—10 frames, and from a cubic soon afterwards.

4.6.1 Curve fitting. Let us recall the ball's equations of motion from Section 2.3.1, Equation 1. Given the velocity components v_x, v_y, and v_z and the spin vector w_x, w_y, w_z, the accelerations acting on the ball are a_x, a_y, and a_z:

$$a_x = C_d v_t v_x + C_m v_t (w_y v_z - v_y w_z) \qquad (82)$$

$$a_y = C_d v_t v_y + C_m v_t (w_z v_x - v_z w_x)$$

$$a_z = C_d v_t v_z + C_m v_t (w_x v_y - v_x w_y) - g$$

$$v_t = \sqrt{v_x^2 + v_y^2 + v_z^2}$$

The constant g is the acceleration of gravity, C_d is the drag coefficient, and C_m is the Magnus Effect coefficient.

Given a stream of ball positions, we must estimate the initial conditions $\vec{p}$, $\vec{v}$, and $\vec{w}$ which best explain the ball positions. We declare the reference time $t=0$ to occur at the time of the trajectory's first data point.

A preliminary investigation into applying nonlinear Kalman filtering to trajectory estimation revealed that the 9×9 matrix operations required would take too long for real-time operation. Kalman filtering might prove useful in off-line analysis to verify the aerodynamic model.

Instead, we fit a quadratic to the data for each coordinate axis, then use Equation 82 to compute higher-order correction terms which are used to pre-correct the sums for the quadratic fit of the following data point. Over several frames, we expect the corrections to converge to match the new data points, such that the corrections and the initial conditions are stable. The corrections make the trajectory appear to be a quadratic, since all the higher-order terms have been compensated. The quadratic fit sees what it expects to see — a quadratic.

Each quadratic fit minimizes the quantity:

$$E = \sum_t \left(x_t - p_0 - v_0 t - \frac{1}{2} a_0 t^2 - \frac{1}{6} j_0 t^3 \right) \tag{83}$$

where p_0, v_0, a_0, and j_0 are the initial conditions at $t=0$, and x could be any of the coordinates. We set $\dfrac{\partial E}{\partial p_0}$, $\dfrac{\partial E}{\partial v_0}$, and $\dfrac{\partial E}{\partial a_0}$ to zero, then solve for the initial conditions minimizing E.

We compute the corrections by evaluating the jerk j_0 $(\dot a)$ of each coordinate given the prior estimate of the initial conditions. Each of the equations to find the minimal E has a right-hand side of the form:

$$\cdots = \sum_t x_t t^k - j_0 \sum_t t^{k+3} \tag{84}$$

where k runs from 0 to 2, so the correction is simply effected. As new data points arrive, we accumulate the terms $\sum_t t^m$ for m from 0 to 5.

It is possible to compute more sophisticated correction terms by simulating the flight of the ball. The trajectory's quartic, quintic, and higher-order nature is then properly compensated. Although computing the corrections by simulation can and has been implemented in real time, the results do not support a prolonged discussion here. The simple jerk feed-forward performs better than the simulated feed-forward; we believe that this is due to the noise characteristics and to a probable mismatch between the equations of motion (Equation 82) and reality.

4.6.2 Estimating spin. Once we have computed the position, velocity, and acceleration estimates, we need to be able to compute the spin estimate, as it is really the velocity and spin vectors which determine the acceleration. The acceleration, jerk, and higher-order derivatives are dependent variables.

A cursory examination of Equation 82 might lead one to try to assign values to the accelerations and velocities and solve for the spin vector. Unfortunately, the equations are singular at all times.

The underlying physical explanation is that the Magnus Effect exerts a force perpendicular to the spin and velocity vectors. At any point in time, only the projection of the spin vector into the plane perpendicular to the velocity is detectable.

We should be able to recreate the entire spin vector by solving a system of equations describing the two components at each instant in time. However, we do not have time to do this. The technique's potential accuracy is unknown, though it is clearly a function of the trajectory. A high looping trajectory which maximizes the range of velocity vectors would give the best spin estimates; these are also the most dangerous trajectories.

In practice, we observe that most of the velocity is along the Y axis (the long direction of the table), therefore w_y is least detectable. By assuming that it is zero, we can solve for w_x and w_z directly from the equations for a_z and a_x respectively. We also use v_t in place of v_y.

As a consequence, the system may be caught completely unaware by balls with a large w_y. Humans have also been observed to exhibit this problem: watching the opponent's stroke can eliminate this surprise.

4.6.3 Extrapolation. We can extrapolate the future path of the ball by simulation, using Equation 82 and the computed initial parameters. A rather coarse timestep (0.1 sec) accelerates the process, resulting in errors of approximately 1 cm when applied to a trajectory the length of the table. The bounce can be predicted from the results of Section 2.3.2.

An undesirable consequence of our trajectory fitting technique is that the system is unable to describe unmodeled effects, such as the inaccuracy of Equation 82 and the residual geometric distortion in the vision system. Instead, the parameters are forced to "walk" in certain directions to attempt to compensate. The spin parameters are especially affected, causing inaccurate predictions of the resulting bounce. To ameliorate this effect, we weight later data points more than earlier points.

4.6.4 Segmentation and higher-level analysis. The trajectory analyzer must segment the ball positions into individual free-flight trajectories. Whenever the ball bounces, is hit by either player, hits a side wire or the net, the trajectory analyzer restarts the curve fitting process.

New data points are checked for consistency with the current trajectory, by extrapolating the current trajectory to the time of the new data point (remember that the data points have different timestamps which are not predetermined). A quite accurate comparison may then be made. The threshold to conclude that something has happened, and that a new trajectory should be started, is determined by a table entry. The table's input is the number of points over which the current trajectory has been accumulated. A single out-of-specification data point will be ignored, but a second outlier will cause a new trajectory to be initiated.

The trajectory analyzer keeps track of the back and forth course of the ball, awarding points as indicated by the rules of the game. A finite state machine with five major states monitors the ball's position: awaiting serve, before the opponent's bounce, after the opponent's bounce, before the robot's bounce, and after the robot's bounce.

At present, the decisions are made "on the spot" without waiting for additional data. Certain circumstances, such as determining if a ball hit a side wire and went left or right, could be more accurately addressed by waiting for further data.

4.6.5 Remarks. It should be clear that interpreting and predicting the motion of even a ping-pong ball is a complex task. We have created approximate ways to perform the task, suitable for our limited computational resources. There are a large number of individually trivial details necessary to achieve a robust performance.

It is our belief that it would be advantageous to apply the expert controller techniques of Chapter 7 directly to this problem. The expert controller could learn to generate actual spin values from the computed values, using an analysis of the resulting bounces to supply the correct answers. The expert controller could also carefully analyze the completed trajectory to assign a winner or loser. The `sai` task has been designated to perform this analysis.

4.7 Vision System Accuracy

In this section we will quantitatively analyze the performance of the vision system. Section 4.4.4 previously presented a description of the residual errors resulting from the camera and lens calibration process. We will present the results of a test of the vision system's static accuracy, then analyze trajectory data from moving targets.

Aside from Figure 14, we have relegated this section's voluminous figures to Appendix 2.

4.7.1 Static accuracy. The vision system's static accuracy was tested by placing ping-pong balls at measured locations in the workspace, then analyzing the balls' observed positions. By computing the average position reported by the vision system and comparing it to the measured position, we can assess the static accuracy. The standard deviation of the measured values reflects the amount of random noise in the process, or repeatability.

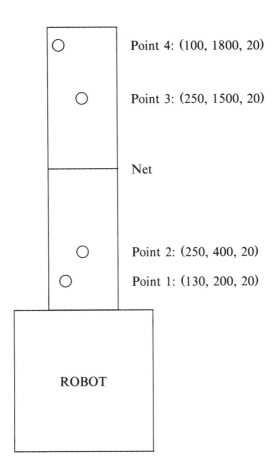

Point 4: (100, 1800, 20)

Point 3: (250, 1500, 20)

Net

Point 2: (250, 400, 20)

Point 1: (130, 200, 20)

ROBOT

Figure 14. Locations of Balls for Accuracy Testing. The view is from above the robot; X is to the right, Y is up.

Figure 14 shows the locations of the balls on the table. Two locations are visible to the top cameras, and two locations to the bottom cameras. The bottom cameras viewed an orange ball rather than a white one, to reduce camera saturation. "O" rings held the balls stationary. The placements have an uncertainty of about a millimeter. The X axis uncertainties are somewhat larger because we did not have access to the laser reference line we calibrated the system with.

Table 2 contains the results of the tests: the average error and standard deviation of the error for each ball placement. The error is defined as

Point	ϵ_x σ_x	ϵ_y σ_y	ϵ_z σ_z	Total σ_t
1	-0.64 ± 0.03	0.05 ± 0.04	-0.72 ± 0.17	0.97 ± 0.13
2	-0.41 ± 0.02	1.47 ± 0.06	-4.37 ± 0.14	4.63 ± 0.11
3	-1.53 ± 0.06	-0.28 ± 0.32	-0.39 ± 0.09	1.63 ± 0.05
4	-0.26 ± 0.11	0.68 ± 0.42	-0.24 ± 0.19	0.79 ± 0.43

Table 2. Static Position Errors (millimeters)

measured position minus actual position. Approximately thirty data points were taken by the system for each position before it correctly concluded the ball would not move again.

The repeatability data (σ) is seen to be quite good in general. The uncertainty increases with range as expected, except for position 1 which is "tucked in" underneath the cameras and is not localized as well.

The absolute accuracy data indicates that the bottom camera pair has residual errors. The errors, especially in Z on position 2, may be accounted for by the saturation that still occurs at that location. The calibration may also have been affected by the anisotropic radiation pattern of the calibration fixture's lights.

The accuracy of the vision system is still quite satisfactory. We have an average accuracy of 1 millimeter on stationary balls; the system's repeatability is better than 0.5 mm.

4.7.2 Vision system accuracy on moving object, no air drag. We will now consider the accuracy of the system on objects in free fall, without the interference of the atmosphere's drag or the Magnus Effect. Rather than evacuate the working area, we use a white steel ball with a diameter of 17.6 mm and a mass of 21 grams. The effect of the atmosphere is thus made negligible. In contrast, a ping-pong ball has a diameter of 37.8 mm and a weight of 2.5 g; it suffers 40 times more drag than the steel ball.

We throw the steel ball in the direction of the robot (with the robot instructed not to hit it). The resulting trajectory may be seen in Figure 56. We display the error between the predicted position of the ball and its measured position in Figure 57. The data reflects both our ability to make short-range predictions and the amount of noise in the vision system.

The vision system's error on a ball in flight at 4 m/sec is quite commensurate with the error when the ball is stationary (see Table 2). We are locating the ball to within half a millimeter. The accuracy is reduced at the beginning and ends of the trajectory, and when jumping from one pair of cameras to the other. A systematic increase in error at the peak of the ball's trajectory is not adequately understood.

We have no accurate, independent measurement of the path of the moving ball, so we can not compute the vision system's absolute accuracy. Instead, we can measure the acceleration of gravity (along the Z axis) and compare it with a reference value (Figure 58). The acceleration is latched at the nominal value, 9806 mm/sec^2, for the first four frames, glitches as the fitting begins, then converges towards approximately 9750 mm/sec^2. The top cameras' last two frames (which should be deleted) cause the estimate to temporarily degrade. The estimate gets very close to the nominal value using the lower camera data, but this is mostly accidental.

We conclude that we have measured g to 0.5%. The air drag may account substantially for the remaining error.

4.7.3 Vision system accuracy with drag but no spin. A catapultlike striking mechanism was used to launch ping-pong balls at approximately 3.5 m/sec with a 1 to 2 Hz spin, as measured with the SP-2000 video system. The trajectory exhibits air drag, but no Magnus Effect.

The errors between the predicted and actual ball positions are shown in Figure 59. The initial frames have higher errors because the ball is initially stationary, and because the curve fitting must settle. The gap in the data signals the transition between the upper and lower cameras; the bounce causes a large peak shortly thereafter. The prediction accuracy from the lower-right-hand "Total" graph is on the order of 1 mm.

The drag may be seen directly in Figure 60, which plots the Y axis acceleration of the ball. The accelerations shown for the first five frames are predicted on the basis of the ball's equations of motion, Equation 82; the subsequent accelerations are from the trajectory fitting process. The actual drag tends to be somewhat higher than the predicted drag on both the initial track and the data after the bounce.

A similar discrepancy exists for the Z axis acceleration, Figure 61. The trajectory fitter consequently believes that the ball is spinning at approximately 10 Hz, as illustrated by Figure 62. The bounce and paddle impact will be incorrectly predicted, resulting in a reduced success rate.

After the bounce, the ball's measured and predicted spin is about 13 Hz or 80 rad/sec, yet the vision system reports approximately 150 rad/sec.

4.7.4 Vision system accuracy with drag and spin. A Sitco RT-III Loop commercial table tennis training "robot" was used to launch balls at 3 m/sec with substantial top-spin. Actual measurements of the ball's spin are not available, but indirect evidence from a model of the trainer and analysis of the bounce agree on a 30 Hz (200 rad/sec) spin.

The observed values in Figure 63 appear to be in reasonable agreement after a settling period. However, notice that the spin starts out substantially above the predicted value, then decays. The decay process may be due to the simplified trajectory fitting scheme.

After the bounce, the spin is computed at approximately 200 rad/sec, yet we predict it to be closer to 160 rad/sec.

Our conclusion is that, regardless of the unknown cause, the spin value is consistently 50 to 60 rad/sec too high. The decay effect exhibited in Figure 63 complicates compensation. We believe that the errors are caused by the lack of adequate physics to describe the trajectory, and the simplified trajectory fitting method.

4.7.5 Operation in play. The final test of the vision system is its performance on live balls in play. We will examine the system's performance from the point of view of the expert controller, which is given the time, position, velocity, and spin at which the ball will cross the robot's end of the table (where Y=0). Because of the sheer volume of the data, we will examine only one shot in detail, and another only quickly. Additional information about the performance of the entire system, which of course involves the vision system, may be found in Chapter 8.

We will examine a stroke from the middle of one volley; we were not especially selective except to insure that it illustrate the features we wish to discuss. The trajectory is shown in Figure 64. The human opponent has hit a reasonably hard 6.1 m/sec shot at the robot (velocities are shown in Figure 65), which the latter has returned. The prediction error data in Figure 66 shows that at this higher speed, the RMS error is higher. Notice that after the robot's return bounces, the vision system can not see the ball until Y=1900. The ball's rapid motion across the image plane causes its brightness to go below the threshold. The error in depth is quite high as expected, since the ball is over 2 meters away.

The time at which the ball will cross the end frame is relatively stable, as shown by Figure 67. Similar curves for the crossing Z position, speed in Y and Z, and top-spin are shown in Figures 68, 69, 70, and 71. These graphs show what the expert controller has to work with.

As a final example of an even more challenging shot to return, consider Figure 72, which was hit with a high side-spin. The resulting lateral acceleration was about 2900 mm/sec^2, or 0.3 G. The curve of the trajectory is clearly visible in the Y vs. X display. From the machine's point of view, the vision system figures out fairly rapidly what is happening, as shown by Figure 73, which plots the predicted X crossing position vs. time.

During the first several frames, spin analysis is disabled until enough data is accumulated for meaningful results. Once the spin analysis begins, a quite accurate final crossing point is generated. At that point in time, the ball was just crossing the net. Some 0.3 sec later, backing off from the table as far as possible, the robot hit the ball back for a successful return, compensating for the reported spin.

4.8 Summary

We developed a stereo vision system which, due to its gray-scale processing and calibration techniques, provides accurate position data at 60 Hz. We found detailed models of the sensor and processing system which are essential to high performance.

Although the vision system was designed from the beginning to maximize processing speed, we have made it clear that speed alone does not suffice to generate accurate position data for rapidly moving objects. We derived explicit compensations for the temporal characteristics of the video cameras.

We developed a complex motion model to be able to generate accurate predictions of the ball's position. The ball's aerodynamics required that an unobservable vector, spin, be detected. By using feed-forward and iteration techniques resembling the expert controller's temporal updating (Section 7.3), we are able to generate accurate predictions of the ball's future trajectory even while it is moving at high speed.

The vision system could be improved by better models of the ball's aerodynamics, and possibly by correcting the camera calibration data to account for the nonuniform radiation distribution from the calibration fixture's lights.

Chapter 5

Robot Controller

We must specially design the robot controller for very dynamic control. In this chapter, we will begin by describing the robot's mechanical hardware, electronics hardware, and software architecture, to provide the reader the background needed to understand the remainder of the work. We will develop a (robot) trajectory generation scheme, analyze the robot dynamics so we can predict the robot system's performance, and finally, examine its performance on actual trajectories.

The robot controller tries to achieve predictable, and reliable, high-performance motions at the envelope of robot capabilities, unlike most systems, which plan conservative motions to avoid having to consider actual manipulator capabilities. We assume the task is sensor-driven (such as robot ping-pong), such that each motion is unique, and that motions will have to be changed while they are in progress. Consequently, we must rule out approaches based on learning or prior knowledge of the trajectory.

The robot controller must be able to evaluate the trajectories' feasibility in advance. It must compute quantitative information about the trajectories that will enable the expert controller to improve them — to increase or decrease their stress level by altering the task. The feedback process is essential to making aggressive use of a manipulator. A conventional system might blow a fuse or surreptitiously overshoot the target. As described, we want high performance we can count on.

5.1 Robot Mechanism

Let us begin the discussion of the robot by describing what it must do, as this will govern our selection of a robot.

5.1.1 Task requirements. The robot must be able to reach throughout an approximately half meter cube. Only five degrees of freedom are required because the paddle can be rotated about its normal vector, but the direction of this degree of freedom varies. A six degree of freedom robot is really required. The range of orientations within the working volume do not have to be isotropic, but need to be useful for the ping-pong task. The expert controller affords some flexibility here, because it can take advantage of whatever orientations are available. The accuracy requirement for proper placement is on the order of millimeters at the instant of contact.

The robot must be moving at 1−3 m/sec at the point of contact with the ball, after accelerating for 0.3−0.6 sec. At a bare minimum, accelerations of 0.5 G are required, though in practice they will be higher because the paddle is not directly accelerating along the final velocity vector, but must take a more circuitous route. Accelerations of 2.5 G are typical; much higher accelerations are sometimes needed. The accuracy of the velocity provides a lower bound on the accuracy of the return shot. An error of 20 mm/sec will cause approximately 1 cm of error after a 0.5 second flight.

5.1.2 Robot selection. As our interests and skills lie in electronics and software, rather than mechanical design, the decision was made early on to use an existing commercial robot, rather than designing one specially. This approach also lends credence to our claim that it is the robot controller, not the robot mechanism, which limits existing systems.

The fastest class of robots available at present are based on the SCARA design, for example, the IBM 7535 or Adept robots. However, they lack the six degrees of freedom required for this task.

Instead, we had access to a Unimation PUMA 260 (among others); with a reach of 0.4 m, it is a smaller and faster relative of the PUMA 560. The specification lists 1.0 m/sec as the maximum tool velocity, but the back-EMF-limited joint speeds range from 350°/sec for J2 (joint 2) to 2000°/sec for J6. For example, spinning J1 at its maximum rate would yield a tool velocity of 3.5 m/sec. Output torque ranges from 5000 oz-in (ounce-inch) for J2, which must bear the brunt of the gravitational load, to 600 oz-in for J6.

5.1.3 Robot configuration. The reach of the 260 is a bit small for the application. For illustrative purposes, the rectangular solid with the largest volume which fits within the 260's workspace is 400 mm in width and height, but only 100 mm in depth (radially from the robot).

In addition, it would be impossible to generate the required paddle speeds over a wide range of positions using the primary joints; the closer the paddle is to the arm, the faster the joints must spin. Most of the time, the paddle would be close to the arm. People have the same problem when ping-pong balls are hit straight at them.

To create a workable robot configuration, we put the paddle at the end of a 0.45 meter stick, mounted perpendicular to the axis of joint six. The stick enhances the reach of the robot, without significantly affecting its ability to tuck the paddle in for close positions. The configuration also allows a relatively slow rotation of joint six to generate the nominal striking velocity, and provides transit speeds of 5 m/sec or more as needed.

One consequence of the stick is that the load inertia, approximately 2 oz-in-sec^2, greatly exceeds the manufacturer's load inertia limit (in bold type, "NOT to exceed") for J6 of 0.5 oz-in-sec^2 and for J4, 1.0 oz-in-sec^2.

The robot is hung upside-down in order to keep the robot base (torso) from getting in the way, and so that the paddle can swing down on the ball, rather than having to be swung up (Figure 15). The paddle can be swung directly underneath the robot base as needed, so the primary working volume is obstacle-free. The robot position informally maximizes the working volume.

5.2 Controller Electronics Architecture

The existing controller for the 260, which was comprised of an LSI-11 and six 6503 microprocessors, was totally inadequate for our purposes. We have retained only the power amplifiers from the original controller. Slight modifications to the amplifiers increased the maximum torque for J4, J5, and J6 from one half the motor rating to nominal. We do not know why the manufacturer had derated them.

Our controller architecture is shown in Figure 16. The main processor is a Motorola 68020-based single board computer with a 68881 floating point coprocessor, currently running at 20 MHz. There are 2 MB of RAM on-board, with another 1 MB off-board. As discussed in Chapter 3, the robot controller contains a network interface and a clock synchronization (clox) board.

Two slave processors, named planet boards (Jupiter and Saturn) each control three joints apiece. The planet board was custom designed for this and other similar control applications. It contains a 68020/68881 daughterboard (in a 68000 socket), 32 KB of RAM, and an interface to another board type, the trident. The 12.5 MHz processor has a 16 bit bus with 3 cycle memory accesses. Since the main processor requires 4.5 cycles per access, the planet is not much slower.

Two trident boards reside in a second Multi-Bus card cage; each trident contains the circuitry to interface its processor to three joints,

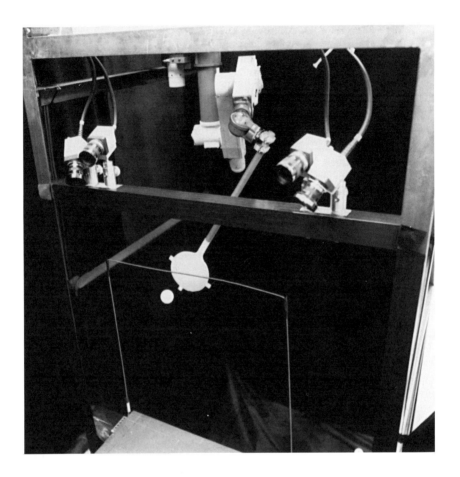

Figure 15. Robot Configuration. The robot is visible hanging upside-down just above the (1 m wide) horizontal camera support bar.

including optical encoder circuits and digital to analog converters. The `trident` boards in turn connect to the original robot controller.

A third specialized `planet` board contains a total of 56 KB of RAM and reduced I/O capability; it is used to execute background kinematics and dynamics calculations. Following the astronomical naming scheme, this processor is the `dwarf` (star).

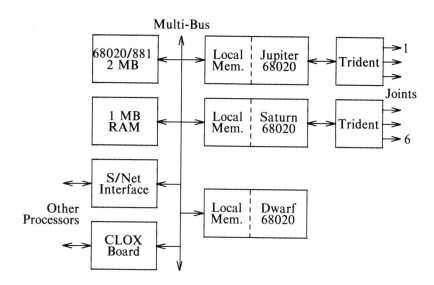

Figure 16. Robot Controller Architecture. The expert controller runs in the processor at top left. The `dwarf` performs background kinematics and dynamics. The slave processors can not access the Multi-Bus, but can be accessed from it. The `trident` boards are located in a separate chassis.

The `planet` and `dwarf` boards each present a portion of their memory as a shared memory area to the main processor. They may also generate interrupts to the main processor and vice versa.

Shared memory makes it easy for the main processor to oversee operations in the slave processors without loading the slave processor, to monitor the joints' average torque or tracking error. Some program variables that must be accessed by both host and slave may physically reside in the slave, reducing the communications cost nearly to zero.

The `planet` and `dwarf` boards have no ability to modify variables in the main processor, or in the other slave processors. Although this means that the main processor has to transfer some data among processors, it makes it impossible for a software error in a slave processor to destroy variables (and debugging systems) in the main processor.

There is no provision for the `planet` board or the main processor to lock out the other processor while it is updating shared variables, so simultaneous access conflicts must be carefully avoided. We must prevent conflict by separating the times during which the processors update the variables in shared memory.

The architecture provides substantial computing power for control, while minimizing the impact of its being spread across several processors.

5.3 Robot Software Architecture

We have built the robot ping-pong system on top of a substantial robot control package, which is implemented as a C subroutine library. The package was explicitly designed to facilitate the addition of new trajectory generators. Pointer-to-function variables make it easy to substitute new code for built-in functions. As this system serves as the basis of the robot ping-pong controller, we will provide an overview of it, even though the ping-pong system significantly alters some aspects of it.

The nominal package produces joint-interpolated and straight-line motions with continuous path interpolation and the ability to alter the robot's present motion in a well-controlled fashion. The motion generators and the servos interact at a synchronous 26 msec major servo rate. The motion generators must deposit a new target location into the servos' shared memory by the end of each major clock period. The joint servos run at an 830 μsec minor servo rate, interpolating the target locations to generate position, velocity, and acceleration setpoints. All three joints on each `planet` board are processed each minor clock cycle.

The Jupiter board (first `planet` board) interrupts the main processor each major clock cycle. The main processor reads some data out of the joint servos, then transfers control to the appropriate trajectory generator. After the trajectory generator has run, it may request a calculation by the `dwarf` processor by depositing an operation code in a control word. The trajectory generator terminates for that cycle. Meanwhile, the `dwarf` processor performs the requested calculations, then interrupts the main processor. The main processor transfers data among the processors as specified by the `dwarf`, for example, it downloads new gains to the joint processors. The main processor will terminate the motion if an error has occurred.

Although the structure appears convoluted, it minimizes the amount of work the main processor must perform. The main processor has good control over just what work is being performed, and can monitor the system's performance in real time.

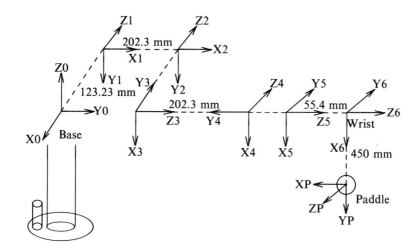

Figure 17. PUMA 260 and Paddle Kinematic Configuration. Each joint revolves about the Z axis of the previous joint. The arm position is (90°, 0°, 90°, 0°, 0°, 0°). We have suppressed some small offsets in the paddle mounting for clarity.

5.4 Basic Elements

We will review the basic computational building blocks used throughout the work, with attention to aspects which are different than standard practice. We will also discuss our motor model and back-EMF limiting.

5.4.1 Kinematics. The PUMA 560 robot's basic kinematic equations are well known [41]; only the joint lengths and offsets are different on the 260. The coordinate systems, joint numbers, and link lengths may be found in Figure 17. The figure also shows the paddle's mounting to the wrist.

We have three primary data types upon which the primitives operate: the Pose, the Transform, and the Config (configuration); each is a C structure. The Pose is comprised of the six joint angles a1 to a6. The Transform contains three unit vectors $\hat{n}$, $\hat{s}$, and $\hat{a}$, plus one unrestricted vector $\vec{p}$; it describes a four by four homogeneous transformation matrix T:

$$\mathbf{T} = \begin{bmatrix} n_x & s_x & a_x & p_x \\ n_y & s_y & a_y & p_y \\ n_z & s_z & a_z & p_z \\ 0 & 0 & 0 & 1 \end{bmatrix} \tag{85}$$

A `Transform` represents a six-dimensional position and orientation, often that of the robot's end-effector. Although the `Transform` contains 12 parameters, the $\hat{n}$, $\hat{s}$, and $\hat{a}$ vectors are mutually orthogonal and of unit length; they may be described by only three independent parameters.

The `Config` contains all the variables needed to quantify the robot's configuration: a `Pose`; two `Transforms`, one for the wrist and one for the tool; six feed-forward torques; six joint inertias; variables describing the arm configuration — above, left, and flip/noflip; the joint sines and cosines; an assortment of combinations of joint angles and link lengths; and a mode word that indicates which of the assorted data is really there. The arm forward kinematics solution produces a `Config` from a `Pose`.

The inverse kinematics routine takes a `Transform` and a prior `Config`, then produces a new `Config` whose configuration matches the prior `Config`. It is essential to match a prior configuration to ensure that the correct values of the joints are obtained: the range of both J4 and J6 substantially exceed 360° and there is no unambiguous *a priori* selection criterion for their values.

Once we have a `Config`, calculations of the gravity, inertia, Jacobian, and dynamics may proceed without recomputing many of the same quantities.

5.4.2 Gravity loads. Gravity torques are normally derived as a by-product of the arm dynamics equations, see [16][36][49]. By deriving the equations directly, we obtain a form which is particularly convenient to implement, even in the absence of full dynamics.

One complexity we will introduce is to derive the calculations assuming an arbitrary load. Most dynamics papers make the simplifying assumption that the center of gravity of the load is along the axis of the last link, however, this does not correspond to the more sophisticated loads now being manipulated by robots. It is a particularly poor approximation for the ping-pong paddle.

The basic equation specifying the torque exerted on a joint due to a single point mass is:

$$T_g = m\,(\vec{r} \times \vec{g})\cdot\hat{a} \tag{86}$$

where m is the mass, $\vec{r}$ is the radius vector from the axis to the mass, $\vec{g}$ is the gravitational acceleration, and $\hat{a}$ is a unit vector along the rotational axis of the joint. We can use the triple scalar product relations as needed to simplify the calculations:

$$T_g = m\,(\vec{r} \times \vec{g}) \cdot \hat{a} = m\vec{g} \cdot (\hat{a} \times \vec{r}) = m\vec{r} \cdot (\vec{g} \times \hat{a}) \tag{87}$$

The torque equation (87) is independent of the coordinate system in which the vectors are evaluated, as long as the vectors are all in the same coordinate system. A judiciously chosen coordinate system will simplify the resulting expressions.

The full derivation is too tedious to present here. However, the crux of the approach is to do the calculations in either the base frame or the frame of joint 1, so that the equations are expressed in terms of the components of the wrist coordinate frame, which is already available. The complete set of equations is summarized below:

$$T_{g2} = -Link2\,C_2 + T_{g3} \tag{88}$$

$$\begin{aligned}T_{g3} = &- Link3\,S_{23} \\ &- LoadX\,(C_1 n_x + S_1 n_y) - LoadY\,(C_1 s_x + S_1 s_y) \\ &- LoadZ\,(C_1 a_x + S_1 a_y)\end{aligned} \tag{89}$$

$$\begin{aligned}T_{g4} = &LoadX\,(a_{3x} n_{6y} - a_{3y} n_{6x}) + LoadY\,(a_{3x} s_{6y} - a_{3y} s_{6x}) \\ &+ LoadZ\,(a_{3x} a_{6y} - a_{3y} a_{6x})\end{aligned} \tag{90}$$

$$\hat{a}_3 = (C_1 S_{23},\ S_1 S_{23},\ C_{23}) \tag{91}$$

$$T_{g5} = (\,-LoadX\,C_6 + LoadY\,S_6)\,a_z + LoadZ\,(n_z C_6 - s_z S_6) \tag{92}$$

$$T_{g6} = LoadX\,s_{6z} + LoadY\,n_{6z} \tag{93}$$

$$Link2 = m_2 gr_2 + m_3 gd_4 + m_L ga_2 \tag{94}$$

$$Link3 = m_3 gr_3 + m_L gd_4 \tag{95}$$

$$LoadX = m_L gr_x \tag{96}$$

$$LoadY = m_L gr_y \tag{97}$$

$$LoadZ = m_L gr_z \tag{98}$$

We directly measured the load (paddle) mass m_L and its position relative to the wrist $\vec{r}$. We obtained values for the robot parameters $Link2$ and $Link3$ by experimentally balancing the motor torques against gravity.

The gravitational torques may be computed at a cost of 46 operations for an arbitrary load, as compared to 18 operations assuming the load is symmetrical such that *LoadX=LoadY*=0. We assume the `Config` supplies the results of the 6 trigonometric functions.

5.4.3 Jacobian. The Jacobian and its inverse are critical to understanding the relationship between changes in the robot manipulator's joint angles and motions in the task's Cartesian space, and vice versa. The Jacobian is the partial derivative of the robot configuration with respect to each of the joint angles; it tabulates how the motion of any specific joint changes the robot's configuration.

We will directly compute the Jacobian in the task space, rather than first computing it in the robot space and then transforming it to task coordinates. Because many vectors are common among the joints and need be transformed only once, the total work load is reduced.

If $\hat{a}_{i-1}$ is the vector about which the ith joint rotates (following the right-hand rule), then the change in position per rotation in joint i is:

$$\vec{d}_i = \hat{a}_{i-1} \times (\vec{t} - \vec{p}_i) \tag{99}$$

where $\vec{t}$ is the position of the end effector (paddle), and $\vec{p}_i$ is a point along the joint's axis of rotation. The differential rotation vector $\hat{r}_i$ equals $\hat{a}_{i-1}$.

The arm's Denavit-Hartenberg matrices [20] serve as the basic resource for defining these quantities, see [41]. We compute the vectors in robot coordinates, then map them to the task coordinates (by multiplying them by a `Transform`), and finally evaluate Equation 99 to get the Jacobian. There are only three distinct $\vec{p}_i$ vectors, since J1 and J2 intersect at a common point, and J4, J5, and J6 intersect at the wrist triple point. One vector is the position of the wrist in task coordinates, which we assume is already known, and one of the other two vectors is zero. Because J2 and J3 are parallel, there are 5 distinct $\hat{a}_{i-1}$ vectors; two are trivial.

The final semantics of the Jacobian we compute are that the $\vec{d}_i$ vectors define how much the paddle tip moves for a unit rotation of joint i, and $\hat{r}_i$ specifies how much a unit rotation of the joint causes a rotation about each of the task coordinate system's axes.

5.4.4 Inverse Jacobian. The semantics of the inverse Jacobian are just the reverse of the forward Jacobian, and specify how much each joint must change for a given motion along the basis vectors ($\hat{i}$, $\hat{j}$, $\hat{k}$ for six dimensions) of the task space.

We follow the approach of [50], inverting the Jacobian in block format. If the Jacobian is evaluated at the wrist, the position and orientation are decoupled. The decoupling leads to a block of zeros in the Jacobian which greatly simplifies the inversion. Accordingly, our Jacobian routine computes the Jacobian at the wrist and at the tool tip simultaneously, at only a slight additional cost.

The Jacobian may be written as:

$$\mathbf{J} = \begin{bmatrix} \mathbf{J}_{11} & \mathbf{0} \\ \mathbf{J}_{21} & \mathbf{J}_{22} \end{bmatrix} \tag{101}$$

so that the inverse is:

$$\mathbf{J}^{-1} = \begin{bmatrix} \mathbf{J}_{11}^{-1} & \mathbf{0} \\ -\mathbf{J}_{22}^{-1}\mathbf{J}_{21}\mathbf{J}_{11}^{-1} & \mathbf{J}_{22}^{-1} \end{bmatrix} \tag{102}$$

We evaluate the inverses of the three by three submatrices numerically.

5.4.5 Inertias. The joint inertias vary as a function of configuration: consider the arm in a straight-out versus tucked-in position. We compute the inertias using a very "lumpy" model. The inertia for each joint is the sum of terms:

$$J_i = \sum_L m_L r_L^2 + J_{self} \tag{103}$$

where the index L is over the lumps, small but massive particles. We combine the self-inertias, including motor inertias, into a single value J_{self}. Rather than have distinct masses and radii which must be determined for the lumps, we have inertialike values that are the product of the mass and relevant link lengths. As the arm moves, we multiply these values by unitless joint sines and cosines, then add J_{self} to obtain the presently effective J_i.

The inertias of joints 1 and 2 are considered to be independent of the configuration of joints 4, 5, and 6. Joint 3 was empirically determined to be sensitive to the paddle configuration, accordingly there are terms dependent on the wrist joints. The inertias of joints 4 and 5 depend heavily on the paddle configuration. Joint 6's inertia is a constant since the paddle can not move relative to it.

The calculations resemble those for the Jacobian, because the same radii are required for both calculations.

5.4.6 Dynamics. A robot's dynamics reflect the relationship between the torques exerted by its actuators, and the robot's motion. The robot's mass distribution, configuration, and velocity all contribute to the dynamics. Technically, the gravity torques and inertias we have previously described are all part of the robot's dynamics, however, we consider the dynamics to be primarily the torques generated by the arm's motion. Just as a car's suspension must produce torques to maintain the car's attitude as it careens around a curve, the robot must counter the torques generated by its own motion.

Section 5.6.1 will present the dynamics equations, but for now we will just describe which parts we use. At present, only the coupling inertias to and from the wrist joints are computed. There are no terms among joints 1, 2, and 3, even though there is a term from joint 1 to joint 6, for example. The equations are based on those of [36].

In the future, we hope to use the full results of [36], including not only coupling inertias but centripetal and Coriolis effects as well. Timing analysis indicates that the dwarf processor will be able to handle the full load; we have simply not implemented it yet.

5.4.7 Motor model. The torque generated by a motor is proportional to the current through it [72]. For this reason, we use constant current amplifiers to drive the motor; the computer then specifies the torque to be generated. The motor's limited power dissipation and demagnetization flux restrict the current, and thus torque, to some upper limit T_{clip}.

During motion, the motor behaves as a generator, creating a voltage or electro-motive-force (EMF) which opposes further acceleration in that direction. As long as the constant current amplifier has an adequate voltage swing, this back-EMF is not a problem. Once the range of the amplifier has been exceeded, the motor can generate only a reduced torque. The maximum voltage is limited by the motor winding insulation and the amplifier's power transistors.

A prototype torque versus speed curve is shown in Figure 18. The curve may be described by T_{max}, T_{clip}, and k, such that the available torque is:

$$T_{avail} = \min(T_{clip}, T_{max} - kv) \tag{104}$$

where v is the joint velocity in rad/sec.

The relevant parameters are computed from motor and amplifier characteristics by:

$$T_{clip} = gK_m I_{max} \tag{105}$$

$$T_{max} = \frac{gK_m V_{max}}{R}$$

$$k = \frac{g^2 K_m K_e}{R}$$

where g is the gear ratio, K_m the motor torque constant, I_{max} the maximum safe motor current, V_{max} the maximum amplifier voltage, R the winding resistance, and K_e is the back-EMF constant (V-sec/rad).

With this information, we can and must plan the trajectories to avoid the back-EMF limitation.

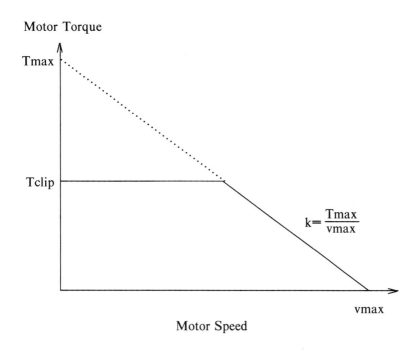

Figure 18. Back-EMF Limited Motor Torque. At low speed, motor torque is limited by the allowable motor current. As the speed increases, the torque begins to be limited by the amplifier's maximum output voltage. At vmax, the motor's generated EMF equals the amplifier's maximum voltage, and no torque can be produced.

5.5 Trajectory Generation

We must choose a representation for the trajectories the robot will follow. A representation's utility is measured by what may be done with it; given an instance of the representation, what properties of it may be described?

In this section, we will describe the requirements for the representation, compare several alternate approaches, including a brief look at biologic trajectories, then describe the characteristics of the chosen representation, quintic polynomials, in more detail.

5.5.1 Requirements. We will do our planning in joint space (rather than Cartesian, for example), because the limits on the robot's performance are expressed primarily in this space. For each joint, the data specifying the trajectory is: the initial position p_i, the initial velocity v_i, the initial acceleration a_i, the final position p_f, the final velocity v_f, the final acceleration a_f, and the time of flight t_f. The initial time is always assumed to be zero. In our case, the final acceleration a_f will always be zero, because we are trying to attain a designated final velocity and position. By maintaining the final acceleration at zero, we minimize the velocity's sensitivity to slight errors in the final time.

5.5.1.1 Degrees of freedom. The representation must have at least seven degrees of freedom to accommodate p_i, v_i, a_i, p_f, v_f, a_f, and t_f. Given these seven values, it must be possible to completely define the trajectory. This bound eliminates some representations with too few degrees of freedom. Extra degrees of freedom are permissible, as long as there is a reasonable way to generate and refine their values under the auspices of the expert controller.

5.5.1.2 Continuity. The trajectory's position, velocity, and acceleration should be continuous. A continuous acceleration not only reduces the generation of higher-order vibrations in the arm, but prevents the planning system from believing that the acceleration can be changed instantaneously.

5.5.1.3 Malleability. As new sensor data arrives, we will be constantly modifying the terminal characteristics of the trajectory. The old trajectory must be continuous with the new trajectory, and must be well behaved even for substantially different targets. We must be able to predict the parameters of the transition. Simple transition-window schemes that linearly interpolate between one trajectory and another are not satisfactory. In some cases, the time between alterations may even be less than any reasonable transition time. The robot ping-pong task generates new trajectories every 50 msec.

Notice that we do not assume that the system simply servos at a sensor-supplied position, which does not require trajectory planning. Sensor-induced updates may arise very early in the motion when the manipulator is still close to the starting point; the trajectory planner must smoothly alter its destination. Sensors may even indicate that an entirely different sequence of motions may be necessary, so we must be able to entirely retract a planned motion if needed.

5.5.1.4 Peak acceleration. Before we have planned the trajectory, we would like to be able to compute an estimated maximum acceleration. Once a trajectory has been planned, we must be able to compute the maximum and minimum accelerations, so that we can determine if the robot will be able to execute the motion.

5.5.1.5 Peak position and velocity. We must be able to compute the maximum and minimum positions and velocities once we have planned a trajectory. The position limits help determine if the robot will collide with any obstacles. The velocity limits may be used to determine if the back-EMF limit may be a problem.

5.5.1.6 Acceleration-minimizing position and velocity. If the maximum actuator performance limit is being approached, the expert controller needs to know how to modify a proposed trajectory to minimize its acceleration requirements. Given a specified motion, we must know what final position would minimize the maximum acceleration (leaving the final velocity unchanged), and what final velocity would minimize the maximum acceleration (leaving the final position unchanged).

5.5.1.7 Back-EMF limitation. A way to explicitly treat the motor back-EMF limitation is desirable, otherwise, a coarser worst-case analysis must be applied, preventing the full use of the machine's capability.

5.5.2 Introduction and comparison of trajectory types. The most fundamental measure of a trajectory type is how far it can drive the robot in a certain period of time, without exceeding any of the constraints. Figure 19 compares four trajectory types by displaying the maximum displacement that may be obtained by starting from rest, moving, and returning to rest. Joint 6, on which the plot is based, has a range of 530°. The trajectories, in order of the distance traveled from farthest to shortest, are as follows: full power, trapezoidal velocity with bang-bang acceleration, quintic polynomials with EMF avoidance, and quintic polynomials with worst-case EMF assumptions. We will discuss each trajectory type, then briefly examine biologic trajectories.

5.5.2.1 Full power. Let us consider applying full power to the motor, allowing it to ramp up to the back-EMF limit, and then, at just the right instant, reversing the torque and decelerating at the maximum rate to a stop just at the end of the allowed time interval. Note that we can always decelerate at the full rate because the EMF is helping rather than hindering the amplifier. The resulting plot reflects the maximal performance of the robot, motor, and amplifier, giving a benchmark for further comparisons.

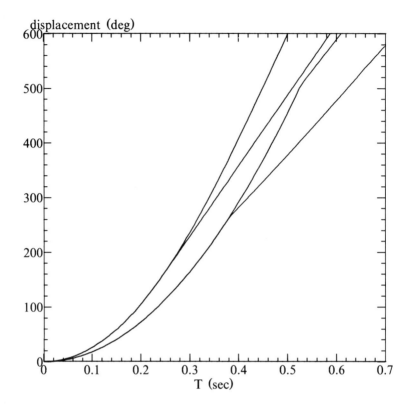

Figure 19. Comparison of Trajectory Types. The distances traveled along various trajectories are plotted as a function of the motion time. The trajectories encounter the plot's top edge from left to right in this order: full power, bang-bang, quintic polynomials with EMF avoidance, and quintic polynomials with worst-case EMF assumptions.

However, this scheme does not have enough degrees of freedom, is maximally discontinuous, and requires iterative approaches to identify key parameters. It has no provision for servoing during the course of execution, and in addition, since all of the actuator torque has already been used in one direction, there is no available correction if the actuator fails to accelerate as fast as expected.

It is a desirable goal to see if these problems could be mitigated without sacrificing too much of the powerful performance advantage. Faster computers and manipulators with more uniform characteristics, such as direct drive arms, would make this goal more feasible.

5.5.2.2 Bang-bang acceleration with trapezoidal velocity. A somewhat restrained version of the full power approach is to accelerate at the maximum rate, run at a constant velocity as soon as the back-EMF limit is encountered, then decelerate at maximum torque until the end of the motion, resulting in a trapezoidal velocity profile. This is the second highest curve in Figure 19.

To be applied, the acceleration must be smoothed by adding linear transition regions at acceleration discontinuities, complicating implementation and reducing performance from that shown in the graph. The allowable acceleration must be derated at lower speeds to allow margin for servoing.

The full generalization of this approach for arbitrary initial and final conditions would require a large number of cases and frequent switching between trajectory segments. The acceleration would not always be equal to the maximum in this case.

5.5.2.3 Quintic polynomials. Polynomials are a natural choice for a motion representation because their properties are well known, and closed form solutions may be derived for many of their properties. The derivatives are easy to compute, and may be represented in the same form.

To match the six degrees of freedom required for trajectory planning, we will use fifth-order, or quintic, polynomials. Others have proposed the use of quintic polynomials and cubic splines [19][49]. Only a single quintic polynomial is needed to represent the entire trajectory, so the trajectory is inherently very smooth and easy to evaluate. Quintic polynomials do not have multiple subsegments, as do quadratic segments or cubic splines.

A quintic trajectory is shown in Figure 20. As may be seen from the figure, the acceleration does not remain at its peak value for very long. There are several important consequences to this.

First, we can not go as far in a given amount of time; the bottom curve in Figure 19 is a quintic. However, since we do not count as much on the trajectory's peak acceleration, we need not derate the motor's peak acceleration to leave room for servoing, but can take full advantage of the computed peak motor acceleration.

Another examination of Figure 20 shows that by the time the velocity curve has reached substantial levels, the acceleration has dropped. We do not need to do back-EMF planning based on the maximum velocity, but can "shoehorn" a larger acceleration under the back-EMF limit. Consequently, the performance of a well-planned quintic can approach that of bang-bang acceleration, as shown by the third highest curve in

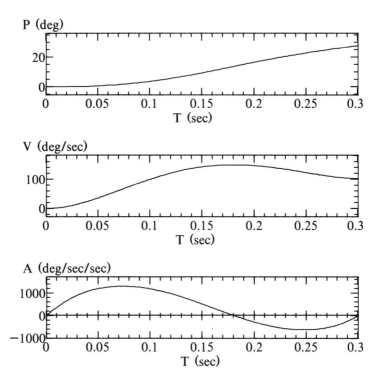

Figure 20. Example of a Quintic Trajectory. The joint moves 30° in 0.3 sec with a specified final velocity of 100°/sec.

Figure 19. We will examine the details of avoiding the back-EMF limit in Section 5.5.3.6.

The quintic attains 70 to 80% of the bang-bang trajectory's displacement for durations between 0.2 and 0.4 seconds. By 0.525 seconds, the two curves (Figure 19) are nearly equal. If T_{clip} is more than 47% of T_{max}, the performance of the quintic will exceed that of the bang-bang over some portion of the trajectory.

Because the bang-bang trajectory generator must smooth its acceleration curve to reduce jerk, the actual bang-bang curve is even lower than that shown, reducing any advantage of the bang-bang approach near zero. In light of the quintic approach's simplicity, it appears to be an excellent choice.

The expert controller will specify the start time, a duration, and a quintic polynomial for each joint. The global `clox` system serves as a reference for the starting time and duration. A temporally sorted queue arrangement in the robot controller allows several quintics to be concatenated to represent different stages of the task, such as wind up, coast during contact, and return to ready. When new sensor data causes quintics to be added to the queue, we flush any part of the planned trajectory that occurs after the new quintic's start.

5.5.2.4 Biologic trajectories. It is interesting to compare our robotic trajectories with biologic ones. Psychologists have studied aiming tasks where a person must rapidly position something (a cursor, arm, finger, *etc.*) within a specified target. The trade-off between motion distance, time, and accuracy may be examined.

Reference [44] proposes a detailed model explaining several observed trade-offs in aiming tasks. The model predicts explicit acceleration profiles which appear similar to measured biologic acceleration profiles, though the authors do not quantify the degree of fit. An example is shown in Figure 21, with an equivalent quintic shown as a dotted line. The equations describing the acceleration curve are too lengthy to justify including here; the interested reader is referred to [44] for details.

Although both trajectories start at the same time, the biologic profile does not begin accelerating significantly for some time, and consequently requires a higher peak acceleration and velocity. The biologic trajectory would suffer back-EMF problems much sooner than the quintic. Of course, the constraints on biologic actuators are much different than for electrical motors.

When the available motion time is relatively long compared to the distance to be traveled, or the accuracy requirements are high, biologic systems use multi-phased motions. Such motions are composed of a sequence of pulses of the shape shown in Figure 21, aligned such that the next pulse starts exactly in the middle of the previous one.

There appear to be many unanswered questions about biologic trajectories. Why do they have the shape exhibited, and what generates it? The equations for Figure 21 are quite substantial; it seems unlikely that a biologic system would be able to accurately evaluate the equations. Alternatively, we might ask if the experimental data justifies such a detailed function. The equations' complexity was necessary to satisfy an abstract model of the motion-time/accuracy trade-offs. A much simpler function might successfully explain the real data, rather than the model.

The biologic model also fails to consider how motions with controlled terminal velocities might be generated, as time-reversible force profiles are intrinsic to the model. Finally, it is not clear how changes may be

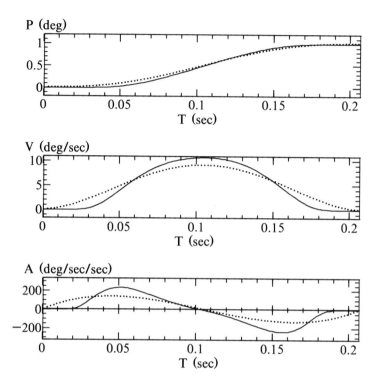

Figure 21. Biologic Motion Profiles. The solid curve is the biologic profile; the dotted curve is a quintic polynomial. Both trajectories start at 0 sec and last until 0.207 sec.

incorporated into biologic motions in progress. It is especially difficult to shorten motions composed of indivisible force pulses.

5.5.3 Properties of quintic polynomials. In this section, we will describe properties and uses of quintic polynomials that pertain to robot trajectory planning, and derive some useful results.

5.5.3.1 Delta position trajectory. The simplest motion is one where the robot begins at rest, translates a specified distance, and comes to a halt. Given a basic equation of:

$$p(t) = a_5 t^5 + a_4 t^4 + a_3 t^3 + a_2 t^2 + a_1 t + a_0 \qquad (106)$$

we apply the boundary conditions:

$$p(0) = p_i \tag{107}$$
$$v(0) = 0$$
$$a(0) = 0$$
$$p(t_f) = p_f$$
$$v(t_f) = 0$$
$$a(t_f) = 0$$

We can directly solve these equations, yielding:

$$a_5 = \frac{6(p_f - p_i)}{t_f^5} \tag{108}$$

$$a_4 = \frac{-15(p_f - p_i)}{t_f^4}$$

$$a_3 = \frac{10(p_f - p_i)}{t_f^3}$$

$$a_2 = 0$$
$$a_1 = 0$$
$$a_0 = p_i$$

The position, velocity, and acceleration curves of a canonical unit step are shown in Figure 22.

We would like to be able to compute the limits on the velocity and acceleration required to execute the motion. For this simple case:

$$v_{max} = \frac{15(p_f - p_i)}{8t_f} \tag{109}$$

$$a_{max} = \pm \frac{10\sqrt{3}(p_f - p_i)}{3t_f^2} \tag{110}$$

The maximum velocity occurs at the midpoint of the motion, but the maximum accelerations occur at $t_{maxa} = \frac{3 \pm \sqrt{3}}{6} t_f$. For simple applications, the inverted relation $t_f = \sqrt{\dfrac{10\sqrt{3}(p_f - p_i)}{3a_{max}}}$ may be of use.

From these calculations, we can see that the acceleration is predictably quite sensitive to the time of flight. The peak velocity is slightly under a factor of two greater than the average velocity.

5.5.3.2 Delta velocity trajectory. We can also define a trajectory which changes only velocity, but not position. Although this does not arise directly in practice, it shows the characteristics of more complex motions which change both position and velocity.

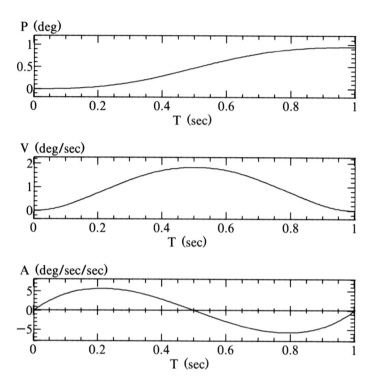

Figure 22. Quintic Unit Position Step. The position moves one unit in one second with zero final velocity and acceleration.

In this case, the boundary conditions on Equation 106 are:

$$
\begin{aligned}
p(0) &= p_i \\
v(0) &= v_i \\
a(0) &= 0 \\
p(t_f) &= p_i \\
v(t_f) &= v_f \\
a(t_f) &= 0
\end{aligned}
\tag{111}
$$

After setting the quintic polynomial and its derivatives to these boundary conditions and solving the simultaneous linear equations, we obtain a new set of coefficients:

$$a_5 = -\frac{3(v_i+v_f)}{t_f^4} \tag{112}$$

$$a_4 = \frac{8v_i+7v_f}{t_f^3}$$

$$a_3 = -\frac{6v_i+4v_f}{t_f^2}$$

$$a_2 = 0$$

$$a_1 = v_i$$

$$a_0 = p_i$$

Unfortunately, the limits on such a trajectory are uninformative unless $v_i=0$, so for the remainder of the section we will assume this is so. The position, velocity, and acceleration curves of a canonical unit velocity step are shown in Figure 23.

The maximum position excursion occurs at $t = \frac{2}{3}t_f$ with an amplitude of $p_{max} = p_i - \frac{16}{81}v_ft_f$. The displacement is linearly proportional to the velocity, and more interestingly, *increases* with the time of motion.

The maximum velocity excursion occurs at $t = \frac{2}{5}t_f$ with a value of $v_{max} = -\frac{64}{125}v_f$. The maximum accelerations occur at $t = \frac{7\pm\sqrt{19}}{15}t_f$, with amplitudes of approximately $-1.95v_ft_f^{-1}$, and $3.94v_ft_f^{-1}$. The acceleration increases linearly with the final velocity and increases reasonably when the available motion time decreases.

5.5.3.3 Matching position, velocity, and acceleration.

We can now examine the case of matching arbitrary positions, velocities, and accelerations at the beginning and end of the motion. The boundary conditions on Equation 106 are:

$$p(0) = p_i \tag{113}$$

$$v(0) = v_i$$

$$a(0) = a_i$$

$$p(t_f) = p_f$$

$$v(t_f) = v_f$$

$$a(t_f) = a_f$$

Once again, we set the quintic polynomial and its derivatives to the boundary conditions to obtain the coefficients:

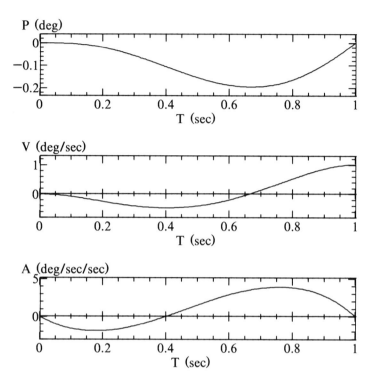

Figure 23. Quintic Unit Velocity Step. The velocity is increased to 1 unit/sec in 1 sec, while leaving the position unchanged.

$$a_5 = \frac{t_f((a_f-a_i)t_f-6(v_i+v_f))+12(p_f-p_i)}{2t_f^5} \tag{114}$$

$$a_4 = \frac{t_f(16v_i+14v_f+(3a_i-2a_f)t_f)+30(p_i-p_f)}{2t_f^4}$$

$$a_3 = \frac{t_f((a_f-3a_i)t_f-8v_f-12v_i)+20(p_f-p_i)}{2t_f^3}$$

$$a_2 = \frac{a_i}{2}$$

$$a_1 = v_i$$

$$a_0 = p_i$$

A fully matched trajectory is shown in Figure 24. Components of both the position and velocity step curves are present; also notice that the initial

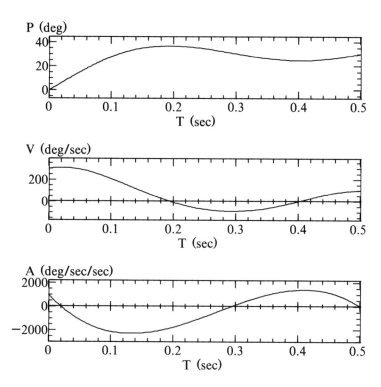

Figure 24. Matched Position, Velocity, and Acceleration. The position indexes 30°, the velocity changes from 300°/sec to 100°/sec, and the acceleration changes from 1000°/sec² to zero.

acceleration is nonzero. We use only trajectories where the final acceleration is zero, though if the task required it, we could easily make the final acceleration a variable.

The limits on the acceleration, velocity, and position curves must be found by numerically evaluating the coefficients (Equation 114), finding the zeros of the derivatives of the polynomial, and then substituting the resulting times back in to get the actual limits. The acceleration limits may be found easily by solving a quadratic, but the velocity and position limits require cubic and quartic roots respectively.

Although the solutions to cubics and quartics are commonly given [58], they tend to gloss over the implementation's details, such as how to avoid having to do all calculations using complex arithmetic, and how to detect and correct the failure modes. A better treatment may be found in [66].

The resulting implementations can pose a significant drain on the CPU resources, especially when they must be performed for all six joints.

5.5.3.4 Acceleration-minimizing final position. Suppose that a joint is near its maximal acceleration, and we wish to find the final position which minimizes the acceleration. Knowing this position, the expert controller can attempt to alter the task so that this final position is attained, thus minimizing the joint's stress. In this case, the boundary conditions are:

$$p(0) = p_i \qquad (115)$$
$$v(0) = v_i$$
$$a(0) = a_i$$
$$v(t_f) = v_f$$
$$a(t_f) = a_f$$

There is no constraint on the final position — we wish to compute it.

A straightforward attempt to compute the maximum acceleration as a function of an arbitrary p_f, and then to minimize this maximum over p_f turns out to be infeasible (using MACSYMA, [74]). The peak acceleration limits must be found using quadratics, and subsequent substitution and differentiation fail to produce useful results.

Instead, we pick an arbitrary time, t_j, to be an acceleration maximum, then find the t_j which minimizes the acceleration at that time. The equations then turn out to be solvable. We will not show all of the intermediate results because of space limitations, but outline the procedure involved.

To force the acceleration maximum to a particular time, we add a sixth constraint to Equation 115, setting the jerk $(\dot{a})$ to be zero:

$$j(t_j) = 60a_5t_j^2 + 24a_4t_j + 6a_3 = 0 \qquad (116)$$

With this constraint, we can solve for the six polynomial coefficients a_5 through a_0. Substituting the coefficients into the acceleration polynomial and evaluating it at $t=t_j$, we get the quantity to be minimized, namely, the greatest acceleration a_{max}. We then evaluate:

$$\frac{\partial a_{max}}{\partial t_j} = 0 = \frac{\mathbf{P}(t_j)}{\mathbf{Q}(t_j)} \qquad (117)$$

such that $\mathbf{P}$ and $\mathbf{Q}$ are polynomials. We can ignore $\mathbf{Q}$, and factor $\mathbf{P}$. The factors specify the times of interest t_j, and include 0, t_f, $0.5t_f$, and a lengthy unfactorable quadratic in t_j. Since the acceleration is prespecified at the end points of the interval (0 and t_f), those roots are not of interest. The root at $0.5t_f$ is the root of interest, because it is right in the middle of the interval, where we wish to minimize the acceleration. We choose to ignore the unfactorable polynomial altogether, although there is some chance that it might produce roots in the region of interest. If the initial acceleration $a_i=0$, then the quadratic is considerably simplified — to one which has no real roots. If worse came to worse, we could always numerically evaluate the quadratic, but there would be substantial calculations to produce a final answer.

The resulting acceleration-minimizing position is:

$$p_{a,\text{min}} = \frac{10t_f(v_i+v_f)+(a_i-a_f)t_f^2}{20} + p_i \qquad (118)$$

The peak acceleration is:

$$a_{p,\text{min}} = \frac{6(v_f-v_i)-(a_i+a_f)t_f}{4t_f} \qquad (119)$$

5.5.3.5 Acceleration-minimizing final velocity. We can similarly find the final velocity which minimizes the acceleration required to get to a final position at a specified time. We leave out the constraint on final velocity, restore the constraint on final position, and repeat the calculation. This time we find the important root at $t_j = \frac{2}{5}t_f$.

The resulting acceleration-minimizing velocity is:

$$v_{a,\text{min}} = \frac{44(p_f-p_i)-20t_f v_i+(3a_f-a_i)t_f^2}{24t_f} \qquad (120)$$

The peak acceleration is:

$$a_{v,\text{min}} = \frac{72(p_f-p_i)-72t_f v_i-(9a_i+2a_f)t_f^2}{25t_f^2} \qquad (121)$$

5.5.3.6 Avoiding the back-EMF limit. We would like to be able to compute the worst-case margin between the acceleration we are planning to demand, and the restricted acceleration that can be generated by the motors due to the back-EMF limit. The margin is:

$$a_{margin} = \frac{T_{max}-kv(t)}{J} - a(t) \qquad (122)$$

where J is the inertia of the joint. The variable a_{margin} will have a minimum at some $t=t_E$, it is this minimum margin we desire. If the margin is less than zero, the motion is unacceptable and must be replanned. Note that we gloss over some trivial details on the signs of the quantities.

The back-EMF limit is difficult to preplan because the time at which the back-EMF limit is most severe is not immediately apparent: it must be determined on a case by case basis.

If we concern ourselves first with a simple motion where $v_i = v_f = 0$ and $a_i = a_f = 0$, we can look at the fundamental principles. Figure 25 shows a variety of displays for the analysis of such a motion.

In the upper-left "Acceleration" plot, the antisymmetrical curve passing through (0,0) is the acceleration, a cubic. Only the central portion between -0.15 sec and $+0.15$ sec is relevant, as the motion is 0.3 sec long. In the bottom left graph, the velocity profile may be seen. Notice how rapidly the velocity and acceleration go to infinity if a software error causes the portion outside the main interval to be evaluated.

Immediately above the acceleration curve is the back-EMF limit, equal to the maximum acceleration $\dfrac{T_{max}}{J}$ (4000°/sec^2), minus $\dfrac{k}{J}$ (15.0 sec^{-1}) times the velocity (see Equation 122). As may be seen, the worst-case back-EMF limit is substantially below the peak acceleration, but this is acceptable since the back-EMF limit always remains above the acceleration.

The difference between the acceleration and the back-EMF limit is shown in the top right-hand graph of Figure 25; the derivative of this curve (jerk) is the bottom right "Peak Finding" display. The curve's zero crossings define the critical times t_E, which allow us to subsequently compute the EMF margin.

Above the back-EMF limit in the top left acceleration display is a quadratic approximation to the back-EMF limit, which is visibly a good approximation in the central region where the back-EMF limiting will occur. The difference between this approximation and the back-EMF limit is also shown in the two displays to the right; they may be seen to be good approximations in the region of interest (about -0.05 sec).

Based on this analysis, the worst-case time is found to be:

$$t_E = \frac{kt_f^2 - t_f\sqrt{\underline{k}^2 t_f^2 + 48}}{24} \tag{123}$$

where $\underline{k}$ is $\dfrac{k}{J}$. The back-EMF margin may be obtained by substituting t_E into Equation 122.

When the initial and final velocities and accelerations are not zero, the quadratic velocity approximation is not available. We are forced to substitute the velocity and acceleration polynomials into Equation 122, symbolically take the derivative, then numerically find the root t_E within the interval 0 and t_f. Since the velocity curve is quartic (the acceleration

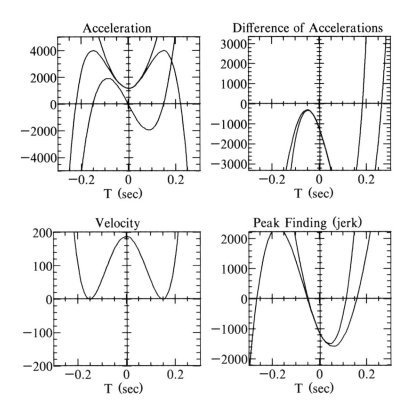

Figure 25. Avoiding the Back-EMF Limit. The figure graphically shows the determination of the worst-case back-EMF-limited time, at −0.05 sec. The trajectory lasts from −0.15 sec to +0.15 sec. See text for a detailed explanation.

is only cubic), we need to solve a cubic polynomial, which we can do fairly directly.

The benefit of this process is that on long motions, we can achieve 75% of the distance the joint would travel if the motors were at maximum torque, while keeping the joint under planned, servoed control.

5.6 Trajectory Following: Prediction and Control

Once a trajectory has been proposed, it must be evaluated to determine if it can be successfully executed by the robot, and then it must be executed as accurately as possible. Both stages draw on some of the same material, so we will discuss them both in this section.

5.6.1 Robot total dynamics. The torque at a joint of a manipulator may be written as [49, with additions]:

$$T_i = \sum_{j=1}^{6} D_{ij} a_j + \sum_{j=1}^{6} \sum_{k=1}^{6} D_{ijk} v_j v_k + D_i - F_i v_i - S_i sgn(v_i) \qquad (124)$$

where D_{ij} are the coupling inertias and D_{ii} includes the actuator inertia. The acceleration of joint j is a_j, D_{ijk} are centripetal and Coriolis terms, v_j is the velocity of joint j, D_i is the gravitational load on joint i, F_i is the viscous damping coefficient for joint i, and S_i is the intercept of the friction at rest (not the same as static friction, see [71]). The calculation of these parameters was discussed in Section 5.4. The function $sgn(x)$ equals $+1$ for $x > 0$, 0 for $x = 0$, and -1 for $x < 0$.

5.6.2 Feed-forward control. Our servo control is based on a PD (position and derivative) controller:

$$T = k_p (p_d - p_a) + k_v (v_d - v_a) + T_{ff} \qquad (125)$$

where p_d and p_a are the desired and actual positions, and similarly for the velocities. The gain constants k_p and k_v are chosen as high as possible to maximize tracking accuracy, but are limited by stability requirements, especially those due to nonlinear elements of the manipulator plant. We will discuss T_{ff} shortly.

An integrating term $k_i \int (p_d - p_a) dt$ is added to Equation 125 when v_d is zero to minimize the steady state error, but the integrator is disabled during motions because the trajectories are so dynamic that the integrator is a hindrance.

When disturbing torques act on the manipulator, Equation 125 is balanced by errors in position or velocity. This is undesirable, since the manipulator is constantly being subjected to such torques.

Instead, we feed-forward as many torques as possible using T_{ff}, so that only torques not so fed-forward affect the accuracy [3]. From Equation 124, we feed-forward terms due to the acceleration of the same joint and the other joints, gravity load, and friction. At present, we do not feed-forward centripetal and Coriolis effects.

We compute gravity loads and D_{ii} inertias at the 26 msec major cycle rate. We also compute the torque due to the coupling pseudo-inertias D_{ij} for $i \neq j$, using the acceleration at the midpoint of the 26 msec cycle. We change the feed-forward torques only once each 26 msec.

The joint servos execute the PD routine every 830 μsec, computing the feed-forward due to friction and acceleration (of that joint alone), then adding the feed-forward for that 26 msec cycle. This approach greatly reduces the computation required of the joint servo and the amount of data that needs to be transferred among the processors. The side effect is a small increase in the apparent disturbing torque.

5.6.3 Performance estimation. During the planning process, we must establish if a given proposed trajectory is feasible: can the robot actuators cause the robot to follow this trajectory, while still maintaining the accuracy required for the task? Knowledge of the manipulator's capabilities is essential to being able to drive the robot at the limits of those capabilities.

In Section 5.5.3.6, we discussed how to determine if an individual trajectory will exceed the actuator capability, based on the simple model:

$$a_{margin} = \frac{T_{max} - kv(t)}{J} - a(t) \tag{126}$$

where J is D_{ii} for this joint (i).

It is apparent from Equation 124 that the situation is considerably more complicated than Equation 126 would indicate. What we desire is that T_i in Equation 124 be less than $\min(T_{clip}, T_{max} - kv(t))$, which reflects the actual motor capabilities.

Following the approach of Section 5.5.3.6 again, we wish to compute the minimal margin against the EMF limit, and we also need to ensure that the margin against the maximum motor torque T_{clip} is not exceeded.

The first observation is that the coefficients D_i, D_{ij}, and D_{ijk} change dramatically with position. We would need to use iterative methods to be able to correctly handle this issue, basically simulating the trajectory. It is a long-term research problem.

Instead, we can simply take the maximum value of each parameter at the beginning and end of the trajectory. If more processor time is available, we could evaluate the parameters at the midpoint of the trajectory as well. We are clearly throwing away system performance by this simplification, and furthermore, we run the risk of not catching actual limit violations.

The terms $D_{ijk} v_i v_k$ result in eighth-order equations, which are hard to solve in real time. It is possible to approximate the octic polynomial with a quartic one, but the equations to compute the coefficients are rather substantial. Furthermore, we must compute the coefficients for all pairs of joints exhibiting significant coupling, aggravating the computational load. When using the full dynamics, it may be preferable to compute the coefficients of the octic product polynomial and use numeric techniques to find the relevant minima and maxima, rather than using the closed form solution we will develop. We are not computing D_{ijk} anyway, so we simply drop these terms. The static friction term is nonlinear and not that significant, so we drop it also.

We are left with the same basic form as the earlier Equation 122 that served as the basis for our description of how to avoid the back-EMF limit, thus justifying it. The only additions are the coupling inertia terms D_{ij} for $i \neq j$ and the gravity terms D_i, so we get a back-EMF margin of:

$$a_{margin,E} = \frac{T_{max} - kv(t) - \sum_{j \neq i} D_{ij} a_j(t) - D_i + F_i v(t)}{J} - a(t) \quad (127)$$

and a margin against the motor's maximum torque of:

$$a_{margin,T} = \frac{T_{clip} - \sum_{j \neq i} D_{ij} a_j(t) - D_i + F_i v(t)}{J} - a(t) \quad (128)$$

The minimum of both equations may be found by computing the coefficients of a_{margin} as a fourth-order polynomial, then solving the cubic to find candidate minima.

It is important to notice that we can solve these equations only because of the regularity and consistency of the polynomial representation.

In practice, we are currently ignoring the coupling inertias and friction terms in Equations 127 and 128, to the detriment of accuracy and benefit of computational speed. Furthermore, we compute the back-EMF limit only during initial planning, not during the subsequent updates (though we continue to check against the motor maximum torque).

Doing these calculations at all is essential, but the advantage of increasing the calculations' accuracy diminishes as their errors approach the errors in our knowledge of the machine's parameters (inertias, masses, frictions). Algorithms for accurately determining robot parameters are also becoming available [45][47], so we need to know how to take advantage of our knowledge of the machine.

We designed the controller architecture so that the expert controller could monitor the torques during arm movement, and tune the trajectory if the performance is less than expected. The comparatively slow rate of the expert controller's updates makes it unlikely that problems could be corrected at present, because a problem would probably not be detected until the acceleration was fairly extremal. The fastest peaking trajectories are most likely to be problems, and require the fastest response from the expert controller.

As robot control computers' performance continues to increase, we will be prepared to translate CPU cycles into increased robot performance.

5.7 Robot Controller Performance

This section's purpose is to give the reader a feel for the performance of the robot controller. We will first take a look at some "off-line" motions, then at the robot's performance on the ping-pong task, using live motions extracted from the data logging system.

We have placed this section's numerous figures in Appendix 3.

5.7.1 Directly specified motions. We will examine in some detail a motion from the joint angles:

$$(-62°, -192°, 160°, -23°, -38°, -8°)$$

to

$$(-14.1°, -225.3°, 185.4°, -89.9°, -58.8°, 23.8°)$$

which was extracted from the robot ping-pong system at one point. The first position is the "get-set" position of the robot between points, the second position was the computed hit position for a ball. Normally, joint six has a nonzero final velocity, but we will consider the motion from rest at one position to rest at the next. The motion's duration is 0.35 sec.

Figure 74 shows joint 1's performance executing this motion. Figure 75 shows joint 1 completing the same displacement, but while the other joints are stationary, eliminating the inter-joint coupling.

For both of these graphs and the graphs to come, the position error is in encoder counts, the velocity error is in encoder counts per 26 msec major cycle, and the D/A (digital to analog converter) value is in D/A units, which can range from -2048 to $+2047$. The position and velocity errors are both the desired value minus the actual value. The horizontal unit is the number of 830 μsec minor servo cycles. The D/A and velocity curves have been filtered twice by a non-causal FIR filter that takes the average of each 3 adjacent samples ($\frac{z+1+z^{-1}}{3}$). The statistics are computed before filtering.

Each joint 1 encoder count is 0.0077°, and 1 encoder count/major cycle is 0.29°/sec. The peak error is lower with all joints moving (Figure 74) than without due to favorable dynamics, but the dynamics result in a larger overshoot at the termination of the motion. From 500 cycles onward the joint settles back towards zero error.

Figures 76 and 77 show the same displays for joint 5. Each encoder count is 0.0114°; an encoder count/major cycle is 0.43°/sec. There is a dramatic difference in the shape of the curves due to the dynamics. Note that the corresponding curves without the inter-joint coupling inertias would be even worse. At the end of both curves, the integrator may be seen working to reduce the steady state position error. The friction appears quite high on this joint, at least in this location, and perhaps should be further compensated. Reference [45] discusses more complex friction calibration schemes that are able to cope with local effects.

Joint 6 is examined in Figures 78 and 79. An encoder tick is 0.014° and one per major cycle is 0.53°/sec. From Figure 79 it may be seen that the joint executes the motion reasonably well in isolation. The positive error before 200 counts in Figure 79 is interesting; it indicates a problem with backlash or joint flexibility. The joint has accelerated farther for a given torque than expected, so the motor/encoder must not be seeing the entire load torque.

Joint 6 exhibits a notable positioning error of approximately 0.78° in Figure 78 and a 13°/sec velocity error. The corresponding disturbing torque must be about 150 oz-in. Dynamics are certainly a major factor, but flexibility may also play a part.

5.7.2 Analysis of an actual hit. Figure 80 shows three orthogonal views of the trajectory of the paddle's center while hitting a ball. The initial position may be identified by the apparent discontinuity in velocity; it is at the bottom of the top view plot. The desired trajectory and the actual trajectory are overlaid. The hit position is identified by a triangle and a delta; the triangle indicates the actual position of the arm at the hit instant, the delta indicates the desired position. Both markers are superimposed in this display. The motion time is 0.3 seconds, somewhat shorter than the motion time in Section 5.7.1.

Figure 81 shows the Cartesian velocity of the paddle's center. Once again, the triangles show the hit instant; in this case the paddle was moving approximately 1.4 m/sec at contact. Most of the velocity is in the Y direction towards the opponent. The peak paddle acceleration is 2.5 G. The sampling rate for these displays is the major sampling rate, 26 msec.

The corresponding joint velocities are shown in Figure 82. Joint 6 can be seen to build up substantial speed while positioning for the hit, then run at constant velocity briefly in the vicinity of the hit. The other joints come to a stop for the hit instant, then accelerate to return to the get-set position in time for the next stroke's initiation.

The joint space position errors are shown in Figure 83 (actual minus desired positions). Although all of the joints have position errors, the errors are rather small. At the contact time, the total position error from all sources was 3 mm, while the arm was moving at 1500 mm/sec. The effective timing accuracy is 2 msec. The position errors of all six joints deflect the paddle normal by 0.25°.

Figure 84 plots the error in velocity. Spikes at 3.27 seconds indicate when a new set of polynomials was downloaded. The error at the hit time corresponds to approximately 40 mm/sec. The position and velocity error graphs may be translated as follows: first, the paddle was moving too slowly, then the paddle was accelerated to compensate, finally, it went past where it was supposed to be. At the contact time, the paddle was too far out in front and moving somewhat slower than planned. Individually, the joints are close to critically damped, so we are seeing dynamics or joint flexibility.

5.8 Summary

The robot control package has emphasized the generation of accurate and predictable motions, even though the desired motion changes every 50 msec. Quintic polynomials were used to great advantage to make a variety of calculations possible in closed form. The implementation's architecture offloads work to the slave processors, making almost all of the main processor's time available for planning. The resulting performance could be improved, but it is certainly adequate. As more processor cycles become available, we will continue to be able to increase the accuracy of the predictions and the resulting arm motions.

Chapter 6

Expert Controller Preliminaries

This chapter begins the description of the generic design of the real-time expert controller at the heart of the robot ping-pong player. Unfortunately, though the system's components are interrelated and integrated, we will have to present them in a linear fashion. In this chapter, we will introduce two elements of the substrate which underlies the overall expert controller. Most of the discussion will be ping-pong-independent, but we will occasionally use ping-pong as an example.

The first major topic to be discussed is the architecture of the program, which was designed to achieve some of the advantages of a rule-based system, while maintaining rapid execution. We will precede the discussion of the program architecture by reviewing the pros and cons of rule-based systems.

The second major topic is a specialized data structure which represents both symbolic and numeric data throughout the program. The data structure interacts directly with the program architecture.

6.1 What is an Expert Controller?

Before we delve into the substance of the chapter, we should consider a fundamental issue of nomenclature: what is an "expert controller?" The term combines "expert system" and "robot controller" to reflect a system that integrates elements of both. However, an expert controller is not a conventional expert system, so calling it an expert system confuses many people with prior expectations.

"Expert systems" are loosely defined. Expertise in some specific, challenging domain is a fundamental requirement. Expertise requires finding a high-quality answer in an efficient manner. In this case, the system's expertise lies in ping-pong. One expert system for speech understanding, HEARSAY-II, achieved the proficiency of a 10 year old, though this performance was still regarded as inadequate [32]. Although it is hard to assign an age to our robot ping-pong player's ability (since it can beat adults), our system certainly seems comparable.

In some sense, we seek a *skilled* performance. As Hayes-Roth, Waterman, and Lenat point out [32], "skill means having the right knowledge and using it effectively." The goal of applying knowledge to gain performance inspired our system. The expert controller's design strives to maximize the application of the (human or machine) system creator's knowledge to the mechanism's real-time control.

We have encountered some other signs of an expert system [32]: symbolic representations, graceful degradation, and introspection. Without having discussed the system in detail, suffice it to say that our system contains elements of these signs as well.

Our goal was not to create an expert system, but to understand the problem domain: how to apply the system creator's knowledge to real-time control. The resulting system may not fit everyone's definition of an expert system, but it combines aspects of expert systems and robot controllers. We call it — an expert controller.

As we described in the chapter's introduction, this chapter explains two fundamental expert controller components. The following chapter will further explicate the overall design. For now, let us regress to uncover some observations that guided the expert controller's design.

6.2 Rule-Based Systems

Conventional AI research often employs rule-based systems. An initial concept had been to try to use compilation techniques to extend rule-based systems into the real-time domain. In this section, we will discuss the pros and cons of rule-based systems in the context of expert controllers, leading up to the features of our system.

A rule-based system represents its information as a large set of IF–THEN rules. The rule-based system scans the list of rules until it finds an executable rule, executes it, then hunts for another rule to execute.

A *blackboard* is a common element of rule-based systems. The blackboard is a central repository for the program's data; any element of the program may examine the entire blackboard at any time. A small set of primitives arbitrates access to the blackboard. By contrast, a conventional program restricts access to program data in a hierarchical manner, such that unless the data is "global," data is available only to modules directly related to the data's creator. A conventional program may erase the data as soon as it no longer appears needed.

6.2.1 Support for rules in conventional systems. Rule-based systems have a number of advantages when applied to certain problems. The rules separate the knowledge base from the inference engine required to use it, allowing each to be developed independently; in particular, inference engines may be reused. The inference engine provides data matching and search algorithms which are task independent.

Global blackboards enable each rule to access any variable without regard to the program's structure (since there is none), so the rule base may take advantage of all available information. The data's longer lifetime (relative to the conventional program) lets more modules take "hints" by examining indirectly related data that might otherwise be deleted. Consequently, the program's output (the swing) can be more optimal. High visibility of program variables is a desirable characteristic.

Because each rule is complete in its own right, it is presumably easy to understand. The preconditions for an operation are not spread across an entire if-then-else hierarchy as in a conventional program, but localized within each rule. The preconditions are easy to understand and modify.

A rule-based system can provide flexible control. By merely manipulating a few variables, a nonlocal goto may be obtained without cries of protest from structured programmers, or the explicit designation of the target of the goto. Sudden changes in control flow are useful in exception handling, when a different activity must suddenly be scheduled.

The amorphous structure of rule-based systems implies the knowledge base may be trivially augmented by adding a few rules. Localized improvement — incremental programming — accelerates the knowledge acquisition process because the program's competence may be slowly increased while maintaining a working, testable system.

From a long-term research perspective, the most important advantage of a rule-based system is that the rules are usually in a machine-understandable form, often a LISP data structure. Future AI programs will want to augment their knowledge base, and to do so, the knowledge base must be in a machine-readable, understandable, and changeable form.

6.2.2 Real-time system characteristics. Transparently, a real-time rule-based system must be optimized for speed. The expert controller problem domain has specialized characteristics that affect the system design. The expert controller is intermediate between the deterministic, closed-form, numeric approach of standard robotics and the symbolic representations and emphasis on static problems in current AI. The expert controller must select among multiple strategies and cope with varying results, rapidly processing both symbols and numbers.

Most expert systems analyze a situation to uncover its causes. An inference engine proposes hypotheses and tests them for their ability to explain the facts. The inference engine works backwards from the possible outputs to the input, recursively exploring different explanations.

Real-time robotic systems require the synthesis of a plan. Because the system creates new data rather than examining old data, it is appropriate to work from the problem towards the solution. The inference engine need not be as complex. The data is known and fixed in quantity, eliminating the need for pattern matching between rules and variables.

On the other hand, a robot system requires more sequencing than a situation analysis system. Data dependencies among subtasks force one subtask after another to be solved, suggesting a data-flow architecture rather than independent parallel tasks. A rule-based system must implement sequencing with goal and state variables that obscure its original advantages of clarity and easy modification. Changing the sequence of a rule-based system can require global searches to find the affected rules, and may nearly require the complete execution of the program.

The expert controller domain also places much more emphasis on numeric calculation. Arithmetic in a rule-based system may require the user to use an "escape" to the language implementing the rule-based system (usually LISP), or the use of less powerful mathematical tools. The interaction between the numeric and rule-based parts of the program may be very restricted. Breaking a program into numerical and non-numerical pieces is detrimental to the program's simplicity, understandability, reliability, and ease of modification by man or machine.

6.2.3 Examples of real-time rule-based systems. Let us briefly examine a few of the trade-offs between speed, symbolic ability, and numeric ability that have been taken by some existing systems, thus highlighting some of the previous section's points.

The R1 system for computer configuration [43], which had no real-time constraint, ran at approximately 5 rules per second on a mainframe DEC KL-10. For real-time control, we would like to execute a rule on the order of every millisecond, two hundred times faster, on a microprocessor.

Depending on the requirements of the task, the expert system may be operated in a loosely coupled mode, where planning can be done in a non-time-critical fashion. Chande and Newcomb [18] proposed the integration of numerical spacecraft operations software, such as trajectory planners, with an expert system for higher-level control. (They also commented that "LISP ... can be embarrassing for real-time decision making.") However, ping-pong requires expertise applied to dynamically changing sensor data.

Foulloy *et al* [23] have prototyped a real-time expert production system for laser cutting. The rule base attempted to encode rules of thumb relating to the quality of cut. The rule base was quite small (30 rules) and was segmented into different classes which were selected situationally, so that only a few rules needed to be considered at a time. The use of states and the small number of rules to begin with made the complexity at any individual time small, so it remains to be seen how this approach would scale to larger problems. The system was largely symbolic with only a minimum of quantitative analysis.

Mamdani has developed a fuzzy production system for the control of cement kilns [42]. Although the application sounds low-tech, it is an excellent demonstration. The system provides a fuzzy interpretation for a set of control rules for the kiln. The rules are evaluated in a fuzzy sense each cycle, and a composite output generated. The system possesses a fixed mathematical framework which is useful for analysis but restricts its extension to more complicated domains. The approach deals with each variable individually, making coordination of multiple outputs difficult. There is no provision for internal state or sequencing.

6.2.4 Rule compilation systems. The concept for an efficient rule-based system was to compile the rules and a limited-function inference engine, commensurate with the capabilities outlined in the previous section, to a finite state machine resembling modern parsers. In any particular state of the finite state machine, only certain rules would be executable. Only the members of this set would be tested to see if they were executable, saving the time to test nonmembers. The compiler could examine the preconditions of the executable rule set to generate an efficient test order to select the desired rule. Most questions associated with test ordering are NP-complete (require exponential time to solve), so heuristics would be necessary. Rules would compute figure of merit values used by the inference engine to select the best executable rule.

In the final analysis, it turned out that an important principle was:

Why discover what you already know?

Even though sequencing constrains the program flow, the number of states can become enormous. The compiler must prune illogical states as they are generated to minimize the number of states. The pruning requires knowledge of the task's flow of control, which the programmer knows but the compiler does not. Rather than forcing the compiler to uncover the flow, it is better to provide the programmer with a way to specify it.

6.2.5 Final reduction. If an expert system's rules are successively divided into smaller and smaller sequential pieces, the finite state machine generated by a rule compiler has extended branch-less threads, and the machine's state becomes increasingly similar to the program counter of a conventional program. One expert system engine already compiles and then interprets its data structures [22].

Why should we not just use a conventional programming language to describe the rules? A single programming system can then describe the rule system and the arithmetic. A fast compiled language can rapidly execute the program. Readability and ease of modification may be obtained by appropriately structuring the program and data (even further than in "structured programming").

Even though the emphasis in this book is on semantics, not syntax, one advantage of a rule-based system is that the program is machine-readable. The possibility of incremental programming by AI programs may appear to be adversely affected by using a raw unconstrained language, as it might appear that the AI program might have to be able to understand a full programming language. However, this is not necessarily so.

First, the AI program presumably wrote the expert controller in the first place, or at least has been taught its structure, so it has significant independent information about the program. The AI program would not write any code it could not read. It can modify the expert controller by top-down synthesis, rather than having to do a much harder bottom-up analysis from the syntactic level.

Humans find it hard to understand unrestricted code, and consequently enforce constraints requiring *comments* in the code. Comments embed high-level information about a program in the same data structure, so that a human does not have to perform a tedious and error-prone analysis to understand what the code does. An AI program can similarly leave machine-readable comments delimiting and describing the program, so that it does not have to be able to read the source code.

6.3 Actual Architecture

We may now outline the expert controller's basic features. The expert controller is implemented in the programming language "C" [40], which provides efficient implementation of standard numeric programs. The architecture of the program and data structures constitutes the knowledge-base-independent inference engine, which still results in a machine-readable knowledge base as described in Section 6.2.5.

To provide the high visibility of rule-based systems discussed earlier, data storage revolves about a central blackboard that may be logically viewed as consisting of tuples:

⟨*symbol, value*⟩

The value may represent either some figure of merit for the strength of the symbol, or some numeric value as in (joint_1, 40.2°).

All possible symbols on the blackboard are unique, so each tuple may be represented by a variable that may or may not contain a value at any particular time, and a *note* that indicates whether or not it presently does contain a value. Notes and the variables are implemented as global data in the C program. Section 6.3.1 describes the note's implementation.

At a macroscopic level, the notes represent the state of the task: what data is available and what subtasks have been completed or need to be done. Notes are added and subtracted as the program executes. The program counter implicitly stores part of the state of the blackboard: program execution may reach a location only after testing some subset of the state. The program does not have to retest the previously tested state to decide what to do next. The program counter acts as a cache of the blackboard, providing a fast way of accessing often-used information. Other than in critical sections [60] which update data structures, the cache may be flushed by resetting the program (program counter) to a known state; the program will then reexamine the blackboard to determine its next activity. The system will continue to run, although the loss of partially completed work will waste CPU cycles. The implementation will be discussed in Section 6.3.2.

The important characteristics of the program flow architecture are:

1. During normal operation, the program runs very fast, with the state encoded in the program counter.

2. Whenever necessary, the system can easily and efficiently be redirected to another task.

The expert controller acquires a distinct data-flow taint since the program flow is controlled by adding and removing data from the blackboard. We can now look at some more details.

6.3.1 Notes. The notes are simple binary flags with three primitives: *scribble*, which sets a note, *wipe*, which clears it, and *visible*, which returns its value; the names reflect their function on a blackboard.

The notes are not directly connected with the associated piece of numeric data by being part of the same structure, or by pointers. If we were to put note and datum in the same structure, it would have to have a

C union data-type, because notes are associated with many different types of data including whole structures, which may contain additional notes. Sometimes notes are not associated with any data. The notes may be ignored by non-symbolic parts of the program, saving typing and simplifying the interface to less intelligent software.

For future flexibility, the notes are embedded in a structure. One thought was to have the notes arranged in a hierarchy, so that deleting a parent note would delete its children at the same time, which is often desirable. For example, if we invalidate a note that designates the presence of a completed robot position, we will want to invalidate a note that indicates that the joint angles have been computed, because the joint angles are derived from the robot position. These semantics are implemented much more efficiently and flexibly by defining subroutine calls such that instead of deleting the parent note, we call a subroutine particular to that note which deletes it and its children. We need more subroutines, but the notes are deleted faster because there are no overhead operations to process the list of children.

6.3.2 Program flow implementation. The program flow is controlled by notes. The basic approach is shown in Figure 26 and Table 3. Did_task_1 and so on are notes indicating just that. After task_1 returns, the program counter implicitly records that task_1 has been performed, so did_task_1 does not have to be retested. Instead, did_task_2 will be tested and task_2 run immediately. This is a simple illustration of how the program counter encodes the blackboard's state. During normal operation, task_1 and task_2 are performed in sequence with only two quick tests of notes as overhead.

Notice that the structure is indefinitely hierarchical as shown with did_task_1a, but that it can not support reentrance or recursion — which are unneeded for robot control. Each task can be divided into smaller and smaller subtasks, until each subtask contains only a sequence of statements which must be executed as a unit, without any control statements.

If the flow of control must be drastically changed, the program configures the appropriate notes, then executes a longjmp. In Table 3, if the test whatever in task_1a passes, the longjmp will be executed. Program flow will resume from the setjmp, and shortly thereafter arrive at task_2, bypassing the rest of task_1.

Longjmp and setjmp (at the head of Table 3) are standard C subroutine library calls which communicate using main_jmp_buf, a C structure containing saved program and register data. Longjmp causes all subroutine calls since the setjmp was executed to be removed from

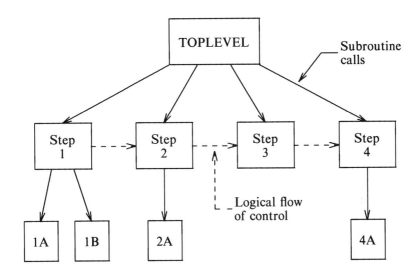

Figure 26. Program Flow Architecture. The TOPLEVEL routine examines the blackboard to decide what routines to call, creating the apparent flow of control shown. By changing the notes, we can easily redirect control.

the stack. The program context is modified so that program flow continues from the `setjmp` as if the `setjmp` had just been completed. Intervening levels of subroutines do not require special coding to check return values from routines they call, reducing complexity, increasing speed, and allowing the exceptions from low-level routines to be changed, without requiring the modification of all the routines that cause the changed routine to be called.

When program flow resumes from the `setjmp`, the expert controller quickly drives back down through the program hierarchy until the right section of code to execute is found, at which point execution continues. The overhead to find the right code is minimal because there are only a few tests at each level of the program hierarchy, and the cost to test a note is very low. This slight overhead is mitigated by the infrequence with which it must be incurred.

The program flow architecture executes quickly under symbolic control, and can rapidly switch tasks when necessary. Clearly `setjmp` and `longjmp` are dangerous if abused, but there is only one `setjmp` in the entire program, so the destination of a `longjmp` is always clear.

```
/* main program */

    setjmp (main_jmp_buf);

    if (invisible (did_task_1))
       task_1 ();
    if (invisible (did_task_2))
       task_2 ();


/* later */

task_1 ()
{
   if (invisible (did_task_1a))
      task_1a ();

   /* do the rest of task_1 */

   scribble (did_task_1);
}

task_1a ()
{
   if ( whatever )
   {
      scribble (did_task_1);
      longjmp (&main_jmp_buf, 1);
   };
}
```

Table 3. Program Flow Fragment. The main program (TOPLEVEL) calls the subtasks selected by the notes. The program executes the normal flow rapidly. A `longjmp` causes control to return to the `setjmp`; the correct routine will be quickly reestablished.

6.4 Model Data Structure

In this section we will describe the "model," a specialized data structure used to store both symbolic and numeric information. By representing as much information as possible in models, we simplify AI programs as well as the expert controller.

6.4.1 Design objectives. The model's basic function is to map a set of inputs into a set of outputs. Depending on the values of the inputs, different outputs may be produced. A simple example is a symbolic/numeric version of square root which maps an input value to one of the tuples:

$$(\text{sqrt\_is}, value)$$
$$(\text{input\_negative}, by\_how\_much)$$

depending on the input.

The model must be able to interact with the global blackboard, though in some cases, especially when the same model is used several times for somewhat different purposes (as in square root above), the interaction will be indirect.

We wish to isolate the model's internal details as much as possible from those routines that use it. Not only does this simplify the clients, but it makes it possible to change the internal implementation of the model as required, without affecting the clients. A model may be implemented by composing or inverting other models, or might be partially or completely implemented by a code fragment.

The accuracy required of a model depends heavily on its function, so the model's structure must be able to provide different accuracies. The accuracy must be hidden from the clients. In addition, the accuracy may be different in different portions of the input space.

Even the number and identity of a model's inputs may need to be hidden from the clients. As the sophistication of a model's implementation grows, it may acquire additional inputs from the blackboard. Some inputs may be used only in portions of the input space that are especially sensitive to that input.

We can achieve this degree of implementation independence by making the client interface a subroutine call. The code implementing the model can then call library functions to access the model's data.

The next several sections (until the chapter's conclusion) relate the model's implementation. Because the details of the model's implementation have been hidden from the expert controller's user, the casual reader may be content to skip these sections.

6.4.2 Implementation — nonterminal nodes. The model data structure is a generalized quadtree or octree. A quadtree has two inputs; at each node in the tree the range of both inputs is divided in half (Figure 27). The notation $x<m>$ denotes the m'th bit of the fixed point representation of x, and $x<m-n>$ denotes a range of bits.

Each node in the model data structure can have a different set of inputs (though an implementation parameter currently limits the number of inputs to a particular node to four). The range of each input can be divided up into any binary power of bins (Figure 28). This design achieves the flexibility desired. The C structures representing a node are:

```
typedef struct IMelement
{
    unsigned char cod, len;
    Adesc ad[MAXSUB];
} ModElement;

typedef struct IAdesc
{
    unsigned char argno, fwid, foff, unused;
} Adesc;
```

The cod element differentiates nonterminal and terminal (data) nodes; for the nonterminals we are discussing, it always contains a special value. The len argument describes the number of inputs to this node, each described by an Adesc. The Adesc specifies which of the model's arguments is to be divided, and selects a field of bits from a fixed point normalized representation. The range and identity of each argument is stored separately in a header structure not shown.

The bits from each input are concatenated and used as an index into a vector of pointers which follow the ModElement; each pointer points at another node. The formation of the indices to access the rightmost node in Figure 28 is shown in Figure 29.

6.4.3 Implementation — data nodes. At the bottom of the tree are data, or terminal, nodes. The data nodes are identified by the cod field, which is used to determine which outputs are contained in the node by lookup into a header. Each output value is represented by an eight or sixteen bit integer which is converted to the appropriate external representation.

The data node must also affect the symbolic information encoded in the notes. Each cod identifies a set of output variables that the node contains, a set of the notes to be scribbled, and a set of the notes to be wiped by the recall of this data element. A bit vector can represent each set since the number of elements affected by a particular model is small. The set of codes is computed automatically during model creation. For each note there are two sets of outputs, noteS and noteW. A note is scribbled (set) if any output in its noteS set is output by the code, and is wiped if none of its noteW outputs are present. The use of two different sets allows a model to implement wired-OR and wired-AND semantics.

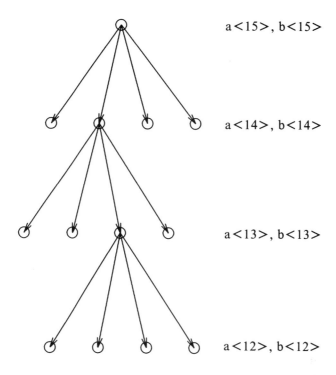

a<15>, b<15>

a<14>, b<14>

a<13>, b<13>

a<12>, b<12>

Figure 27. Quadtree Graph Structure. One bit from each input is tested at each level of the tree.

For example, a note may be scribbled by the main routine, several models run, and the note rechecked to see if any model has wiped it.

6.4.4 Technical considerations. The representation determines a model's storage requirement. Using large amounts of memory to store detailed multi-input models is no longer the limitation it once was. Extrapolation of current VME-bus memory boards to megabit chips gives 16 MB/board; 48−64 MB could be achieved with 4 Mbit chips. A 100 MB system is not unreasonable.

We should turn a robot on and leave it on permanently, accumulating more accurate models all the time. Since experimental robot systems have been known to crash literally and figuratively, we can implement a quasi-permanent memory by checkpointing it to disk. New robots can be downloaded from experienced robots.

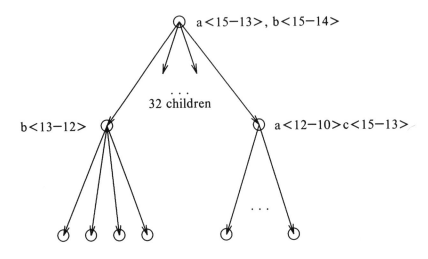

Figure 28. Model Graph Structure. Any number of bits of several inputs may be tested at each level.

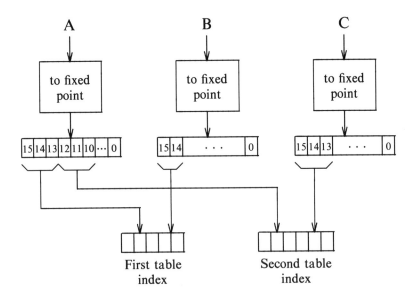

Figure 29. Rightmost Node Index Formation. The generation of the two table indices to locate the rightmost node of Figure 28 is shown.

The model data structure was designed to be loaded and unloaded repeatedly from main memory to disk. Pointers are carefully controlled and represented as relative offsets while on disk. Models are restructured to a breadth-first form when written (nonterminal nodes before terminal nodes), as they may have undergone arbitrary changes while in memory.

The read/write primitives for models also account for the different byte orders of the 68020s the models run on during operation, and the micro-VAX used during program development.

6.4.5 C interface. The model is contained in a data file on disk or in a block of memory, yet it must still present a C interface to the clients that will use it. A specialized program, `autoface`, reads the model's data file (summarized in Table 4), and automatically produces the interface subroutine that is compiled into the program. A sample `autoface` output is shown in Table 5.

This model evaluates return strokes from the robot. It has a single input, which happens to be passed as an argument. Globals can be directly accessed without being passed as arguments. `TOSCINT` is a macro which converts the input to a scaled integer. The scaled integers are passed to a function, `model`, which looks up the appropriate data node in the model. `Model` may be called with as many arguments as the model requires.

The type of the data node determines the appropriate block of code to return outputs and modify notes. Outputs can be either globals as shown or returned through arguments. Notes are scribbled or wiped as described earlier according to the outputs generated.

The `autoface` program precompiles the information about which outputs ought to be written and what notes should be modified. At run time, the model executes quickly with minimal overhead and no data structure scanning.

6.4.6 Model creation. Data must be entered into each model. There are three possible data sources:

1. humans,

2. off-line programs, and

3. real-time programs.

The human data source is just that, a person coaching the program with a mixture of quantitative and qualitative information. Off-line programs are simulations that exhaustively explore some input space and compute responses, often with both symbolic and numeric components. Lastly, the expert controller may autonomously modify the models, or learn.

```
1 inputs, 2 outputs, 5 codes used, 2 notes
1820 bytes of data, root at 778
Inp zfar (<a1>) min 0.0 max 750.0
Out crit_underfar (crit_underfar) min 0.0 max 100.0 (short)
Out crit_overfar (crit_overfar) min 0.0 max 300.0 (short)
Code 0(NIL),
    scribbles; wipes suspect_underfar suspect_overfar
Code 1, crit_underfar*,
    scribbles suspect_underfar; wipes suspect_overfar
Code 2, crit_underfar,
    scribbles suspect_underfar; wipes suspect_overfar
Code 3, crit_overfar*,
    scribbles suspect_overfar; wipes suspect_underfar
Code 4, crit_overfar,
    scribbles suspect_overfar; wipes suspect_underfar
Code 255 is TABLE_CODE
Note suspect_underfar, scribble on crit_underfar,
    wiped by lack of crit_underfar
Note suspect_overfar, scribble on crit_overfar,
    wiped by lack of crit_overfar
Code 0 used 123 times
Code 1 used 4 times
Code 2 used 31 times
Code 3 used 6 times
Code 4 used 92 times
1 tables
```

Table 4. Model Header Data. The table summarizes the data in Zfar_eval's header. The notation <a1> indicates that zfar is passed as an argument; the outputs are to globals.

Each data source has different requirements. The human requires an easy-to-use interactive interface. Both types of programmed data sources require subroutine packages to simplify the interface, and hide at least some of the details of the implementation. The details of the subroutine package are not that interesting and we will not discuss them further, aside from confirming the package's existence. The needs of learning are quite a bit more substantial; we will devote Section 7.5 to it.

The program used by humans to specify models, builder, is a mouse-driven, graphics-oriented, interactive program that currently runs on an AT&T Teletype 5620 DMD terminal. Models with one input and any number of outputs may be constructed. Cubic splines interpolate between human-specified data values. Builder's graphic display when creating the Zfar_eval model of Table 5 is shown in Figure 30. The model was defined using the mouse and a few keystrokes to type the variable names.

```
Zfar_eval (a1)
   double a1;
{
   short inparray[1];
   ModCElement *mep;

   TOSCINT (a1, 0.0, 750.0, &inparray[0]);
   mep = (ModCElement *)model (MZfar_eval, inparray[0]);
   switch (mep->cod)
   {
case 0:
      wipe (suspect_underfar);
      wipe (suspect_overfar);
      break;
case 1:
      FROMSCINT (*(short *)(mep->c + 0), 0.0, 100.0,
         &(crit_underfar));
      scribble (suspect_underfar);
      wipe (suspect_overfar);
      break;
case 2:
      FROMSCINT (*(short *)(mep->c + 0), 0.0, 100.0,
         &(crit_underfar));
      scribble (suspect_underfar);
      wipe (suspect_overfar);
      break;
case 3:
      FROMSCINT (*(short *)(mep->c + 0), 0.0, 300.0,
         &(crit_overfar));
      wipe (suspect_underfar);
      scribble (suspect_overfar);
      break;
case 4:
      FROMSCINT (*(short *)(mep->c + 0), 0.0, 300.0,
         &(crit_overfar));
      wipe (suspect_underfar);
      scribble (suspect_overfar);
      break;
   };
}
```

Table 5. Automatically Generated Interface. Autoface produces this code for the Zfar_eval model (Figure 30), which writes the underfar and overfar evaluators on the blackboard. SCINT stands for scaled integer.

The markers in Figure 30 indicate data points directly specified by the human; the rest were generated automatically. The codes marked with an asterisk (*) in Table 4 (codes 1 and 3) internally denote the human-specified data points, but are otherwise identical to codes 2 and 4.

The `builder` program makes it easy for the human programmer to add certain types of information to the knowledge base without having to write much code. Later sections (see 7.2.2, 7.2.3, and 7.3.4) will describe the use of models for this purpose.

6.4.7 Possible minor enhancements. A few simple enhancements to the modeling process have been conceived, but not implemented because of the lack of a need, and are pointed out here in the interest of completeness in case the need should arise.

The `autoface` program currently does not support notes as output arguments from the interface subroutine, though this is just a matter of adding a small amount of additional code. `Autoface` would be more general if it could input and output integers rather than exclusively `doubles` (the C data-type for double precision floating point) as at present, though this has never proven necessary. On occasion, it has appeared as if the facility to automatically specify that a `longjmp` be executed when certain notes are scribbled or wiped would save typing. However, this feature would make the expert controller harder to follow, so it remains unimplemented.

At a somewhat more sophisticated level, it might also be useful to be able to specify automatic linear interpolation within the bin corresponding to a given range of inputs. Interpolation would reduce the memory requirements for slowly varying continuous functions where accuracy is essential. Interpolation could also be implemented by enhancing the `autoface` program.

The model data structure currently can not support very unstructured data. Certain outputs could be tagged as pointers rather than as `doubles`, so that arbitrarily complex data structures could be constructed within the model framework. This might prove especially useful for learning programs. The primary difficulty is to add the tricky code to chase and flatten the pointers (to the model input/output routines).

The most complicated enhancement would be to construct a two-dimensional model builder based on contour maps. The semantics and algorithms for editing the contour maps would be non-trivial, but feasible. As will be discussed in Section 7.2.5, in practice, two-input models have been decomposed to two single-input models. Multi-input models have only proven necessary for machine-generated models, and would be quite complex for a human to specify and input, even with a good tool.

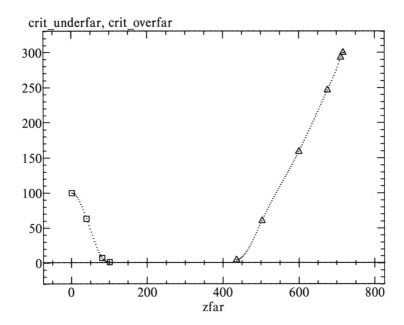

crit_underfar, crit_overfar

Figure 30. Graphic Display of `zfar_eval`. The model indicates whether, and by how much, a Z value (`zfar`, mm) is too low (`underfar`, squares), or too high (`overfar`, triangles). In between, it returns no value.

6.5 Summary

In this chapter, we have described the architecture underlying the expert controller. The architecture follows a data-flow paradigm, but implicitly caches the blackboard's state in the program counter to speed execution by eliminating redundant tests. When necessary, the program flow may be rapidly redirected to an indirectly specified target.

We introduced the "model" data structure, which represents both numeric and symbolic information. Model instances may be created by specialized programs, or more often, by a human-interface program. These tools and the regular program organization facilitate coaching by high-level programs, as well as flexibility during development by humans. The ensuing Chapter 7 will make use of the model data structure throughout.

Chapter 7

Expert Controller

This chapter continues the description of the generic design of the real-time expert controller at the heart of the robot ping-pong player. We will begin by investigating the system requirements. Discussion of initial planning, temporal updating, and exception handling follows. Finally, we conclude with a discussion of learning's applicability to this domain.

7.1 Functionality Required

To understand why something should be organized the way it is, we must first understand what it must do. We will review the specific capabilities required of the expert controller.

7.1.1 Initial planning. The expert controller must select initial values for program variables whose values are not directly determined from the sensor data. For example, the return velocity of a ping-pong ball can be arbitrary within certain bounds. The values of these "free" variables will greatly influence the values of other program variables. A poor choice of the initial values may cause the plan to be infeasible. For example, the choice of a particular return velocity may result in there being no kinematic solution to the robot configuration, if the consequent wrist position is too far away from the robot's shoulder.

We have to avoid problems whose existence can not be detected until we have committed them. The expert controller must intelligently pick values for the free variables to minimize the likelihood of subsequent problems, before much information is available to guide the selection.

7.1.2 Temporal updating. Once an initial plan has been formulated, the expert controller must update it as new data becomes available at 60 Hz. We will refer to the modification of the plan as temporal updating. Changes in the input data must be mapped into appropriate degrees of freedom in the plan so that the resulting plan continues to be feasible.

In addition, the expert controller must evaluate the current plan, and modify it preemptively to avoid problems. For example, if a particular joint is getting close to its maximum torque output, the expert controller should begin to change program variables in advance to compensate.

Finally, the expert controller must be able to trade off constraints between task and robot. A robot-related problem may be solved by adjusting robot-related degrees of freedom, or by adjusting task constraints. If the wrist is getting too far away, we could adjust not only the stick angle, but the ball's return velocity. The expert controller must understand the relationship between task and robot variables.

7.1.3 Exception handling. The expert controller must recognize Murphy's Law: anything that can go wrong, will. Robot ping-pong exemplifies this point. Especially when the ball bounces or hits the net, or the spin suddenly becomes understood, dramatic changes in plan are required. A variety of problems can arise: the ball may hit a side wire marker, the net, or fly off the end, the robot kinematics may no longer be solvable, or a joint limit may be hit. In addition, the expert controller must handle exceptions that inevitably arise during the initial planning process.

The expert controller must rapidly identify a strategy to solve the problem. It must have a means for causing changes in the program's existing flow of execution; such a method was developed in Chapter 6. The implementation of the strategy must be monitored, subsequent errors handled in the context of the original problem if necessary, and alternative strategies chosen if the initial approach proves infeasible.

7.2 Initial Planning

In this section, we will discuss the initial planning problem, that is, how to go from the first data point to the first plan. The main emphasis is on how temporal updating simplifies this procedure, and on some operators to allow strategy to impact the process.

7.2.1 Problems and objectives. The reason that we have an initial planning problem is that the problem is underconstrained, that is, we have more degrees of freedom than equations to determine values for them. However, we do have many constraints on the entire set of variables, though not necessarily directly upon the free variables. The angle of the stick supporting the paddle is one example of a free variable. Its value dramatically affects the kinematic and dynamic reachability of the resulting configuration.

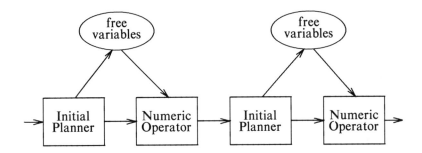

Figure 31. Initial Planner Organization. The inputs are evaluated and used to pick values for a few free variables. These variables allow further computations which will create additional free variables, and so on.

During the initial planning process, we will alternate between performing initial planning for some small set of free variables, and performing numeric calculations based on those free variables. The results of these calculations let us form an initial plan for yet a different set of free variables (Figure 31).

The constraints on the initial plan tend to be highly nonlinear, for example, those derived by mapping constraints on the robot's joint angles (limit stops) into constraints on the robot's (Cartesian) position and orientation. Some may not be computable in closed form and require extensive search techniques to discover, such as the constraints on acceptable launch trajectories when including the effects of spin and drag. Once we have an initial plan, we can form locally linearized estimates of the constraints, but initially, we can not even do this.

The solution to this conundrum comes with the realization that the initial plan need not be perfect. The subsequent temporal updating process will improve the global optimality of the plan. It will be much easier to solve problems during temporal updating when all the constraints are visible, than it is to solve them during initial planning when they are not.

To further justify this approach, notice that the initial sensor data is similarly flawed, and is essentially guaranteed incorrect. We should not devote excessive effort and, especially in the real-time context, time, to finding the optimal plan based on suboptimal data (garbage in, garbage out). The ability of temporal updating to reduce the complexity of initial planning is an important point.

If the details of the initial planning process excessively affect the generated initial plan, it indicates a poorly designed initial planning system.

Other researchers have reached a similar conclusion about the desirability of minimizing sensitivity to numeric parameters [32, p. 265].

One way to view the combination of initial planning and temporal updating is as an iterative solution to the initial problem. Iterative algorithms are quite common in many fields. Two factors distinguish simple iteration from the planning and updating process: the input data changes each iteration, and the output data is used immediately each iteration (Figure 32).

We will discuss the effects of the first point in the discussion of temporal updating (Section 7.3). The rationale and necessity behind the second point, even if the input data was not changing, is that we must keep the system latency low, so that the robot has adequate motion time.

As a consequence, we must avoid overcommitting the system to a poor plan, since the use of a plan results in an irrevocable change in the system's physical state, namely, the robot will be in a different position with a possibly substantial kinetic energy. The planning process must evaluate the robustness of alternatives it is considering, so that the system has the maximum possible flexibility to compensate for later changes in sensor data. As is pointed out in [21], knowledge of sensor uncertainty is very important. The use of robustness evaluation is a matter of choice in application design. We will describe one example in Section 8.2.1.

7.2.2 Selecting among alternatives. The first type of initial planning decision we will consider is how to select among several alternatives, given any number of continuous or discrete input variables. For example, we might decide whether to make a forehand or backhand shot (though our system always uses forehand). We assume there are few alternatives, or we would use the continuous technique described in Section 7.2.3, and quantize its results.

We begin picking an alternative by subjectively evaluating all applicable input data over the possible alternatives. Models are used to map input data to one or more figures of merit, usually between ±2. Not all figures of merit need be generated all the time, in keeping with the symbolic/numeric nature of models. Failure to produce a figure of merit indicates a "don't care" with respect to that alternative and input.

Unlike other work which tries to assign true semantics to the figures of merit: certainty measures [15], fuzzy sets [38][61], Dempster-Shafer structures [69], and evidential theory [15], we claim that such efforts are largely extraneous in this context.

Probabilistic and certainty factors explicitly assume that the problem domain is one of analysis, not synthesis. Such factors reflect knowledge

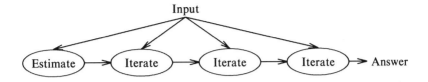

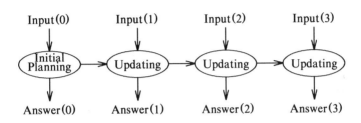

Figure 32. Iteration vs. Planning and Updating. At top is the data flow for an iterative algorithm. At bottom, we see the similar structure of initial planning and updating, but we get new data each cycle, and use the output each cycle.

about the probability that the disease is pneumonia, or the certainty with which we know the source of the oil spill.

In a system devoted to synthesis, the semantics may be: "Is it a good idea to try to hit the ball when it is dropping at 1.4 m/sec?" It is very hard to make a probabilistic estimate of the impact of this variable on the system, if one is to do it initially during system construction, or especially if one attempts to do it based on learning during system operation. The real probability is obscured by the effect of many, many other possibly unmeasurable variables. We will discuss learning in Section 7.5.

Our approach is to make the evaluators display the right characteristics, to include as many factors as possible, then let the group statistics and robustness of the system operate. There is no *right* answer.

Once we have evaluated all the available inputs, we "decide" on an alternative, using a routine of that name. The `decide` operator squares all the factors for each alternative, preserving their sign, then sums them up to obtain a figure of merit for the alternative. The alternative with the highest figure of merit is selected. `Decide` designates the selected alternative either by scribbling a note associated with the alternative, or by returning an integer code, depending on which is easiest to use.

```
int decide (double final_fom[], int n_altern,
        double fac1[], fac2[], ..., 0L);

int decidew (double final_fom[], int n_altern,
        double wei1, fac1[], wei2, fac2[], ..., 0L);

decideN (Note *notes[], double final_fom[], int n_altern,
        double fac1[], fac2[], ..., 0L);

decideNw (Note *notes[], double final_fom[], int n_altern,
        double wei1, fac1[], wei2, fac2[], ..., 0L);

int decide2 (double final_fom[], int n_factors,
        double fac1, fac2 ...);

int decide2w (double final_fom[], int n_factors,
        double wei1, fac1, wei2, fac2, ...);
```

Table 6. Forms of `Decide`. Based on numeric factors (`facn`) and weights (`wein`), an alternative is selected. The index of the selection is returned, or a specified note for each alternative is scribbled.

Squaring the figure of merit (with preservation of sign) is semantically nonfunctional, but makes the figures of merit easier for a human to generate and understand. It has the effect of increasing the importance of borderline factors, and reducing the importance of nominal ones.

Optionally associated with each factor is a weight which is multiplied by the factor's value for each alternative, allowing high-level specification of the factor's importance.

A special routine, `decide2`, selects between only two alternatives, using a single set of evaluators to indicate the relative merits of case A versus B. `Decide2` reduces the number of evaluators and makes the semantics clearer. The `decide` routines are implemented as subroutine calls (Table 6).

`Decide` is fast, predictable, and useful: it captures the essential intent of the specifier. It does not try to attach too much significance and accuracy to data which is inherently loosely specified. `Decide` directly creates symbolic information for the blackboard.

7.2.3 Selecting a continuous value. In this section we will consider how to select a value for a continuous variable. One possible continuous variable, the ball's post-hit speed, might be determined by the ball's incoming speed and height in a complex manner. We will select values of continuous

```
double combine (int n_evaluators, double eval1,
      eval2, ...);

double combinew (int n_evaluators, double wei1, eval1,
      wei2, eval2, ...);

double combinev (int n_evaluators, double evaluators[]);

double combinewv (int n_evaluators, double weights[],
      evaluators[]);
```

Table 7. Syntax of Combine. A consensus value (weighted average) is chosen for a free variable; that value is returned from combine. The evaluators (eval*n*) are possible values.

variables with the same attitude with which we select among alternatives, but we clearly can not evaluate an infinite number of alternatives to select a value for a continuous variable.

Instead, our approach is to explicitly compute optimal values from restricted views of the problem (and correspondingly small numbers of inputs). For example, we might compute an optimal return speed from the incoming speed, and another return speed from the ball's height. We will then combine the values together to get a consensus.

The evaluators used to choose values for continuous outputs produce not figures of merit, but values in the output space. They are the semantic equivalent of "If x, then do y." We refer to these evaluators as *absolute*. Rules are still with us, but increasingly camouflaged. The rule produces real numeric data, and in addition may produce symbolic data: "I do not care," or "Do something else."

The combine operator is a simple average; evaluators may be passed as arguments or stored in an array. A second set of routines allows weights to be specified for each evaluator (Table 7). The weights can express such semantics as: "I definitely want x=39." The weights are often generated at the same time as the primary evaluator by the same model, but separate meta-models can alternatively specify the relative weighting of the evaluators.

It is also possible to have *relative* evaluators. Relative evaluators indicate that under the circumstances, it is best to shade the output in some particular direction: a ball with much spin might suggest a softer shot. The relative evaluators are combined, then added to the combined result of the absolute evaluators.

Absolute evaluators are correct by construction, that is, they can never produce an illegal result. Combinations of relative evaluators may produce illegal results, for example, a value of 600 for a variable that must be between 0 and 500. A secondary model may compress the range to ensure that the value stays well behaved.

7.2.4 Planning from large models. We occasionally need to generate outputs from very complex, nonlinear functions of several inputs, for example, what initial velocity would cause the ball to cross the table's far end at a particular height after bouncing. These requirements may be addressed by using multi-input models generated off-line by simulation and analysis programs. These programs can use iterative and search techniques to find solutions that would be prohibitively time consuming during system operation.

The multi-input model must quantize its inputs, and especially for models with many inputs, the quanta may have to be relatively large to keep memory requirements within reason. The quantization has the effect of lowering the resulting model's accuracy.

The accuracy of the estimate can be improved if the model outputs not a final result, but descriptive information about the output in the region of interest. In the case of individual outputs, the model may supply the coefficients necessary for a linear interpolation of the desired output.

In another case, the output to be generated has bounds that are a function of the inputs. We can use normal planning techniques to select a value within the range retrieved by a model (Section 8.2.3.2).

In complex situations, it is a distinct possibility that there may be no acceptable solution for some combination of inputs — an unreachable ball, perhaps. The situation can be easily represented using the model structure, however, it is important to go a step further by communicating as much additional information as possible. At the least, models of lower resolution and complexity can be used to provide very rough estimates of any feasible solution to serve as a seed for recovery efforts. More information on this subject may be found in Section 7.4.3.

7.2.5 Remarks. As described, our emphasis has been to capture the major effects required to generate good initial plans. We have matched the complexity of the process to the inaccuracy of the sensor data presented to it, and the quality of results demanded of it, taking advantage of the robustness afforded by the temporal updating process. As we will see in Chapter 8, the result is simple and fast planners that are robust to numerical nuances, and produce fundamentally sound plans.

Nearly all of the evaluators used in the initial planning process have only a single input, and may be built using the `builder` program (one of the reasons for not creating a higher-order-model builder). Why can we get away with only one input?

Each individual model is intended to capture only a single effect. When we think we need to use a model with several inputs, it usually indicates that we just do not understand the single underlying effect. If we can identify, understand, and isolate that underlying variable, we can numerically compute it, then use our single input models. By understanding the fundamental issues, we get a better, more feasible solution, and can predict additional effects.

It has appeared on occasion that additional semantics in `combine` and `decide` might be necessary. For example, one group of evaluators might indicate one response, and another group a different response. Should `decide` and `combine` try to consider this, instead of presenting an average value? The evidence so far suggests not, that when such cases arise they signal deeper problems. Sometimes the averaged response works out all right, other times exceptions occur, but it is likely that they would have occurred in any case.

We need not have any visible concrete justification for picking the evaluators. The evaluators can and do include effects that are beyond the scope of modeling known to the system. High-level programs can coach the behavior of the system without justifying changes in detail to the lower-level system, which may not be capable of the representations, modeling, and level of analysis necessary to arrive at a coached strategy.

By using the common model data structure throughout the system, we make it easy for the coach to control the system's strategy.

7.3 Temporal Updating

Once we have formulated an initial plan and begun its execution, we must continue to update it as additional sensor data becomes available. The temporal updating process will be the subject of this section.

7.3.1 Objectives. The temporal updating process has two primary objectives: to change the plan in response to new sensor data, and to propagate information about the later stages of processing up to the earlier ones, and so achieve a more globally optimum solution to the problem. However, global optimality is a loosely defined criterion, and we need not have any formal measure. Instead, we shall try to ensure that no problem becomes severe enough to endanger the task, or at least, that if problems are to become worse, they all do so at the same rate, so that no individual problem occurs prematurely.

An important advantage of the temporal updating process is that we can try to avoid exceptions altogether. It is vastly preferable to avoid a problem by correcting it in many small steps than to try to correct it in one big step. By the time an exception occurs, there may be insufficient reaction time to make the necessary corrections.

The temporal updating process must have knowledge of the plan in progress as it is formulating a new one. The motion in progress alters the manipulator's capabilities. The robot's position and velocity cause torques and inertias which determine its maximum acceleration. Once the robot has reached substantial velocities, its possible destinations at a given future time are heavily constrained. Knowledge of the past plan is required to generate continuous transitions between the old plan and the new one.

At a macroscopic level, knowledge of the prior plan is essential to provide hysteresis, that is, to ensure that decisions are made on the same basis as they were made in the past. If a decision is borderline, we do not wish minor numerical effects to cause the system to flip-flop back and forth among alternatives on succeeding updates. Such behavior swiftly results in problems as the robot system tries to track the unstable plan. As the time until the ball must be hit dwindles, the system will be unable to track the plan, and will have to give up.

The temporal updating process has an advantage that the initial planning process did not: estimates of program variables and the relationships among them. However, we must be careful that changes in the input data or plan do not render the estimates harmful rather than helpful.

7.3.2 Program and data structure. Before we go into the details of the temporal updating process, we must describe the program and data structures necessary to support it.

We must carefully separate the higher-level planning and temporal updating code from the lower-level, numerical code, as shown earlier in Figure 31 for initial planning. This will enable us to have the correct semantics later during exception handling, and has the additional benefit of often enabling the lower-level code to be used for initial planning and updating.

We will refer to the planning routines that comprise the heart of the temporal updating process as *tuners*. The tuners are run once each temporal updating iteration, after new sensor data arrives. The tuners adjust the program's free variables in response to global program conditions. Low-level numeric calculations process the free variables and sensor data to formulate the revised plan.

The free variables must be carried over from one iteration of the program to the next. As described, once values have been chosen, they should be maintained in place to aid other decision processes, including the selection of their own next value. We must not purge these values at the end of each iteration as we might be inclined to do at first glance. Logically, we need two sets of notes per variable: one to signify its presence or absence, and another to signal that it has been updated. During the initial planning process, both notes are equivalent. During temporal updating, the presence/absence notes are left unchanged, but the looked-at notes control program sequencing in a data-flow style.

Similarly, we must carry over from one iteration to another the data used to evaluate the task state. The evaluating data is derived from the free variables. The data's presence is strictly determined by the presence or absence of the last-computed input to the routine that computes this data, so no additional notes are needed. We recompute derived data when its inputs change (the data-flow model again), rather than on demand. This strategy makes sense because it is likely that we will use the data more than once, and unlikely that the data will be thrown away.

Some routines must know the true state of the robot, independent of the state of the temporal updating process or exception handling. Previous sections have described the "plan" vaguely as an entity, without providing details. The `plan` data structure provides this information; its contents are determined by the needs of the routines that will use it. A `plan` records the required portion of the system's state when a motion is initiated. The `plan` is not logically equivalent to the data on the blackboard, since the blackboard changes arbitrarily during temporal updating and exception handling. The data in a `plan` is logically consistent and complete.

`Plans` could also be employed to implement backtracking as part of AI search strategies, but backtracking has not proven necessary for our problem domain.

7.3.3 Requirements for numeric routines. During the first stage of initial planning, the input data was evaluated using models. Similarly, during temporal updating, as many program variables as possible and reasonable ought to be evaluated.

The low-level numeric routines (or a small software envelope around them) that compute the outputs must evaluate them by calling the evaluating subroutines, in keeping with the data-driven approach. Although the evaluators appear to be extra work, they are well worth the trouble.

The evaluators must be run during the initial planning stage as well as during updating, so that the evaluators are available during the first updating pass. This is facilitated by using the same numeric routines for both initial planning and updating wherever possible. The numeric routines must also check for errors, and invoke the exception handling mechanism as appropriate.

7.3.4 Design of evaluators. The evaluators used in updating are again implemented as models, but with yet a third output semantics. The model stores, for each possible state, our preferred change in state. For example, consider the model shown in Figure 33, which evaluates the value of joint 3 of the robot (the elbow). As may be seen, the same evaluator can produce several evaluations, conveying symbolic as well as numeric information.

To the far left and far right of the model are the limits on the motion of joint 3 (marked with squares). The joint evaluator's value increases well in advance as the joint approaches the joint limit. The sign of the evaluator indicates the direction of travel desired. Away from the extremities of the evaluator, the value is not zero, but nonexistent, exploiting the symbolic nature of the model.

The interior of the evaluator contains a completely different output, though it has much the same result. It evaluates whether the robot is nearing the end of its reach, at which point joint 3 would equal $\pi/2$ radians. (The too-far evaluator is marked with triangles.) We are able to directly represent that there are two symbolically different outputs, one indicating that the joint is near its limit, the other indicating that the position is nearing the limit of the machine's reach.

The shape of the curves (the distance from the limit versus the correction desired) allows us to specify the behavior of at least this aspect of the system versus time. For example, if the correction exactly equals the distance to the limit, the output will jump to the point where the correction equals zero in one iteration, assuming no other factors are operating.

Normally, we choose a correction less than the distance from the limit, except in the vicinity of the input space where the input becomes no longer objectionable. Under these circumstances, the output will walk down the curve until it "jumps off the end" and becomes completely acceptable (Figure 34). By this method, we can prevent undesirably large jumps in the output, which might cause other problems, while still moving in the right direction. The correction is larger in the vicinity of the hard limit because an exception is more likely; we are therefore willing to make a larger, riskier, correction.

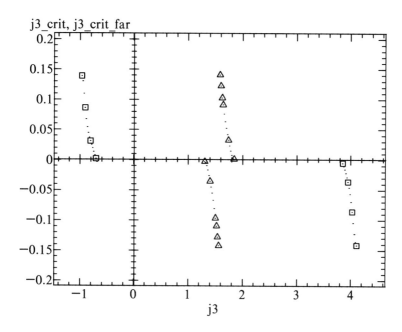

Figure 33. Updating Evaluator for Joint 3. The horizontal axis of this model represents the position, in radians, of joint 3. The vertical axis specifies a proposed correction to joint 3. The central curve, marked with triangles, proposes a change when the wrist is becoming too far away from the shoulder. The curve marked with squares keeps the joint from hitting the limit stops.

It is important to notice that we have encoded a time-varying strategy without requiring any additional state, making the implementation simpler and more robust. In the full operating environment, the variable is subjected to other pressures due to changing sensor data and the problems of other variables, so it would be difficult to define semantics for maintaining additional state.

7.3.5 Constructing tuners. In this section, we will comment on the general design principles necessary for building successful tuners. At present, tuners remain an art, subject to many demands from the varying task requirements. Our experience has been that the hardest part of creating a new tuner is to decide what it should do; once that is done, the coding and definition of the models is straightforward.

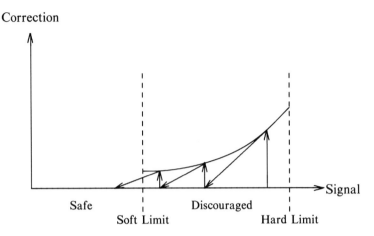

Correction

Safe   Discouraged

Soft Limit   Hard Limit

Signal

Figure 34. Dynamic Behavior of a Correction. The value of the variable being evaluated (joint 3 for consistency) has an initial value close to the joint's hard mechanical limit. If exactly the correction specified by the evaluator is applied to the joint's value, it will jump to the left. After three corrections, the joint's value is outside the discouraged region, and no further corrections are made.

7.3.5.1 Tuner architecture. Rather than have a single massive tuner, we partition the task into tuner modules operating on individual or related free variables. Partitioning makes the system more manageable, and the granularity it imposes is necessary during exception handling.

A tuner alters its output variables to attempt to correct problems. The tuner does not have to examine all possible problems, only those it believes it can solve. Each correction is described by what amounts to a rule. At the end of each tuner, a relative or absolute `combine` (the same routine from initial planning, Section 7.2.3) generates the new value.

7.3.5.2 Choose appropriate variables. It is important to pick the free variables so that the rules for updating them may be easily expressed. The choice of variables should minimize unnecessary coupling between variables. The variable should have a linear relationship to other variables of interest, so that linear interpolations do not cause distortion. For example, a polar (r,θ) representation may be preferable to an (x,y) representation for aiming tasks; it may be easier to specify adjustments to solely the range, rather than x and y simultaneously. The requirements of the task force the final choice.

7.3.5.3 Use symbolic information. The need to use symbolic information arises trivially, when notes signal the presence or absence of evaluators. This subsection's point is to encourage the definition and use of symbolic information, versus implicitly representing the symbolic information by allowing the value of numeric indicators to vanish (go to zero or some other change-inhibiting value) in part of the input space.

A tuner adjusting the ball's horizontal crossing point at the table's far end might evaluate the current crossing point to yield either a desired left or right correction, or a symbolic datum indicating that no adjustment is required. For a similar example, see Figure 34. By using symbolic information, we dramatically reduce the number of rules that a tuner must process on any given pass, improving speed.

7.3.5.4 Use prior information. Data from the previous iteration can aid the computation of updates. During the main-line computing routines, when substantial ancillary information is available, it is desirable to save extra information for later use by the tuners. This point applies particularly to robot-position-related data. Often, we compute quantities that are quite good, or exact, partial derivatives. Rather than computing a particular value from scratch, we can often use a value computed during the previous iteration, even though we will introduce some slight error and inconsistency by doing so.

7.3.5.5 Do no harm. True to the ancient physician's dictum, a tuner must try to ensure that by solving one problem, it is not making another much worse. We might think twice before correcting a 1 cm error in ball placement with a 60° change in joint angle. Partial derivatives are an excellent way of comparing the scale of the problem and solution. We have some expression of the form:

$$symptom = \frac{\partial output}{\partial input} \times cure \qquad (129)$$

If the partial derivative is much greater than 1, we must be careful to avoid overcorrecting the symptom. If the partial derivative is much less than 1, the cure will be significantly larger than the symptom. The best tactic under these circumstances is to not make the change at all, but to let a different tuner solve the problem.

Often we do wind up comparing apples and oranges, and the value "1" in the discussion above ought be replaced with some more appropriate value. When relating angles and distances, the radius arm serves as a normalizing factor. A model can always provide a qualitative interpretation of a specific partial derivative.

7.3.5.6 Do your own job. Individual tuner rules should not try, or need, to examine the consequences of their actions. A change made to one variable will affect many others, but a tuner should not have to consider this. If it had to, the tuning system would become unworkably complex.

Suppose we are tuning a variable T which has an effect on variables A and B; both A and B are stressed. If we tune T to reduce A's problem, we may make B worse. However, B will also be requesting a change in T (that would make A worse). The two changes will cancel; T will remain unchanged and A and B must be mitigated by a different tuner. If problem A is much worse than B, T will improve A at the expense of B until both problems are equally serious (or cured).

It may occasionally prove useful to take an entirely different course of action when we symbolically detect the simultaneous presence of particular conflicting problems. For example, if the ball is in danger of hitting the near frame's top bar, and also of striking the net, rather than trying (futilely) to find the right Z velocity, we should hit the ball harder (by increasing the Y velocity).

7.3.5.7 Types of tuning rules. The tuning rules must be designed to ensure that extreme values for the free variable are not inadvertently produced, and that extreme values generated by an individual rule do not overwhelm other more sensible rules.

The most common type of rule specifies a weight based on the partial derivative of the problem versus the free variable; the value is computed from the criticality of the problem (supplied by an evaluator) and the partial derivative. The rule is well behaved because a small partial derivative gives the resulting outrageous value little weight. These rules follow directly from the Section 7.3.5.5 and Equation 129. To find a joint angle's adjustment to induce a specified change in paddle position, we divide the change in position by the partial derivative (from the robot's Jacobian). A model generates the rule's weight from the partial derivative, ensuring that an unfavorable derivative disables the rule.

Rules may also specify a weight based on an evaluator, and a value based not on the evaluator, but some simple function or constant. The rules are as well behaved as the value, which is usually well behaved by construction. Such rules maintain the current value of a variable, or force the value towards a desired equilibrium position. A similar rule forces the ball's point of contact on the paddle towards the center of the paddle, as long as the time of contact remains remote.

7.3.5.8 Local optimization. A system of tuners can overcorrect, because each tuner tries to correct the entire problem. In practice, the entire desired correction is not usually made anyway due to the influence of other rules, and only one or two variables are positioned to do something about a particular problem at any given time. The other variables are orthogonal to the problem.

Recall that we are not under any obligation to make a change at all, let alone some "optimal" correction. The tuner's behavior is loosely specified; our objective is to create tuners which exhibit the desired effects.

7.4 Exception Recovery

In a complex, dynamic environment, problems occur regularly, as new sensor data forces responses of which the robot is incapable (despite the temporal updating), or as a result of unimplementable initial plans. It is not acceptable for a real-time system to crash, or even to give up. We must at least attempt to actively solve the problem. This section will describe how we can accomplish this.

7.4.1 Detection. Normally, machine exceptions occur as the result of such operations as accessing invalid memory, dividing by zero, or taking the square root of a negative number. Whereas the first case reflects a programming bug, we are interested in the other cases where the exception is the result of a problem in the task.

For example, dividing by zero may signal that the system is currently physically incapable of moving in a certain direction. If we let a machine exception (trap) occur, additional effort will be required to even identify the failing instruction, let alone the semantics.

Other exceptions can arise when particular constraints are violated, for example, that the joint angles of the robot stay within certain bounds. Such restrictions must be enforced by software, though we will refer to both hardware and software detected problems as exceptions.

We will assume that the program contains tests that detect exceptions before they occur, and that a test's failure causes the exception handling mechanism to be invoked. Exceptions that are not pre-detected are considered program bugs, and may cause a crash. The checks that are needed are well known, not overwhelmingly numerous, and good programming practice.

7.4.2 Correction strategies. Even though exceptions must be detected at their point of occurrence, we wish to centralize strategies for correcting the problems. This approach simplifies implementation, lets the problem be evaluated in its full context, and allows us to use more sophisticated, global, problem-solving strategies.

The primary objective during exception recovery is to solve the problem causing an exception and return to the normal task as rapidly as possible. The exception handler must decide upon the best correction to make; a poor choice will prolong recovery.

We will use the tuners to determine and execute the correction. The tuners have the necessary information to do the task, as they are already performing a quite similar one.

When we recover from an exception, we must re-execute part of the program. We have wasted the CPU cycles initially expended executing that part of the program. Selecting the wrong tuner wastes more CPU cycles than necessary, and the tuner may make the situation worse, if it tries a less than clear-cut correction. Even though a given problem may be solved in several ways, the exception handler should use a correction which is unlikely to cause further harm.

Wasting CPU cycles is always bad because it reduces the time for motion. At the end of a motion, this can be a critical effect, and one that is alien to less than true real-time programs and programmers. The exception handler must attempt to minimize the time required to recover.

Once a single error has occurred, the likelihood of an additional error is substantially higher. If the attempted correction was unsuccessful and the same problem immediately recurs, it is important that the exception handler recognize this to avoid going into an infinite loop. The exception handler must try different strategies until it succeeds.

If a new, different exception occurs, it may be best interpreted in the context of the original problem, as the original cure is most often the current cause. By saving state from one problem to the next, we can recognize pathological cases and use alternate solutions.

7.4.3 Requirements for numeric routines. The strictly numeric routines must be enhanced to enable exception recovery. As previously described, exceptions must be intercepted before they occur, causing a subroutine call to the exception handler. The numeric routines must produce error description information that will be useful in recovering.

Normal numeric programs produce *symbolic* error descriptions: "divide by zero" or "sqrt argument < 0," a reversal from what one would expect of a supposedly numeric program. The system architect must establish a correspondence between each such low-level failure condition and a task-level problem. For example, we might establish that a particular square root of a negative number corresponds to the robot target position being out of reach. Subsequently, we can refer to the much more informative error "arm too far" instead of "minus sqrt in backward arm solution."

Numeric data about the degree of error is required as well. If the arm is too far away, we would like to know additionally that it is 11.4 mm too far, as this combination of symbolic and numeric information will allow us to solve the problem. Obtaining this information can require additional work, but it allows us to solve the problem, and does not slow down normal task execution.

Finally, the numeric routine must generate an estimate of the degree of change required to correct the problem. The desired correction is somewhat larger than the error, to ensure that we eliminate the problem in a single iteration. However, excessively large corrections will cause problems in other variables, possibly causing an avalanche.

A single model can conditionally generate a temporal updating tuple, an exception tuple, or no correction tuples (all's well) with a single invocation, simplifying and speeding the implementation.

7.4.4 Architecture for exception recovery. In this section we will describe the architecture of the exception handling system, following the logical flow of events from the time of occurrence of a single initial error. The architecture is shown in Figure 35.

7.4.4.1 Invocation. After an implementation routine has determined that an exception has occurred and characterized the type and degree of the problem, it initiates the exception recovery process by calling the master exception handler, which for reasons that will become apparent, is called *CEO* (for Chief Executive Officer).

At the same time, the implementation routine specifies a note that roughly characterizes the problem. Although it may seem that the note is redundant, since the CEO could simply look at the blackboard, the directly specified note enables the CEO to easily determine the most recent problem, since there may be several at any given time.

The CEO will record the type of problem and that exception recovery is now underway. The CEO also executes global checks on the recovery process that will be discussed in Section 7.4.4.9.

7.4.4.2 Selection of a VP. The CEO will then choose a VP (as in vice-president) capable of handling that particular class of problems. For example, one VP responds to predicted rule violations in the ping-pong ball's flight after the robot hits it. The symbolic information about the problem's classification suffices to make this selection. Once it has been made, it is recorded using additional notes, and the VP can be initiated.

7.4.4.3 Selecting a strategy. The VP is responsible for picking the tuner to attempt a correction. The two most important factors affecting this selection are:

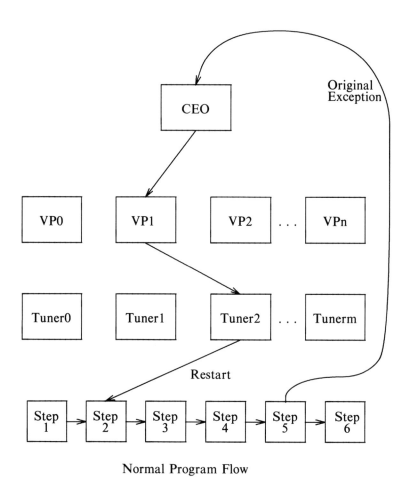

Normal Program Flow

Figure 35. Exception Handling Architecture. An exception occurs in Step 5, causing CEO, VP1, and Tuner2 to be invoked in that order. After Tuner2 has run, VP1 adjusts the blackboard and does a `longjmp`; TOPLEVEL causes control to pass to Step 2.

1. that the problem be sensitive to the attempted correction, and

2. the length of time required to effect a correction.

The length of time required becomes more important as the available time becomes smaller.

The VP must determine exactly what problem should be solved, as the note specified to the CEO is generic. Often, multiple errors occur at once, for example, several joints becoming performance-limited at once. In this case, the VP should be sensitive to the worst error. The tuner will minimize the additional errors as well.

The selection of the tuner may be done using the decide routine, with weights to control the importance of the factors. We run a measure of the exception's sensitivity to the tuned variables through an evaluating model to form the factor values. Once the VP has decided on a tuner, the decision is recorded on the blackboard.

7.4.4.4 Running the tuner. The selected tuner is called directly by the VP to find new values for the selected variables. Notes signal that exception recovery is underway; the notes may selectively disable rules useful only during temporal updating. We want to execute rules that force the variable towards a nominal value only once per updating cycle.

7.4.4.5 Restarting execution. After the tuner has been run, thus updating some free variables, normal program execution can resume. The VP erases enough notes to cause program flow to resume at the point of use of the just-tuned variables. Proper partitioning of the numeric routines and the initial planners and updaters is required so that the latter routines are not rerun, which would interfere with the correction.

A longjmp causes the contents of the machine stack to be erased, including the subroutine call history of the exception handler. The top-level routine then identifies the proper point to continue executing. The wipes and longjmp needed to return control to common locations can be placed in subroutines to simplify programming.

7.4.4.6 Successful correction. An attempted correction is successful if the main-line program succeeds in formulating and initiating a viable robot trajectory. When this occurs, the exception handling process's state is erased, so that the following temporal updating cycle will start with a clean slate. It is debatable whether some information should be saved in case of an exception next iteration, but then the relevance of the old data to the new exception would have to be carefully evaluated.

7.4.4.7 Additional exceptions. Once a single exception has taken place, additional exceptions may occur, especially when the sensor data changes late in a motion. For example, bounces and collisions with the net cause unpredictable changes in the ping-pong system's sensor data. Additional exceptions may also result from an earlier exception's cure. When a subsequent exception arises, the conditions resulting from an earlier exception may indicate that an unusual strategy may be preferable.

The notes allow the exception handling process to rapidly reestablish its original subroutine calling sequence, which was destroyed by the `longjmp` at the conclusion of the first exception. During the initial exception, the CEO and VP recorded which routine they called; during the second exception, since there is prior state, they call the same routine again. A collection of notes can straightforwardly encode the path, as long as there is no recursion (cycles). Once the original context has been reestablished, the VP might encounter one of several cases.

If the same problem has recurred, the criticality of the problem may be examined and compared to the value at the original occurrence. If the problem has been mitigated, the VP should call the same tuner again to let it finish the job. This test is embedded in an algorithm that Section 7.4.4.8 will present. Otherwise, if the tuner did not help, a new strategy should be selected with that tuner excluded from consideration.

If the problem is new, it may or may not have a special treatment in the current context. If it does not, or if the special strategy has been tried and has failed, the VP should give up, and allow its caller to determine further strategy. A VP gives up by clearing its own state and returning. The caller can then select a new strategy, excluding failed approaches from consideration (possibly more than one), much as if a tuner had failed.

If a special case has arisen, the VP may do whatever is indicated to solve the problem. The VP may change the system's state as required, or cause much of the system's state to be discarded and rebuilt from scratch.

A last possibility arises when an exception occurs that the VP is not prepared to handle by itself, yet the VP wants to retain its authority over the situation. A relatively minor problem in the midst of a major one might suggest these semantics. The VP may delegate the problem to another VP, forming a hierarchical structure. The first VP trivially examines the status of the second VP to prevent cycles in the hierarchy. The second VP may then attempt to solve the problem, but the first retains the ability to review and redirect subsequent exceptions.

7.4.4.8 The `worthwhile` *algorithm.* The test "Is it worthwhile to rerun tuner X?" is implemented by a generic algorithm. This simplifies the VP's, and by using a global database, also prevents different VPs from reusing the same tuner. Before a VP uses a given tuner (both the first and following times), the VP asks the `worthwhile` algorithm for permission, citing the problem to be addressed, the proposed method, and the problem's severity (desired correction).

If the approach has not been previously tried, `worthwhile` records the information in its data base, and signals the VP to proceed. If the approach has been tried, `worthwhile` can then compare the stored old and the new criticalities. If the criticality has not been significantly improved, `worthwhile` prevents yet another retry. To catch situations where the error is being reduced by a constant ratio each pass, `worthwhile` limits the number of times an approach can be tried. Unless this is the case, the new criticality is recorded and a retry ensues.

The `worthwhile` algorithm makes it easy to ensure that the error recovery process will not result in an infinite loop, even across a collection of VPs with overlapping correction strategies.

7.4.4.9 Global recovery strategies. At the beginning of every exception handling sequence, the CEO has the opportunity to exert global control. It eliminates the necessity for each VP to test the same things, and provides a place to consider further-reaching strategies.

The CEO can test for upcoming deadlines (such as the ball-to-paddle contact time) to ensure that they will be met. The length of time before a viable plan is created is indeterminate, and occasionally infinite. The CEO can continually monitor the available time, and, when necessary, break off processing to meet the deadline, using the last completed plan as a guide.

The CEO can cause a new data point to be read if exception processing has continued for too long. The decision can be made conditional upon the presence of a new data point, and on its deviation from the existing one. In the absence of a new data point, processing can continue for as long as possible. When reading a data point, effectively starting a new temporal updating cycle, the CEO may preserve or eliminate the current state, depending on how similar the new data is, and on whatever other higher-level information is relevant.

If major exception handling activity has been induced by a drastically new input point, and there is a significant amount of time available, the CEO has the option of completely terminating the current plan, and redoing the initial planning from scratch. To do so, initial planning elements must be capable of recognizing that part of the state that can not be canceled — especially the robot position and velocity. The robot would be returned to its initial position and stopped only if the available time was very large.

If the consequences of breaking a particular constraint are not particularly severe, the CEO can choose to ignore a rule, and allow execution to continue. The main-line computational routines must be compatible with this option. Ignoring the constraint can be as simple as returning from the CEO, or can be achieved with notes.

At this point, it should be clear that there are many options for both CEO and VPs. The application determines what they must do, rather than some recipe. We have strived to create an architecture in which we can express complex strategies effectively, and can continue to improve them as we coach the system towards higher performance.

7.5 Learning?

The role of learning is an important question in the design of large, complex real-time robot systems. Learning is a field in its own right, and we have no desire to duplicate work done there. Instead, we need to consider exactly its applicability to dynamic robotic systems — when to apply it, and how to implement it.

We will consider a specialized form of learning, where the detailed characteristics are learned, but the form of the relation is known in advance, or supplied by an essentially off-line artificial intelligence system.

7.5.1 What could we learn? We can distinguish between the learning of structures, and the learning of parameters.

Learning, without prior information, that moving a light switch causes a light to go on, is an example of learning a structure. An entirely new logical connection between the action and effect must be formed.

On the other hand, we also need to learn the force required to trip the switch. We might want to learn the coefficient of restitution of a particular ping-pong paddle, given that we already know about coefficients of restitutions in general, and may already have values for other paddles.

Humans can learn the rules of ping-pong in one presentation. However, we require substantial practice to achieve and maintain skilled play, even when we fully understand the fundamentals. It is thus our claim that learning may be divided into a high-level, symbolic, artificial intelligence category, and a lower-level but no less important numeric variety. The numeric variety best falls within the domain of this work.

The learning of structures properly belongs in the domain of the controlling AI system, as the task is temporally decoupled. It does not rely upon or produce information directly required by the real-time system, though it may affect the real-time system's structure and algorithms.

We assume that the learning of parameters takes place in the presence of models that define the characteristics of the data to be learned. The model for turning on the light switch might indicate that force is required only along the Z axis; the numeric content must indicate only the magnitude of that force (the parameter).

It seems very unlikely that humans are hardwired to learn all the things they are capable of learning. (Humans are apparently preprogrammed to learn some things, such as language.) Are people preprogrammed to learn to play ping-pong, or in what direction and how hard to push a light switch? Certainly not. The AI system must generate models such that the numeric learning process may take place; they operate synergistically.

Parameter learning is driven by data from the real-time system, and requires no "reasoning." The expert controller applies the learned data in real time. Therefore, the learning of parameters ought to be implemented by the real-time system. The learning may still be at least partially decoupled from the execution of the task; only the *use* of the learned data must be done in real time.

7.5.2 What should we learn? The need to learn implies a lack of knowledge on the system designer's part. Why don't you know whatever it is to be learned? The designer's failure to understand the problem will result in an incorrect parameterization for the model, and almost certainly in a dysfunctional learner.

Repeatability is crucial to effective learning, to ensure convergence, and to prevent the development of excessive, "superstitious," complexity in the material being learned. Coaching procedures for humans emphasize the development of repeatability even at the expense of quality of play during learning. Design for repeatability has been studied in industrial settings [37]. We can increase repeatability by eliminating excess degrees of freedom and the corresponding variability in them. Human skill learning has been described as a process of reducing the number of degrees of freedom to a tractable level, then gradually increasing them [24].

The best candidates for learning appear to be either internal program characteristics, or physical events which require unobservable internal information to predict, but which are well behaved with no discontinuities or regions of extreme parameter sensitivity. A bounce off the paddle's rubber surface is believed to be nonlinear, but locally linear. We could increase the accuracy of the hit prediction by making the linear hit model's parameters functions of the ball's incoming velocity.

The point of this section has been that learning ought to be considered only when really required, not as a crutch for failing to understand the situation, or as an attempt to compensate for irreproducibility by "learning" the causes.

7.5.3 Elements of learning parameters. The process of learning is not monolithic, but requires several substeps, as shown in Figure 36. The software implementing learning must have access to the source data, processor cycles to examine it, and a means of effecting changes. An implementation substrate for these steps (using demons) was previously presented in Section 3.4.3, as part of the data logging system's discussion.

7.5.3.1 Event detection. The first step towards learning is to identify occasions in which learning is possible. Although this may seem a trivial point, it is not. In a complex task, many activities are happening at once, any of which may be candidates for learning different pieces of information.

We will assume that the learning of each piece of information is mediated by a separate agent, a "demon." The demon has the responsibility of identifying appropriate circumstances for its particular parameter or parameters to be learned, and doing the learning.

It is difficult to construct a demon that is capable of recognizing exactly when it should learn, when it would be best to ignore some corrupted data point, or when a data point is being acted on by influences beyond the demon's knowledge.

Instead, we must take advantage of the *active* characteristics of the robot domain. Rather than being passively subjected to stimuli to be learned, the robot actively generates them. The demon's implementation can be considerably simplified by *predicting* events to be learned, rather than trying to identify them.

Of course, this requires some collusion between the program components that plan activities and the demons that subsequently analyze them, but there is no reason why they ought not do so.

7.5.3.2 Interpreting the event. The initiation of a demon constitutes an implicit description of the environment the demon will have to examine. The same opportunity may be taken to explicitly describe the environment, especially if the parameters may be hard to observe subsequently.

The demon has available to it later and better information about what occurred than the initiator. The data driving the learning process must be what actually happened, not what was supposed to happen. If we use only data about what was supposed to happen, a substantial noise component can be introduced into the learning process. Of course, if the observed data has a high noise component, it is best to learn from the expected data instead.

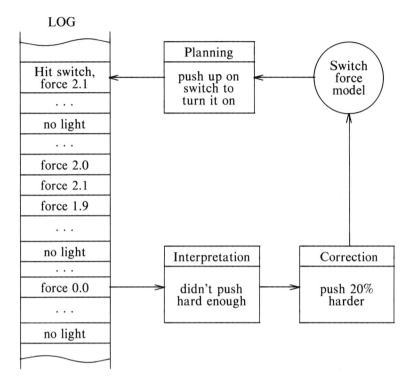

Figure 36. Steps in Learning. The system's history is interpreted to decide that the switch wasn't pushed hard enough; a model is then corrected so that the next time, the planner will cause the switch to be pushed harder.

7.5.3.3 Ascertaining the correct response. The correct response for a specific situation must be ascertained, given the observed stimulus and response data. For example, if we hit a ball at 2 m/sec, resulting in a flight of 1.2 m rather than the 1.5 m desired, we must compute a new paddle speed that would have sent the ball 1.5 m. The complexity of finding the right response is problem dependent, and may range from simple linear relations to iterative simulations. We presumably already have good approximations to the correct results, so low-order local approximations may be successfully used, simplifying the problem.

7.5.3.4 Making the correction. Finally, the demon must make an appropriate correction. The model and the inputs we used initially to generate the output were specified at the initiation of the demon, so the cause of the problem is obvious. The cure is not. It is hard to define good semantics for the change to the model as a whole. There are two effects that must be dealt with: data scarcity and noise.

Any particular data point we learn applies only to exactly the same situation for which it was originally learned, yet every run is different. We must interpolate among the data points available to construct new values.

Furthermore, no data point is perfect — each has noise. The interpolation method must not be dominated by the noise, but filter it out. For example, two closely spaced data points with noise can cause major problems (Figure 37).

Polynomial fits, where the degree varies as a fraction of the number of data points, and low-pass-filtered Fourier reconstructions are possible interpolators. The interpolator must be able to process parameters with substantial numbers of inputs.

As a technical point, it is undesirable to have to execute the interpolator at run time, instead, the interpolator can generate values over the entire input space when a new data point arrives. The model data structure may be used to distinguish between primary data points and the synthetically generated interpolated values. This distinction is already made by the `builder` program, which uses spline interpolation and must therefore remember the human's knot points. (It does not have to operate in the presence of noise and is thus not subject to the problem shown in Figure 37.) Large models may have to be updated only locally to save processor time.

The learning process has the same iterative feedback characteristic of temporal updating. It is not essential that we behave optimally, but only that we eventually converge to the right answers. The quality of our solutions are measured by how quickly they do this.

7.5.4 Remarks. Learning is a difficult technique to apply, and is certainly not a "magic wand" or panacea for poorly understood problems. When learning must be applied, it will be subject to "errors" due to many unknown or unmeasurable factors. Even the best available model of a learning machine, a person, requires many repetitions to master a skill. Convergence will be slow, and performance approximate. However, the initial planning and temporal updating processes operate similarly; the system is well prepared to take advantage of inaccurate data from a slow learner.

Output

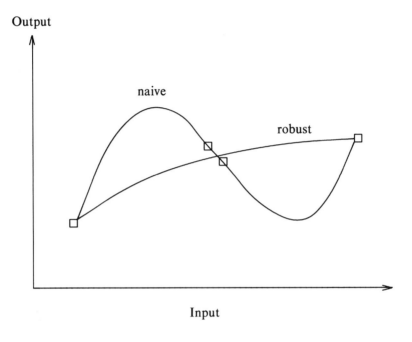

Input

Figure 37. Interpolating with Noise. The two closely spaced points can force simple interpolators to make wildly inaccurate predictions.

7.6 Summary

In this chapter, we have described an architecture for constructing complex and robust real-time systems that are able to process continuous streams of sensor data to solve poorly specified problems. The presence of a continuous stream of sensor data greatly affected the design of the expert controller.

It allowed us to simplify the initial planning process, and concentrate on obtaining initial plans which are "good guesses." Though only a limited amount of data is available during initial planning, we can take advantage of whatever data is available.

The temporal updating process modifies the plan in response to changing sensor data. It also allows information from the later stages of processing to propagate to the early stages, so that the plan can be globally optimized.

The temporal updating process minimizes the likelihood of serious exceptions, yet they can still be forced by the sensor data. We introduced an exception handling scheme to rapidly assess and correct exceptions as they occur, enabling execution to proceed. The architecture allows the old flow of execution to be erased, and a new flow to be efficiently initiated.

The "model" (introduced in Chapter 6) was used throughout the program to represent both numeric and symbolic information. Two operators, `decide` and `combine`, were used to combine information from disparate sources. These tools and the regular program organization facilitate coaching by high-level programs, as well as flexibility during development by humans.

Learning was discussed and methods outlined, but the most significant point is that learning must be judiciously applied, and is best omitted from a well-characterized system.

Chapter 8

Robot Ping-Pong Application

This chapter will describe the expert controller's application to robot ping-pong. We will begin with an overview of the `striker` program. The design of selected program components will be described in Section 8.2. Section 8.3 will present case studies of sample volleys to illustrate the program's performance. Finally, in Section 8.4 we will describe some limitations in the program implementation.

8.1 Program Overview

In this section, we will catalog the program's elements: free variables, tuners, and VPs. Each element will be described in detail later; we do not intend to provide a self-sufficient description here. We will describe the top-level routine in some depth.

The free variables reflect the expert controller's latitude in defining the robot ping-pong task:

1. `hpdno` — the hit plane's index,

2. `depth` — the hit plane depth, possibly offset from nominal,

3. `pad_con_xgen` and `pad_con_ygen` — the position on the paddle's surface where the paddle will hit the ball,

4. `target_alpha, target_vy, target_vz` — the components of the ball's velocity after the paddle hits it (`target_vx` is encoded in `target_alpha` as atan (`target_vx/target_vy`)),

5. `stick_angle` — the angle about the Y axis of the stick that supports the paddle, and

6. `settle_time[6]` — the length of time each joint's arrival at its destination will precede contact with the ball.

Although eight free variables does not seem numerous, remember that we are picking from a space of dimension ∞^8 (counting the settling times only once). The ping-pong task is analogous to controlling a 14 degree of freedom robot.

We have a tuner for each group of related free variables:

1. `tunealpha` — tunes `target_alpha`,

2. `tunecontact` — tunes `pad_con_xgen` and `pad_con_ygen`,

3. `tunehpd` — tunes `depth`,

4. `tunestang` — tunes `stick_angle`, and

5. `tunevyz` — tunes `target_vy` and `target_vz`.

The small number of tuners belies their great importance.

We need a VP to handle each major class of exceptions:

1. `hitVP` — no hit plane depth,

2. `impVP` — a problem with the ball's return flight,

3. `conVP` — no stick angle or an impossible configuration, and

4. `accVP` — a joint EMF limitation.

There are 48 models, too many to describe. The `autoface` program (which generates C front-ends for the models) wrote 16% of the `striker` program. The numerous models illustrate the success of using models to encode strategy.

Appendix 4 lists the `striker` program's top-level loop, fortunately, it is only a few sparse pages long. The `setjmp` may be found at the top of the program; all the code blocks that examine the blackboard must follow it. An early, high-priority, block stops the robot at the stroke's end.

The real code starts with the test "`invisible (robot_moving)`," which looks to see if the robot is moving. If it is not, the following code block performs initial planning. Each subroutine call is prefixed by a test to see if the task has already been performed. A short block removes leftover ball trajectories from previous strokes; it should probably be somewhere else. `Reconsider` is a euphemism for the `longjmp` call.

Once the initial plan has been completed, a transition code block records the plan and the system begins temporal updating. The "`while(1)`" loop encapsulates the updating process; the code resembles initial planning. The routine `tuner` calls all the tuners.

As long as everything goes well, `hit_the_ball` executes the same as any other routine. If an exception occurs, the recovery process will force `hit_the_ball` to be restarted from the `setjmp`; it will then fall through the "`if`" statements until it encounters the right place to resume execution.

8.2 Examination of Program Components

In this section we will describe different parts of the program, roughly organized by the type of activity they control. We will show the expert controller's use, and consequently, outline the ping-pong strategy it implements. The ping-pong-related information is necessary to be able to understand the expert controller's performance, which will be described in Section 8.3. To give a feel for the actual code, we will list some code fragments early on.

8.2.1 Hit plane depth selection. The robot ping-pong player must choose the position along the ball's trajectory at which the robot should hit the ball. The *hit plane depth* (HPD) defines this location by the Y-axis value of the point of contact (Figure 38). We consider three possible HPDs, corresponding to up close, nominal, and far back. The HPD is a free variable which must be selected during initial planning. Figure 39 outlines the process of selecting an HPD.

Table 8 shows the code for evaluating the HPDs. Each HPD has two notes, `examined_depth` and `usable_depth`, which indicate whether the HPD has been tested yet and whether it is a possible HPD. We flag an HPD as unusable if the ball's intersection with the HPD is unreasonably out of the nominal area, putting the robot at risk of running into its cage. `Hit_details` simulates the ball's trajectory to the point of intersection with the hit plane, then evaluates the intersection point to create numeric factors we will use to pick the HPD; if the position is unusable, the evaluator clears the `usable_hpd` note. The same procedure computes a tentative new hit position (see Section 8.2.2) during temporal updating. Figure 40 shows the X direction evaluator. The central curve is the evaluator; the additional curve at each end of X's domain indicates that the hit position is unusable, and by how much.

Once an HPD has been identified as feasible, additional evaluators are called into play. `Glide_eval`, `hitT_eval`, and `reach_model` evaluate the dropping angle, time until intersection, and general reachability of the point, respectively, the latter using a large model generated off-line.

The `CumErr_eval` model evaluates the time from when the ball crosses the end of the table to when it reaches the HPD. If this time is

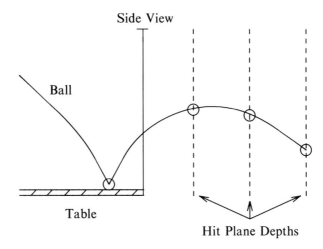

Figure 38. Hit Plane Depth. The system initially plans to hit the ball, traveling from left to right, at one of three nominal hit planes spaced 150 mm apart.

```
for (hpdno = 0, chit_desc = hit_desc;
     hpdno < YH_BUSED; hpdno++, chit_desc++)
{
   chd = chit_desc;
   if (visible (chd->examined_depth) ||
       invisible (chd->usable_depth))
      continue;
   hit_details(cnch);              /* sets examined_depth */
   if (invisible (chd->usable_depth))
   {
      scribble (chd->examined_depth);
      continue;
   };
   Glide_eval();
   hitT_eval();
   reach_model();
   CumErr_eval ( chd->t0depth + InYB_penalty (ball_yb) );
   scribble (chd->examined_depth);
};
```

Table 8. Hit Plane Depth Evaluation. The `hpdno` variable is the index of the hit plane.

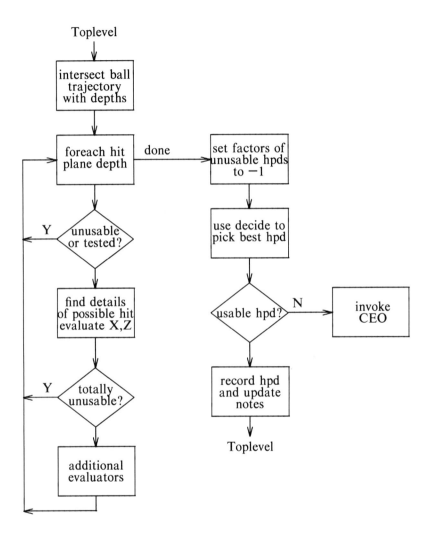

Figure 39. Hit Plane Depth Selection Flow-chart

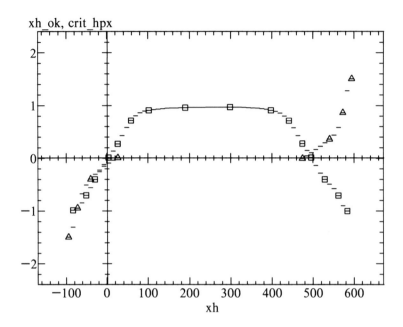

Figure 40. X Hit Position Evaluator. The input to the model is the X position at which the ball might be hit. The central curve, marked with squares, generates a figure of merit for the position. The outer curves, marked with triangles, indicates that the position is too far to the side, including a numeric severity.

excessively long, any error in velocity (especially velocity, though position as well) will have built up to unacceptable levels. On a very deep bounce, we will not obtain post-bounce trajectory data, making the trajectory data even more uncertain. `InYB_penalty` adds an additional penalty to the time of flight before it is used in `CumErr_eval`, depending on the expected position of the bounce on the table.

To ensure that `decide` does not inadvertently select an unusable HPD, we must reset all factors for unusable HPDs to −1 before the HPD selection (Table 9). In the absence of any feasible HPDs, the identifying note `no_hpd` will be set, and the CEO called to initiate exception handling.

The `examined_depth` and `usable_depth` notes make the code restartable, allowing rapid selection of a new HPD if the existing one fails. The HPD selector makes effective use of models, allowing easy specification of qualitative effects which are undeniably true, but for which

```
hpdno = decide (SQhpd, YH_BUSED, SQt, SQx, SQz, SQth,
    SQcum, SQoverall, OL);
printlog (HITDECIS, hpdno, SQhpd[0], SQhpd[1], SQhpd[2]);
if (hpdno < 0)
{
    printlog (NOHPDS);
    scribble (no_hpd);
    ceo (&no_hpd);
};
chit_desc = hit_desc+hpdno;
scribble (valid_hpd);
wipe (no_hpd);
```

Table 9. Hit Plane Depth Selector. We pick a hit plane based on evaluations of the time of flight, X position, Z position, descent rate, time of flight while out of the cameras' views, and reachability.

it is hard to specify justifiable details. As well as hit-related effects, we have also modeled the effects of sensor uncertainty, although precise data is similarly hard to come by.

8.2.2 Tuning the point of contact. During temporal updating, hit_details generates a new ball trajectory and computes a new point of intersection with the previously selected HPD. A tuner then computes a modified hit plane depth in the vicinity of the original one. If the ball is rising or dropping especially rapidly, a new depth can reduce the apparent change in ball location. This correction also keeps the contact point above the table when the ball will drop just over the table's end.

Given the prior paddle position and the new ball position, we can compute the ball's point of contact on the paddle (Figure 41). We can intentionally force the contact point away from the center of the paddle. The tunecontact tuner, the subject of this section, controls this function. As may be seen from Figure 41, tunecontact must tune two degrees of freedom (X and Y) at once, complicating an otherwise pedagogically simple tuner. Tunecontact has three rules:

1. keep the generated point of contact near the computed one, but on the paddle;

2. unless there is little time left, the ball is far away, or exception recovery is in progress, stay at the center of the paddle; and

3. if the point of contact approaches the edge of the table, make contact at the very tip of the paddle.

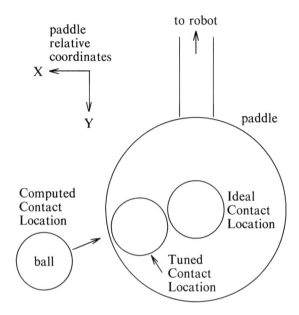

Figure 41. Ball and Paddle Contact Point

The rules are not justified to the program (Section 7.2.5), but they have the following purposes:

1. to minimize the change in arm position due to the new sensor data,

2. to minimize the probability that sensor data errors might cause a clean miss, and

3. to ensure that the paddle does not hit the table at high speed.

Making the program rigorously understand these justifications would be extremely complex and reduce it to apparent catatonia, while probably having no measurable change in performance (discounting execution time).

The rules are not mutually consistent. `Tunecontact` will have to make a reasonable decision using `combine`.

Tuning will be performed in X,Y space, but the constraint to keep the ball's contact point on the paddle is a function of the distance from the center of the paddle. The `Clip_paddle` model computes the desired radius given the computed radius, then the X,Y values (Table 10).

```
/* head towards a clipped version of the
      expected values pad_con_[xy]e */

ract = sqrt(pad_con_xe*pad_con_xe + pad_con_ye*pad_con_ye);
if (ract != 0.)
    t1 = Clip_paddle (ract, &center_wei) / ract;
else
    t1 = 1.;
weip[mfact] = 1.;
valp[mfact] = pad_con_xe * t1;
mfact++;
wei[nfact] = 1.;
val[nfact] = pad_con_ye * t1;
nfact++;
```

Table 10. Radial Contact Rule. The radial position of the contact point is clipped
to be less than the paddle radius, 6.25 cm. The `Clip_paddle` model
is shown below.

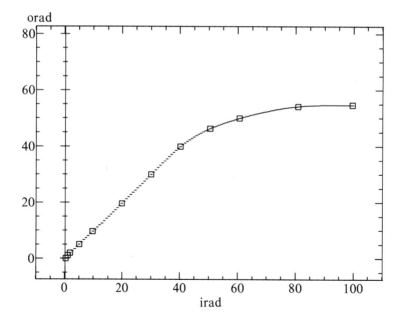

Figure 42. `Clip_paddle` Model

```
/* if we're down close to the edge of the table, make sure
      we keep to the outer edge of the paddle */

if (hpdno == 0)
{
   wei[nfact] = Avoid_table (sqrt (chit_desc->P.y*
      chit_desc->P.y + chit_desc->P.z*chit_desc->P.z));
   val[nfact] = 62.5;            /* radius of paddle */
   nfact++;
};

/* now pick 'em */

pad_con_xgen = combinewv (mfact, weip, valp);
pad_con_ygen = combinewv (nfact, wei, val);
```

Table 11. Table Avoidance and Combine. If the hit plane closest to the table is being used, the point of contact is forced to the tip of the paddle, with a weight determined by proximity to the edge of the table.

The form of Clip_paddle (Figure 42) determines what really happens: how close the ball will be allowed to come to the edge of the paddle, and at what radius the ball should start to be held towards the paddle's center.

Clip_paddle also generates a weight (not shown) for the second rule, such that if the ball is very far from the paddle, there is less tendency to try to center the contact point. Logically this weight is part of Rule 2, but for speed we compute it in Clip_paddle.

Table 11 shows the rule for avoiding the table and the code for combining the rules. Rule 1 has a fixed weight and a variable (though well-behaved) value, whereas Rules 2 and 3 have varying weights and fixed values. Notice that the rules are simple and direct; we have embedded most of the rules' real form in the models, which are easy to understand and modify.

8.2.3 Arm configuration planning. After the point of contact has been identified, we can select a return trajectory, but we will defer discussion of the return trajectory to Section 8.2.4. We proceed to consider the generation of the robot configuration at once.

8.2.3.1 Robot geometry. The return trajectory planning process results in a contact point and orientation in the "world" (table) coordinate space. We must convert the position and orientation to the six joint angles that will drive the motion planning process. The relation among table and robot coordinates may be represented by homogeneous transformation matrices:

$$\textbf{P} = \textbf{W} \ \textbf{T6} \ \textbf{S} \ \textbf{C} \qquad (130)$$

where **P** is the matrix representing the robot configuration in table coordinates, **W** is the matrix transforming robot coordinates to world coordinates, **T6** is the configuration of the robot in its base frame, **S** represents the configuration of the paddle, stick, and its mounting on the robot wrist, and **C** indicates the point of contact of the ball on the paddle. **T6** drives the arm kinematic solution; to find it, we compute:

$$\textbf{T6} = \textbf{W}^{-1} \ \textbf{P} \ \textbf{C}^{-1} \ \textbf{S}^{-1} \qquad (131)$$

However, we have ignored a difficulty: the paddle position and orientation, which have five degrees of freedom, do not uniquely determine **P**, which has six degrees of freedom. We need to specify an additional degree of freedom, the stick angle, which is a free variable in the expert controller. From the paddle orientation $\hat{o}$ and the unit vector $\hat{\imath}$ along the X axis, we compute two orthogonal ancillary vectors that are in the plane of the paddle, such that one $(\hat{u})$ is also in the YZ plane:

$$\hat{u} = \frac{\hat{o} \times \hat{\imath}}{|\hat{o} \times \hat{\imath}|} \qquad (132)$$

$$\hat{v} = \hat{u} \times \hat{o} \qquad (133)$$

The components of the transformation matrix **P** are then:

$$\hat{n} = \cos(stang)\hat{v} - \sin(stang)\hat{u} \qquad (134)$$

$$\hat{s} = \cos(stang)\hat{u} + \sin(stang)\hat{v} \qquad (135)$$

such that

$$\textbf{P} = \begin{bmatrix} n_x & s_x & o_x & p_x \\ n_y & s_y & o_y & p_y \\ n_z & s_z & o_z & p_z \\ 0 & 0 & 0 & 1 \end{bmatrix} \qquad (136)$$

where *stang* is the stick angle (`stick_angle`) and $\vec{p}$ the ball position at the hit. Roughly speaking, these equations define the stick angle as the angle between the stick holding the paddle and vertical $(\hat{k})$, about the Y $(\hat{\jmath})$ axis. The definition breaks when the paddle orientation is along the X axis, but the orientation is always within a small number of degrees of the Y axis in the horizontal plane.

We can measure the robot and its environment to determine the **W** and **S** matrices. The ball's point of contact on the paddle (Section 8.2.2) initializes the **C** matrix:

$$\mathbf{C} = \begin{bmatrix} 1 & 0 & 0 & pad\_con\_xgen \\ 0 & 1 & 0 & pad\_con\_ygen \\ 0 & 0 & 1 & 0 \\ 0 & 0 & 0 & 1 \end{bmatrix} \qquad (137)$$

From **P**, **W**, **S**, and **C**, we can find **T6** from Equation 131. The joint angles can then be determined by the arm inverse kinematics [41].

8.2.3.2 Stick angle initial planning. We are now in a position to consider the initial planning of the stick angle. The geometry of the robot drastically constrains the stick angle, such that only narrow ranges are feasible for any combination of position vector $\vec{p}$ and orientation vector $\hat{o}$. Figure 43 shows the constraints due to the maximum and minimum reach of the arm, and the limitation due to the shoulder offset. The constraints' impact on the stick angle may be directly visualized by transforming them into a plane orthogonal to the paddle's orientation vector that also passes through the paddle's center; the results are displayed in Figure 44. The intractable effects of the angular limits on the wrist joints are not shown.

As may be seen from Figure 44, there are two ranges of possible stick angles that are within the outer reachability limit, but outside the inner reachability limit. Depending on the exact configuration, there may be several possible ranges (especially when joint limits are considered), or there may be none.

If there is not much time available, the selection of the stick angle should favor an angle that can be reached quickly. If the width of a range is small, we should select the region's center to minimize the probability of an infeasible robot configuration.

The stick angle initial planning process proceeds in three stages:

1. find possible stick angle ranges,

2. select one of the ranges,

3. select a stick angle within the range.

The possible stick angle ranges are supplied by a model, `stmodel`, which has five inputs: the hit location (vector) and two orientation angles. Each input is quantized depending on the sensitivity and requirements: sixteen bins for X, Z, and rotation about $\hat{t}$; three bins in Y, one for each HPD; and four bins for rotation about $\hat{z}$, which has a comparatively small

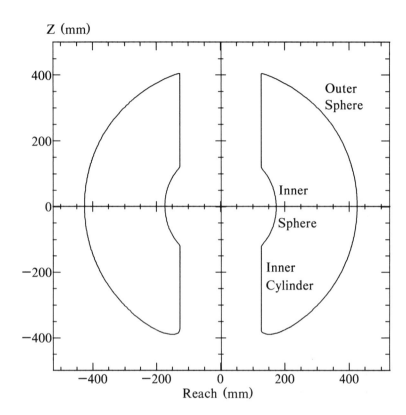

Figure 43. Arm Reach Constraints. The robot's working volume is shown. Roughly, the outer sphere is determined by the total length of the links, the inner cylinder is determined by the shoulder offset, and the inner sphere is determined by the maximum elbow bend.

range. The model is generated by an off-line simulation program which exhaustively tests configurations, including the effect of the joint limits. The simulator looks for stick angle ranges which are common to the bin's sixteen corners (each bin is a four-dimensional hypercube). The two largest ranges are stored in `stmodel`.

At run time, the stick angle initial planner uses `stmodel` to produce the ranges, then evaluates each range using two other models. Each region's width and an expected travel time is evaluated; the travel time is supplied by `stmodel`. `Decide` then selects the best region.

The width of the selected region and the time available are evaluated a second time to create two weights for `combinew` (Table 7, Section 7.2.3).

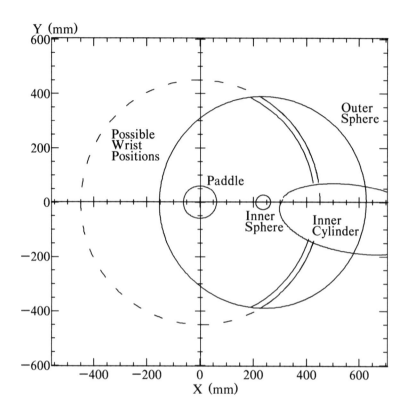

Figure 44. Stick Angle Constraints. The display shows a slice through the robot's workspace in the plane of the paddle. The robot's wrist could lie anywhere along the dashed circle, but to be reachable it must be on a double solid section. In this example, the constraints result in two possible regions for the stick angle.

The width evaluation weights the center of the range. The time evaluation weights the stick angle that is fastest to get to, which is supplied by stmodel.

The stick angle selection process illustrates how decisions can be made using a combination of precomputed and run-time information. Ranges help isolate factual constraints (kinematic limits in this case) from other more subjective factors. This *normalization* ensures that the final result will fall within the specified range, but the position within the range is determined by a process that can be (desirably) independent of the actual range.

8.2.3.3 Tuning the configuration. Once temporal updating is under way, or if an exception occurs, the arm configuration must be optimized; we must reduce the stress on the individual joints, and prevent the position from becoming unreachable. The arm configuration is controlled indirectly by the free variables: the stick angle and (especially) the ball's return velocity vector, which will be discussed in Section 8.2.4. In this section, we will discuss the evaluators that make configuration adjustment possible, and describe two interesting rules from `tunestang`.

As described in Section 7.4.3, numeric routines must describe any error with quantitative error information. Our inverse kinematics routine has been augmented to compute the distance from the outer reachability sphere if a generated position is too far, or the distance from the inner reachability cylinder if the position is too close (recall Figure 43).

After the arm solution has been computed, each joint is evaluated (see Figure 33, Section 7.3.4) to see how close it is to a limit stop. In addition to the normal "hard" joint limits, we check joints 4 and 6, which have ranges over 360°, against their prior value as well. If the new value is more than 250° away, we induce a soft limit error. When very large iteration-to-iteration changes are indicated, lower-level software is attempting to avoid a limit stop by switching to a different 360° band. Unless we catch it, the arm will swing the entire 360°, crashing the robot.

Any joint value outside its range must be compared with its prior value to make sure the correct principal value (from the `atan` in the inverse solution) is obtained; we must get the proper sign of the joint's error. We defer generating the joint limit exceptions until we have computed the Jacobian of the configuration, which is needed by some tuners.

We must also evaluate the configuration for its dynamic feasibility, to make sure the motors will be able to accelerate and decelerate the arm fast enough to arrive at the right position at the right velocity and time. The peak accelerations (positive and negative) required to execute the trajectory may be compared to the computed motor capabilities (Section 5.6). If necessary, we estimate the change (`crit_emf`) in the joint's final position necessary to reduce the joint accelerations to more reasonable values and compute a similar estimate for the final velocity (Table 12). The `best_pf` and `best_vf` routines compute the acceleration-minimizing terminal position and velocity as discussed in Sections 5.5.3.4 and 5.5.3.5. The `Pkclip_factor` model which controls the rating process is shown in Figure 45. The `Pkclip_factor` model is one of the few that we could simplify if we could pass a note as an argument, eliminating the need for the global `critical_power_rating` note; the need is less than overwhelming.

```
eval_stress (j, jtd)
   int j;
   register struct Jnt_traj_desc *jtd;
{
   double pwr,pwrrat,Pkclip_factor(),best_pf(),best_vf();

   pwrrat = jtd->al/jtd->aclipm; /* acceleration low */
   pwr = jtd->ah/jtd->aclipp;     /* acceleration high */
   if (pwr > pwrrat)
      pwrrat = pwr;
   wipe (critical_power_rating);
   pwr = Pkclip_factor (pwrrat);
   if (visible (critical_power_rating))
      {
/* compute the actual distance as a fraction of the
         deltaposition, corrected to account for
         initial velocity, in the opposite direction;
         crit_emf = number of radians to move to correct
         the problem. Similarly for final vel. */
      crit_emf[j] = pwr * (best_pf (jtd) - jtd->pf);
      if (jtd->vf != 0.)
         crit_vemf[j] = pwr * (best_vf (jtd) - jtd->vf);
      else            /* keep stopped joints stopped */
         crit_vemf[j] = 0.;
      scribble (suspect_emf[j]);
      }
   else
      wipe (suspect_emf[j]);
}
```

Table 12. Joint Stress Evaluator. The trajectory's peak accelerations are evaluated
to form crit_emf and crit_vemf, the desired changes in position
and velocity. If the joint is unstressed, no change is proposed, and the
suspect_emf[j] note is cleared.

To tune the stick angle, we will assume that a change in the stick angle
is equivalent to a rotation about the (table) Y axis. We can then use the
inverse Jacobian to find the change in stick angle that causes the desired
change in joint angle.

Accordingly, the code to tune the stick angle in response to a motor
EMF limitation is:

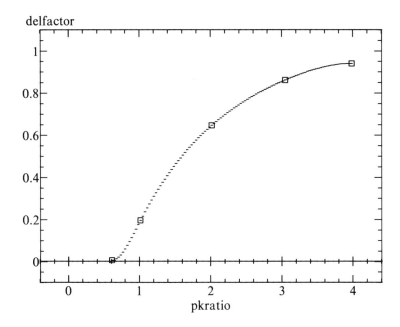

Figure 45. Joint Stress Model. The model evaluates the ratio of the trajectory's peak acceleration to the motor's maximum acceleration. The proposed correction is a fraction of the distance to the acceleration-minimizing position or velocity.

```
if (visible (suspect_emf[i]) && jacob_dthdr[i].y != 0)
{
    wei[nfact] = Edgy_wei (jacob_dthdr[i].y);
    val[nfact] = -crit_emf[i] / jacob_dthdr[i].y;
    nfact++;
};
```

where `jacob_dthdr[i].y` is $\frac{\partial \theta_i}{\partial \delta_y}$. When the Jacobian is small, the `Edgy_wei` model derates the resulting large changes. The same code is used to avoid the joint limit stops.

A more complicated rule tunes the stick angle when the wrist position is too far away from the base to be reachable. The geometry is shown in Figure 46. The basic idea is to cause a change which results in the wrist moving towards the base.

The change in wrist position due to a change in stick angle is represented by the `dposdstang` unit vector, which is equal to $-\hat{n}$ from

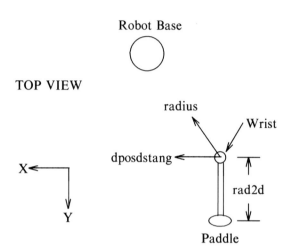

Figure 46. Geometry to Tune TOOFAR. We wish to move the wrist along the radius vector. A change in the stick angle will move the wrist along dposdstang.

Equation 134. The radius vector points from the wrist to the base of the robot coordinate system, which is located inside the shoulder at the center of the robot's reachability spheres. A model evaluates the dot product of the two vectors to create a weight for the rule. If the vectors are approximately collinear, a change in stick angle will significantly improve the situation; the weight will be higher than if the vectors are not collinear.

The stick's effective radius of revolution is rad2d. Rad2d contains no contribution from the Y direction, because the rotation is about the Y axis. The stick angle correction is the recommended linear correction (from the arm inverse kinematics) divided by rad2d.

The rule is implemented by about 20 lines of code; the same basic idea corrects the stick angle when the wrist is too close, and compensates for changes in the intersection of the ball trajectory and hit plane.

The joint EMF and too-far tuners are highly representative of the rest of the rules in the stick angle tuner. Using these rules, the stick angle may be profitably exploited to improve the quality of the arm motion being generated. The resulting programs are quite robust.

8.2.4 Return velocity planning. We can now return to the problem of planning the ball's return velocity and the paddle's orientation; the planning is complicated by the indirect relationship between the ball's return velocity and the robot's configuration and joint angles.

8.2.4.1 Initial velocity planning. The basic resource for initially generating trajectories is the `safehit` model, which generates the optimally safe trajectory in the YZ plane as a function of the hit position and a launch angle control knob. An off-line program exhaustively simulates ball trajectories to create the `safehit` model.

The control knob is normalized, varying from zero to one while sweeping through the range of launch angles feasible for the given location. A separate model generates values for the launch angle knob from the incoming ball's angle of ascent or descent.

The launch angle knob is intended for future use by higher-level strategists to select high lobs or low line drives, by combining a strategic (normalized) control with the one based on ascent angle. By this tactic, the higher-level program need not be familiar with the numeric details, or even be running at the same temporal rate.

The return velocity must also be planned in the XY plane. The first part of our strategy is to hit the ball directly across from where it is now, but displaced somewhat towards the middle of the opposing frame if the ball would be close to an edge horizontally. We could implement this strategy with two separate rules, but it is faster and easier to understand if we do it with only one model. The horizontal target is also varied depending on the XY angle of the ball.

The rationale for this strategy, versus aiming at the middle of the opposing frame for example, is to reduce the sensitivity of the XY paddle angle to the incoming ball's X position, increasing the system's robustness and stability.

After playing the machine for some time, it was discovered that additional semantics were required. If the ball is near one of the side markers, we must aim at the opposing corner to avoid running into the side marker at the robot's end of the table. These semantics were added in a few minutes by modifying the aim point to the opposite corner when the ball is near a side marker, and additionally, generating a weight that causes the opposite corner aim point to dominate the value determined from XY angle (Figure 47 and 48). The code required is simply:

```
w = Aim_lr_xh();
Aim_lr_al();
aim_xc = combinew (2, w,aim_lr_xh, 1.,aim_lr_al);
```

The return trajectory is simulated to verify its correctness and to generate evaluators for subsequent tuning. The simulation models the effect of air drag and also the effect of the spin put on the ball by contact

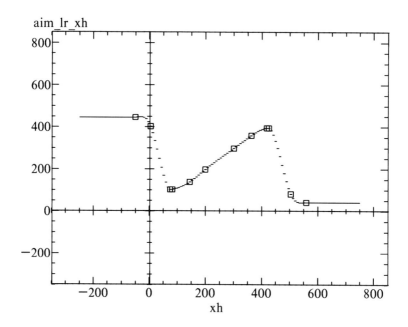

Figure 47. Horizontal Aim Point Value. The model generates an X position at which to aim from the X position at which the ball will be hit.

with the paddle. Even if spin is not intentionally generated, significant amounts are generated incidentally. Since the spin is not known until runtime, it can not be included in the initial `safehit` model without making it another input with several bins, increasing the size of the model by a factor of ten or so. We exploit the updating and simplify the models.

8.2.4.2 Simple tuning. The simulator records intermediate data to aid in tuning, especially the times required for the ball to reach the near, net, and far frames. This data serves as partial derivatives during tuning.

For example, the flight of the ball is evaluated to verify that it will clear the net. The return velocity tuner operates separately in the YZ and XY planes. The YZ tuner tunes the Y and Z velocities simultaneously. The XY plane tuner affects only the X velocity. The YZ velocity tuner's rule for adjusting the Z velocity based on a desired height correction at the net is:

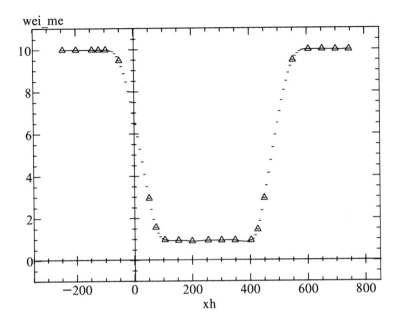

Figure 48. Horizontal Aim Point Weight. The horizontal aim point from Figure 47 is given a high weight when the ball is near a side wire and must be hit cross-court.

```
if (visible (suspect_net))
{
    weiz[zfact] = 1.;
    valz[zfact] = crit_net/(0.9*flight_desc.tmiddle);
    zfact++;
};
```

The variable `flight_desc.tmiddle` is the time of flight until the ball reaches the net; we have simply applied $d=vt$. The factor of 0.9 compensates for air drag, which reduces the apparent effect of changes in the velocity at the beginning of the trajectory. Internal constants of this type are candidates for learning, since the input and output data are simulated and thus noise free. However, the effect of this individual rule can be masked by the other rules, making learning harder.

The presence of an accurate forward simulator greatly reduces the need for accuracy in these inverse correction generators. The simulator is a valuable source of information for tuning.

8.2.4.3 Arm configuration to velocity tuning. The return velocity must be tuned in response to problems in the arm configuration, as well as problems with the flight of the ball. As an example, we will consider tuning the configuration in response to the wrist being too close to the base. The geometry may be seen in Figure 49. A change in the ball's return velocity will cause a change in paddle orientation, $\Delta\hat{o}$, which in turn results in a wrist position change, proportional to the radius of the stick in the YZ plane.

To do this tuning, we must know the relationship between the paddle orientation and the return velocity, as derived in Section 2.3.3. However, we will use a somewhat different formulation. The ball's final velocity may be represented as the product of several matrices. We can evaluate the effect of a change in paddle orientation using a differential rotation matrix about the X axis to rotate the apparent world coordinate system. By symbolically evaluating and simplifying the result, we get a useful result: the change in final velocity for a change in the paddle orientation. We use an exact formulation for the part of the derivative due to the ball's spin, but use an approximation for the rest, as the exact equation's complexity exceeds its utility.

The paddle parameter P_{vivo} is the ratio of the ball's incoming to outgoing velocity parallel to the paddle surface. If P_{vivo} is zero, the bounce is always normal to the paddle, and a change in paddle normal causes an identical change in the ball's final direction. If P_{vivo} is one (light reflected by a mirror), the change in the ball's direction is twice the change in orientation. Accordingly, we use the approximation that

$$|\Delta\vec{v}| = (1+P_{vivo})\,|\vec{v}|\,\Delta\omega \qquad (138)$$

such that $\Delta\vec{v}$'s direction is perpendicular to $\vec{v}$ in the YZ plane; $\vec{v}$ is the outgoing ball velocity, and $\Delta\omega$ is the change in the paddle's YZ orientation.

From the wrist's linear distance to be traveled and the YZ radius, we can compute a desired change in paddle angle, then compute the change in final velocity. We assume the distance to be traveled is small compared to the radius. The rule contains:

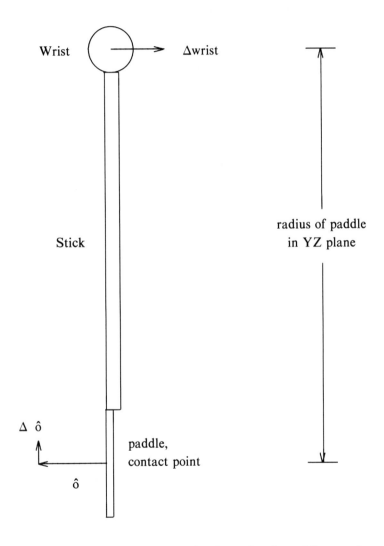

Figure 49. Tuning Arm Position by Velocity. By tuning the paddle normal, we can force the wrist to move in a desired direction.

```
SETYZ();
lv = outward.x*paddle_O.x + outward.y*paddle_O.y;

tw = Dot_eval (lv);
if (lv >= 0)
   sct = -crit_tooclose/yzstick * tw;
else
   sct = crit_tooclose/yzstick * tw;
weiy[yfact] = tw;
valy[yfact] = sct*dydw;
weiz[zfact] = tw;
valz[zfact] = sct*dzdw;

printlog (VYZFACTYZ, TOOCLOSE, weiy[yfact], valy[yfact],
   weiz[zfact], valz[zfact]);
yfact++;
zfact++;
```

The outward unit vector points from the robot base towards the wrist in the XY plane; it is the direction in which we would like the wrist to move to rectify the too close problem. The variable lv is the dot product of outward and the vector along which the wrist moves as we change the paddle angle — the paddle normal (paddle_O). The dot product is evaluated to form a weight for the rule such that if the magnitude of the dot product is small, the weight will be also, thus eliminating an unreasonable correction. The weight is factored into the correction so that if the weight is low and this is the only rule active, the entire increment will not be executed. The sign of the dot product is tested to select the sign of the correction. The variables dydw and dzdw contain the approximate derivatives of the Y and Z velocity with respect to a paddle rotation about X.

As we have seen, even complex relationships can be reduced to simple implementations. We must exploit local linear approximations, and not worry about what happens when the required corrections do not make this assumption entirely justifiable. The system will continue to operate, because the tuning process will correct for any error.

8.2.5 Exception handlers. In this section we will describe the CEO and VPs, and illustrate how they may be organized using the robot ping-pong system as an example.

8.2.5.1 CEO organization. The functional organization of the CEO (Section 7.4.4.1) is as follows:

1. preamble and initialization,

2. global supervisory rules,

3. reestablishment of existing delegation,

4. selection of an initial VP, and,

5. last-ditch recovery rules.

We will describe each block with descriptive text and code fragments.

The CEO gets called with the address of a note as an argument. The note identifies the major classification of the problem, and is saved for later use in determining the appropriate VP for the problem. For example, there are notes to indicate the lack of a hit plane depth, or that some joint is EMF limited.

A note indicates whether this is the first exception to occur, if so, a variety of bookkeeping notes are initialized. Recursive initialization simplifies the implementation by making it much easier to assure that all notes are initialized at the right times. The VPs also use recursive initialization.

Only one global supervisory rule is implemented at this time. It examines the joint trajectory data, and determines if there is sufficient time before the end of the motion to both fix the problem and to execute the code that generates the follow-through and return motions. If there is not enough time, the CEO will cause exception handling to cease, and follow-through planning to commence at once.

If this is a secondary exception, the primary exception has already been delegated to some VP. The CEO will delegate the second exception to the same VP, in case the exception requires special consideration in light of the original problem. If the VP wishes to refuse to handle the new exception, it may simply return; in this case the delegation of the problem is erased. The CEO will continue and pick a new VP as if the first problem had not occurred. A code excerpt is shown in Table 13. A regular naming convention for the notes is apparent. The `del_ceo` (and later, `del_xxxVP`) note indicates that the CEO (or `xxxVP`) has already delegated the problem; a `del_ceo_yyyVP` (or `del_xxx_yyyVP`) note indicates to what VP the problem has been delegated.

If the exception is new or a previously delegated VP has refused to handle the new problem, the descriptive note passed as an argument to CEO directly specifies the VP to handle the exception. The code to delegate control to the `hitVP` is:

```
if (visible (del_ceo))
{
   if (visible (del_ceo_hitVP))
   {
      hitVP();
      wipe (del_ceo_hitVP);
   }
   else if (visible (del_ceo_accVP))
   {
      accVP();
      wipe (del_ceo_accVP);
   }
   . . .
   wipe (del_ceo);
};
```

Table 13. CEO Redelegation Excerpt. If authority has previously been delegated, the CEO will reauthorize the same VP. If a VP returns, it is passing up authority, so the delegation is wiped.

```
if (this_problem == &(no_hpd))
{
   scribble (del_ceo);
   scribble (del_ceo_hitVP);
   hitVP ();
   wipe (del_ceo);
   wipe (del_ceo_hitVP);
};
```

If a VP has exhausted the methods available to it to correct the problem, a VP may refuse to handle the exception, even if the exception is the one only that VP is designed to handle. In this case, the CEO's last-ditch rules will attempt a recovery.

The last-ditch rules attempt generic solutions to problems. For example, after repeated exceptions during initial planning, the ping-pong CEO will attempt to use any other hit plane which is at all feasible.

The final and most general rule for any exception handler is to throw away as much information as possible, read in a new data point, and start over. This is not a bad rule even before we have run out of strategies; if the new data can be previewed and is found to be substantially different than the current data, we might consider throwing away at least some information. Side-spun balls induce this response.

The strength and advantage of the CEO (versus direct calls to specific error handlers) is that it provides a means for new exceptions to be evaluated in the context of the prior history, and allows global error recovery strategies to be implemented without redundant copies. The CEO and VPs can exploit the program's architecture during exception recovery to redirect control to arbitrary points within the program.

8.2.5.2 VP implementations. In response to a particular exception, a VP must rapidly pick a tuner which will maximize the probability of a rapid recovery (Section 7.4.4.3). The VP may reuse the same strategy on subsequent exceptions, but must monitor the success of the strategy to prevent the tuner from making the situation worse, and to prevent infinite loops. The organization of the VPs is similar to that of the CEO.

The exception type must be examined to make sure that it is addressable by the VP. If a VP intends to handle some exceptions that are not the primary exception type for the VP, any prior delegation by the VP must be decoded to see if the exception requires special treatment. If the VP can not address the exception, it must return control to the CEO so another VP can be selected.

The VP attempts to minimize the worst problem, which it must identify by scanning the evaluators under the jurisdiction of the VP. For example, accVP has a subroutine that scans the six joints and identifies the joint with the worst EMF limitation; further efforts by the VP are directed towards making that particular joint feasible, though the tuner will take the other joints into consideration as well.

If a tuning strategy is already in place because of a prior exception, the worthwhile algorithm (Section 7.4.4.8) determines if the strategy ought to be continued. AccVP uses the following code to evaluate whether or not to continue using the YZ velocity tuner (tunevyz):

```
else if (visible (del_acc_vyz))
{
    if (worthwhile (tunevyz, critp, *critp))
    {
        tunevyz ();
        backto_impact ();
    };
    wipe (del_accVP);
    wipe (del_acc_vyz);
    scribble (ign_acc_vyz);
}
```

The call to worthwhile is apparent; the argument critp and its value are the EMF evaluator of the offending joint. If worthwhile decides that continuing to use tunevyz is acceptable, tunevyz is called. The `backto_impact` routine then configures the notes to cause the impact planning process to recur. `Backto_impact` never returns.

`AccVP` explicitly calls `tunevyz` so that an exception recovery indicator note, `Recovering`, is visible to `tunevyz`; it disables updating rules that force the outputs towards steady state values. `Recovering` is cleared by `backto_impact`.

If `tunevyz` has already been tried, the note `ign_acc_vyz` informs `accVP`'s initial strategy selector, disabling `tunevyz` from further consideration. Consider the rule which initially delegates control to `tunevyz`:

```
if (invisible (ign_acc_vyz) &&
    worthwhile (tunevyz, critp, *critp))
{
    scribble (del_accVP);
    scribble (del_acc_vyz);
    tunevyz ();
    backto_impact ();
};
```

To be usable, `tunevyz` must not be ignored, and `tunevyz` must not have tried and failed to correct the problem previously. The `worthwhile` call mainly initializes the `worthwhile` process, since it will rarely fail. Symbolic information can be used to select among alternate strategies, for example, `impVP` uses either XY or YZ plane tuning depending on the type of problem exhibited by the return trajectory.

As is visible from this example, we are not using `decide` to select the best tuner to solve each problem. As described originally, the choice of the tuner should be based on the expected length of time required by the tuner to solve the problem, and the sensitivity of the exception to the tuner.

We sequentially try the tuners from fastest to slowest, wasting execution time on needless tunes; usually the right tuner gets called eventually. This is not a serious limitation except when an EMF exception occurs close to the end of the available time and the stick angle tuner gets called when `tunevyz` would be appropriate. The stick angle tuner takes a substantial amount of time because we must compute the Jacobians and joint trajectories; there may be no time left for the correct tuner.

The importance of including sensitivities as a significant factor in the choice of the tuner was not foreseen until it was observed in practice. Once identified, the proper tool (`decide`) was at hand to rectify the problem. At this time, we are not using `decide` because of the bookkeeping complexity to gather the sensitivities.

8.3 Execution Case Studies

In this section we will study the program's performance by examining its behavior in response to a variety of actual situations. The saved data logs will be our primary resource. We will also summarize the program's performance against opponents.

8.3.1 Understanding log data. Appendices 5—7 contain log data we will reference in our description of the examples. We will overview this data and point out some highlights, but must leave many details for the reader's analysis. First, we will briefly describe the data itself; the reader may consult Appendix 5 for an example.

The log entries' units are seconds, radians, and millimeters. Decimal times are in seconds, but integer times are in microseconds. The data's leftmost column is the global system clock time in microseconds. Time zero has no particular significance. Many execution times may be found by comparing the time stamps of corresponding log entries; some times are computed and displayed by the program.

The 26 msec major cycle interrupt may be seen interspersed with the normal log data, identified by the entry "robot intrpt at" and three additional lines. The time cited for the interrupt is the precise hardware time; the messages are not produced until much later after the dwarf processor has run. The average torque numbers listed are a factor of 8 greater than the fed-forward values because of internal scaling, and the fed-forward values are divided again by 4 before being applied to the D/A. The actual and target positions are 32 times the value in encoder counts.

8.3.2 Initial plan. Appendix 5 contains the log data from an initial planning cycle and the first and last subsequent update cycles. The ball was sighted at approximately 800000; the first five frames have been processed to form a trajectory estimate. The expert controller receives a predicted trajectory at 910532, but because there is no hurry, it decides to give the vision system time to generate more accurate data.

The path of the ball from the end of the table past each hit plane is computed by erif in 2855 μsec; the data is tabulated for each depth in several succeeding lines from 933671 on. The variables beginning with "q" are evaluators, for example, qth evaluates the Z/Y slope of the ball. The slope is the primary factor in deciding to use hit plane depth number 2 at −400 mm from the edge of the table.

The ball's return trajectory is then planned, culminating in a trajectory simulation at 948126. The trajectory is acceptable, though the bounce may be seen to occur at 1956 mm, quite close to the end of the table. The bounce is deep because the ball will have a significant chop-spin after the robot hits it (see wf at 940254).

A stick angle close to the middle of the acceptable range is chosen; "L, O, H" at 949034 indicates the lowest, time optimal, and highest feasible stick angle at this hit position and orientation. The Jacobian and its inverse are computed in 3.6 msec. The joint angles listed at 959306 take longer because the time includes several homogeneous transform multiplications, generation of the evaluators, and other miscellaneous operations.

The program then begins planning the motion, finding the limiting accelerations for each joint up until 963616. The actual limitations are the two innermost ones, ±61 for joint 1. At 963962, the program commits to initiating the motion at time 982598, asserting that its execution time will be less than 18.6 msec. The trajectory will last 0.466 seconds.

Each joint is evaluated from 964909 onwards to find the maximum accelerations and EMF margins. Most joints are lightly stressed except for joint 6, which is only 25% stressed. Joint 6 will be traveling at 5.47 rad/sec at the time of contact. The maximum velocity calculation has been disabled to save time, but off-line calculations show the maximum velocity to be approximately 10 rad/sec.

The completed polynomials are transferred to the joint servos and the dwarf processor beginning at 972663. The initial plan is complete by 974503, 8 msec ahead of schedule. At 982598, the joints will swing into action. The total system latency from when the ball first appeared through all sensors and processing is 0.2 seconds.

8.3.3 Update cycle. Once the initial plan has been completed, striker goes on to update it starting at 975231, using the most recent trajectory description from tranal. The ball will arrive 2 msec later than expected at a slightly different position on the hit plane, rising slower than expected. The depth of the hit plane will be left unchanged (though one rule would move it forward to eliminate the change in height), because the ball is near the peak of its trajectory: changes in the hit plane have a negligible effect.

The ball's point of contact on the paddle is altered to bring it closer to the center at 983519. The XY plane direction of the return, alpha, is tuned at 983880 to bring the ball's X crossing coordinate at the far end of the table (176 mm from 948126 during initial planning) more towards the center of the table. The stick angle is adjusted at 984436 such that the change in the wrist position is minimized; the stick angle is used to absorb the change in the horizontal position of the ball.

The ball's return velocity vector is corrected at 984955 to reduce the depth of the bounce, which was pointed out to be too deep during the discussion of the initial plan. The Y velocity is reduced to achieve this; as may be seen from the results of the flight simulation at 996122, the new depth is 1870 mm.

The remainder of the updating follows the same scheme as the initial plan. The polynomials' position, velocity, and acceleration are planned to be continuous with the polynomials being executed at the cutover time, 1029049 (see 1009544). By 1022904, the polynomials have been transferred to the joints, 6 msec ahead of time.

The elapsed time for temporal updating is 48.4 msec, so we are using only one in three ball trajectory estimates. Notice that this does not reduce the importance of being able to process 60 frames per second, because that stream of data is crucial to forming accurate trajectory estimates. By supplying new trajectory estimates to the expert controller every frame, we ensure that the expert controller is working with the most recent data, without requiring that it spend the time to request it.

8.3.4 Final update and follow-through. Striker continues through five more update cycles before the final one, which we have also included in the appendix, beginning at time 1261475. The initial ball crossing prediction was reasonably accurate, though the ball is now expected to be traveling faster and arriving sooner than originally determined, because the top-spin is understood to be larger.

The return trajectory has now been substantially adjusted; the Y velocity correction (1270750) has been reduced almost to zero because the location of the bounce is now satisfactory. The bounce will occur at 1800 mm, 20 cm from the end of the table, then the ball will cross the end of the table 163 mm from the edge (1280920).

Once the update has completed at 1306350, the program awaits further input. The ball has bounced at Y=275 mm; a new post-bounce trajectory is being built. Unfortunately, the ball will go out of view before enough data has been accumulated for a meaningful prediction.

At 1377173, striker determines that it must begin planning the follow-through, as there would be insufficient time to perform another temporal update cycle. Joint 6 will coast for 38 msec in the vicinity of the intended time of contact, while the other joints remain at rest. (There are 26 msec after the time of contact and 12 msec of settling time before, see 1304048). All six joints will then be returned to their get-set position.

At 1402185, the demon reader begins scanning the stored log. It has been told to stop processing by 2008388, when the ball is expected to cross the opponent's end of the table, and be hit back. Striker does not presently contain any learning functions. The only demons we have implemented compare the predicted motion planning time to the actual value, as an aid to debugging. It would be straightforward to enable the demons to modify the predictions, but since the predictions do not change often, it has not appeared worth the trouble.

8.3.5 Post-mortem analysis. The observed incoming and outgoing shots are shown in Figure 50. The expected return from the last update cycle at 1280920 predicted a Z of 346 mm at the net and a bounce at Y=1800 mm. The return arced much higher than anticipated, though the X intercept at 170 mm was quite accurate: within 7 mm of predicted. Even though there was not enough data for a full post-bounce trajectory analysis, there is enough for an approximate hand analysis. The trajectory analyzer was expecting the post-bounce Y velocity to be approximately 3200 mm/sec, but the actual velocity was apparently about 2600 mm/sec. The ball's arrival at the hit plane would therefore have been 40 msec later than expected; by this time, the arm was already decelerating and 10° past the expected hit point. Since the paddle swings upward on a circular arc, a "high fly" trajectory resulted.

8.3.6 Complex exception recovery — flight path. The next two sections will show two interesting exception recovery sequences which involve multiple steps. Normally, an exception is corrected and the program proceeds in a single step. For example, a noticeable fraction of the strokes require exception handling after initial planning to compensate for the chop-spin the robot normally imparts. The initial trajectory generator should be given an estimated spin, but the exception handling trivially corrects the problem in about 10 msec.

Appendix 6 and Figure 51 display an exception recovery sequence where the ball must be carefully guided horizontally. From 1060292, the ball has a high spin about the Z axis, −190 rad/sec, causing it to curve into the X=0 wire as may be seen in 1062954. The robot assumes that the ball will eventually miss the wire since this is the fail-safe assumption. The robot must guide the ball back to the other side, missing the X=0 wire itself, while compensating for the spin. It is a difficult shot for a man or machine.

The program takes an exception at 1073725, when the return trajectory simulation shows the ball hitting the near side wire (X=Y=0) on the way back. The `worthwhile` algorithm gives permission to the `impVP` to tune `alpha`, where `alpha` is the XY plane angle of the return at the hit; there is no prior evidence to suggest that `tunealpha` ought not be tried.

The `alpha` tune takes place at 1074390, but unfortunately the ball will now travel wide right at the other end of the table, due to the

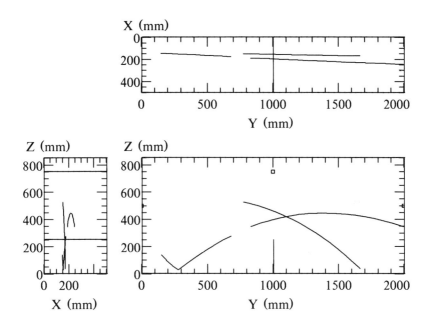

Figure 50. Incoming Shot and Return Trajectory. The ball was served from right to left; the robot's return is from left to right. The gap in the serve marks the transition from the far to the near camera pair.

interaction of the spin and the paddle (almost 1 m/sec horizontally as reported at 1077653). The `alpha` tune can be tried again since a different problem has occurred. The hexadecimal value of `critp` in 1085330 is the address of the problem, which is different than that in the first `worthwhile` call. `Alpha` is tuned again at 1085750, based only on the latest problem because the first was entirely solved. Had there been a very tight squeeze, `tunealpha` would have made its decision based on evaluators of both the near and far problems.

As may be seen at 1096500, the second tuning succeeded, 23 msec from the original exception.

8.3.7 Complex exception recovery — acceleration limit. Recovery from an acceleration limit exception is always time consuming, since it requires that the arm configuration and Jacobians be recomputed. Appendix 7 presents a particularly difficult recovery. The exception first occurs at 5126452 when joint 6 must have a peak acceleration of 157 rad/sec, but can produce only 139 rad/sec.

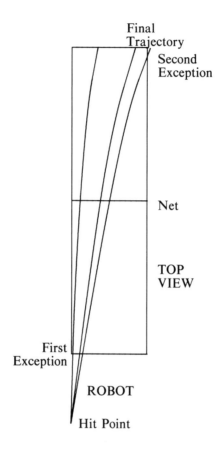

Figure 51. XY Plane Correction. Once an exception occurs, we must tune `alpha` twice before we succeed. The ball's spin and proximity to the near side marker complicate recovery.

Exception recovery begins by tuning the stick angle. The weight 0.49 in 5127696 indicates that the problem is not very sensitive to the stick angle. By 5154036, the problem has recurred, though the evaluator has been reduced from 0.353 to 0.210. A complete correction was not achieved because of the low initial sensitivity and because the available motion time has dwindled 25 msec during the attempted correction.

`Worthwhile` is satisfied with the progress so far, so it allows another stick angle tune to take place. Unfortunately, the exception is still not cured, but nearly so with an evaluator of 0.078. At 5183630, worthwhile gives permission for another attempt, which finally succeeds at 5208131, 82 msec after the original exception.

Careful examination of the \peak acceleration at 5208131, the acceleration limits at 5198181, and the initial limits at 5115670 shows that an important reason we have been able to succeed is that the available acceleration has increased. As the arm moves toward its destination, the effect of the higher gravity loading at the arm's initial position is reduced to that at the final destination, increasing the common acceleration range in between. The program must still work hard to compensate for the loss of motion time while this happens.

Even though the exception was recovered successfully, it clearly could have been done better. As the low weight given to the stick angle correction and the multiple iterations indicate, an alternative correction would probably have been more efficient. If the stick angle tuner had been slightly less effective, it would not have been reused. The tunevyz routine could have modified the angle of the paddle and its final speed to reduce the stress on joint 6. We should use the decide algorithm to select a tuner, as described previously in Section 7.4.4.3.

8.3.8 General play. The robot can play a reasonable game against human opponents. The machine keeps score, making mistakes only when particularly bizarre situations occur. Some mistakes could be eliminated by minor additions to its score-keeping analysis, but others would take much more substantial analysis using all available data, especially the ball's path after an event on which a point must be assessed. Ultimately, we observe that human players do not always agree.

Human players find the robot's small table and high net challenging at first, then gradually adapt. Figure 52 shows a short volley where the robot has returned the ball three times. On the fourth hit, the human (the author, who has much improved his game by substantial practice on this table) made a mistake, hitting the ball into the side wire at the robot's end of the table.

The bounce prediction is probably the single element that most degrades the system's performance at the current time. The prediction error causes too many balls (relatively — the absolute number is not large) to collide with the top wire at the robot's end of the table, or go off the end of the table. Part of the problem is clearly attributable to the overestimation of the ball's top-spin. Even spin-less balls are not predicted correctly; they bounce shorter than expected by substantial amounts. We believe that better understanding of the bounce's physics will correct this

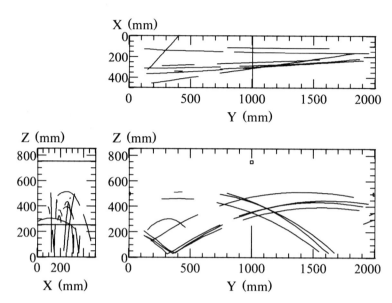

Figure 52. Short Volley. The robot (at left) hits the ball three times, then the human hits the ball into the side wire at X=500, Y=0.

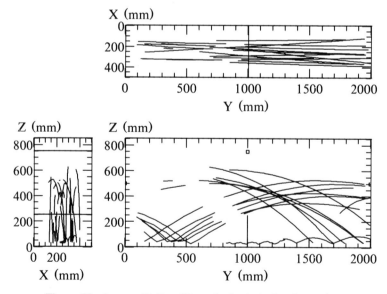

Figure 53. Longer Volley. The robot's sixth shot is too far.

problem (empirical study, not theoretical — our theory is justifiable). The expert controller behaves correctly in response to the inputs available.

Figure 53 shows a longer volley. The robot hits the sixth shot too far, crossing Y=2000 at Z=150. The human lightly tapped the ball back towards the robot, causing the numerous low bounces from right to left. The robot's shots exhibit the high-arc problem due to the inaccurate bounce prediction.

The longest volley we have observed was 21 strokes apiece by the human and the machine. The performance was as much a consequence of the human's lack of mistakes as anything else. The data is no longer available, caused totally illegible plots, and was incomplete because it overflowed `tranal` and `striker`'s log areas.

8.4 Implementation Limitations

In this section, we will discuss some issues which were not addressed by the robot ping-pong system, but are within the scope of the existing system. Long-term research issues will be discussed in the conclusion, Chapter 9.

8.4.1 Collision avoidance. The robot kinematic workspace intersects objects in the robot's environment, making collisions a real possibility. There are few obstacles within the limited reach of the robot arm (from shoulder to wrist), and they are in directions the robot does not usually move. The main danger is that the paddle may hit something at several meters per second. Particularly vulnerable targets include: the table, the wire frame at the robot's end of the table, and the camera mounting bar, which are all in the possible path of the follow-through, and the rear and side parts of the robot's supporting cage, which may be hit during windup.

The expert controller has been instructed on strategies to minimize the chances of collisions. For example, the contact position tuner, `tunecontact` (Section 8.2.2), will force the ball's contact point out to the very tip of the paddle to avoid hitting the table on the follow-through. The XY return planner acts to minimize the XY angle of the paddle's line of flight, so that most of the backswing is directly towards the rear of the cage where there is the most space available, rather than to the side where there is much less. The motion planner allows only a limited angular swing at the final paddle velocity (before contact).

The robot frame has strategically mounted stiff foam blocks to mitigate the effect of collisions. (The blocks are for the benefit of the robot, not the iron frame!) Plastic breakaway screws mount the paddle to the stick and the stick to the robot, to hopefully avoid transmitting collision impulses to the robot. Nevertheless, there is a steady flux of collisions, especially during program development. Unfortunately, most of the high-speed impacts are borne by the robot and cause various internal couplings to slip, consequently, we must periodically recalibrate the joint zeros.

Obviously, it would be better to prevent the collisions in the first place. The paddle's safe working volume may be described by one or a small number of rectangular solids, making it easy to render decisions on a particular XYZ location's safety.

The kinematics and dynamics processor has access to the position of the robot every 26 msec, and is well positioned to implement a collision detector. Regrettably, a projected collision signal from the kinematics and dynamics processor would occur too late for any useful response, even if the working volume was contracted somewhat to provide more look-ahead.

The proposed method of pre-detecting collisions is to find the maximum and minimum points of each joint trajectory, use the forward kinematics to find the Cartesian position, then check the Cartesian position against the bounding box. This algorithm could be applied before initiating a motion. The paddle's arcing trajectory can take it out of the bounding box at positions which are not the maxima or minima of a joint, but with a limited excursion.

Finding the maxima and minima of the joint trajectories requires finding the roots of six quartic polynomials. We can evaluate all six joint trajectories at each maximum or minimum to drive the forward kinematics. Early in the motion, most maxima or minima would occur at the beginning and end of the motion; since those positions are correct by construction, they would not have to be tested. Joints with nonzero final velocities, especially J6, will have interior minima and maxima that do need to be tested.

The quartic equation solver and the forward kinematics required to implement the algorithm are already available. At this writing we have not implemented the algorithm, in the belief that at present, the collision probability does not justify the substantial expenditure of processor cycles. As additional cycles become available, this viewpoint may well change.

8.4.2 Post-hit motion. The robot system tries to maintain a constant velocity during a small interval of time (approximately 25 msec) after the intended moment of contact. Subsequent to the follow-through, the robot will return to its inter-stroke get-set position, such that it will arrive at that location at the time the ball is arriving at the other end of the table. The return motion is unplanned, both in the sense of where the paddle will travel, and in whether or not the robot will be capable of executing the motion.

Quintic joint trajectory polynomials are constructed that describe the desired motion, but they are not checked. The paddle may travel forward into the wire frame, or out into the playing area, where it is sometimes observed by the video cameras. The wire frame marking the robot's end of the table has coiled springs (from car antennas) that are able to withstand repeated impacts.

The robot will not follow the return trajectory precisely if it requires more acceleration than the motors can provide, but we are not particularly concerned with the robot's accuracy during the return trajectory. The return accelerations tend to be feasible, because the robot has been able to get to the hit position from the get-set position in less time than is usually available to return to the get-set position. When the robot is hitting a ball, the vision system's latency must be subtracted from the available motion time. During the return motion, the latency may be added, because the robot must have reached the get-set position only by the time new vision data describing the return stroke becomes available.

A conventional robot trajectory generator checks a requested motion for feasibility by checking that the joint angles do not exceed their ranges, and by planning the motion's duration conservatively so as to not exceed the capabilities of the arm. When a conventional motion planner detects a motion that ought not be attempted, it stops, displays an error message, and awaits intervention.

Although it would seem desirable to have a generic robot motion planner (that could be added to the standard library of joint and Cartesian motion generators) to handle the return motion and ensure that the motion is safe and within manipulator capabilities, it is not possible.

Clearly, the motion generator must not cause the system to stop. As discussed, it is not even possible to halt the robot when an imminent crash is detected, due to the long stopping times. The follow-through must be evaluated during the initial planning process to be effective. We do not test the motion before the hit either, nor do we want to let the consequences of the hit compromise the machine's shots. Humans tend to operate in this fashion as well, following through into the marker wires.

The robot controller may not change the duration of the motion to unstress motors unable to generate the required torque. The only variable available to the return motion planner is the final position of the arm, which could be modified to reduce the required torques. Since the final position is the initial position of the following shot, and it is used in the precalculation of estimated motion times for stick angle planning, changing the get-set location endangers the accuracy of this process.

In view of these factors, we simply live with, and mitigate the effects of, the unplanned return motion.

8.4.3 Drastic changes in time-of-flight. Substantial overshoot may result if a motion's initial or final velocities are large compared to the distance to be traveled. The trajectory specifies the overshoot explicitly, regardless of how well the robot executes the motion. Figure 54 shows a typical trajectory to stop the paddle after a hit. As shown in Section 5.5.3, the overshoot increases with the available time of flight, a counter-useful result.

The proper approach to eliminating the overshoot is to decrease the motion time, increasing the stress on the motors up to some nominal level. If the initial velocity is zero, the motion may be delayed. If the final velocity is zero, the motion may be shortened, reducing the follow-through after the hit.

If both the initial and final velocities are nonzero, we may insert a delay at the point of maximum overshoot, where the velocity is zero. Such a point is guaranteed to exist, since overshoot by definition takes the joint outside the initial and final positions, then brings it back to the final position: the velocity changes sign, passing through zero.

At present, the robot ping-pong system takes no such countermeasures on either the windup or follow-through motions. If the available motion time increases by more than a factor of two to more than 1 sec, the system will give up on the ball to avoid a certain crash; this is one of the few cases where the robot intentionally gives up.

This situation arises occasionally when a ball hits the net and continues on towards the robot along a high arc. The correct response is to stop the motion in progress and replan from scratch, which the program could do.

8.4.4 Allowing nonzero final velocities. Joints 1—5 of the robot are held stationary at the conclusion of the motion, at the instant when the robot hits the ball. The successful solution of the ping-pong impact equations originally depended on this situation. The robot forms a stable platform for the striking motion of joint 6. However, suppose the task is capable of supporting nonzero final velocities for the other joints.

It turns out that as long as the velocities of the other joints are predetermined, the impact equations may be solved in the moving reference frame. Nonzero final velocities may be used to intentionally control the ball's spin. Joints 4 and 5 are especially well positioned for this purpose; we have already written some low-level code to take advantage of this. It is not theoretically possible to generate balls of arbitrary spin; however, a tuner can cause the spin to migrate toward some desirable value. We can pick the desired value after the shot's initial planning.

An important generic capability is to use a joint's terminal velocity (not just J6) to reduce the joint's peak acceleration, as discussed in Section 5.5.3.5. The acceleration requirement can be cut in half by

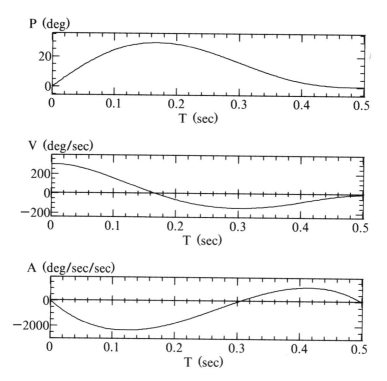

Figure 54. Quintic Trajectory Overshoot. To smoothly reduce the initial velocity to zero, the joint position must travel past the intended final position.

selecting an appropriate final velocity. For example, compare Figure 54 with Figure 55, which has a substantial negative final velocity.

It remains to be seen whether multiple joints can be controlled accurately enough to take advantage of these benefits.

8.4.5 Strategy. The robot ping-pong system begins planning each shot without reference to the game's prior history. The system does not attempt to beat the opponent, but simply tries to return each incoming shot.

The system should record the outcome of each shot: whether the opponent could not return it at all, generated a weak return, or made a smashing return that the robot could not return. This strategy analysis is a logical place to introduce and experiment with learning techniques.

The strategist's objective is to create evaluators and correctors that the basic ping-pong system may use to maximize its chances of success. The strategist may run on its own processor, temporally decoupled from the

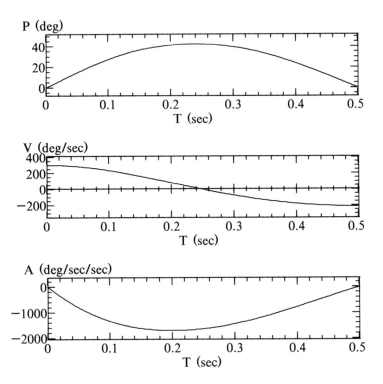

Figure 55. Less Acceleration by Nonzero Final Velocity. By choosing the right final velocity, we reduce the peak acceleration of Figure 54.

real-time system. The strategist can send updates to the robot processor whenever necessary, using a remote procedure call protocol.

Each of the robot's shots may be characterized by its position, velocity, and spin when it crossed the opponent's end of the table. We wish the system to learn the opponent's strengths and weaknesses as rapidly as possible, preferably in only a few volleys. The strategist must be able to work with sparse data and make meaningful predictions about shots which have not been seen before. Even if the learning system is not optimal, we can never do worse than we would at random, since to do worse, we would have to actively detect and aim for the opponent's strengths.

Throughout the work, we have emphasized the importance of making the system alterable by higher-level AI systems. Learning the opponent's characteristics is an excellent starting point for further work in this area. Because the task is well defined, the strategy analyzer would be able to operate solely on the robot ping-pong system's models, without having to modify any code. The separation of the information describing the strategy (in the models) from the code implementing the strategy is a validation of the expert controller's design.

8.5 Summary

In this chapter, we have shown how the expert controller architecture developed in Chapter 7 was applied to the robot ping-pong task. Table 14 catalogs the sizes of the program's components: lines of C source, bytes of program text (no data included), and approximate size when running. The entire system and the expert controller, `striker`, are quite large. Despite the size of the program, we were consistently able to improve the sophistication of the machine's play. The program remains amenable to further enhancement.

The expert controller's architecture is the reason the system could be constructed in the first place, and the reason it has remained tractable.

Program	Function	Source (Klines)	Program (Kbytes)	Running (Kbytes)
`striker`	expert controller	10.7	152.6	1600
	robot control package	7.8		
	slave processor code	2.5	29.0	34
`tranal`	trajectory analysis	3.4	41.6	512
`eye`	low-level vision	2.1	28.6	512
`rtd`	debugger	7.5	157.7	300
`chief`	sequencing	0.7	19.5	256
`sai`	strategy, speech	2.4	32.1	192
`sp2000`	videotape driver	2.0	19.5	896
	miscellaneous	3.2		
Total	robot ping-pong	42.3	480.6	4302

Table 14. Program Sizes

Chapter 9

Conclusion

9.1 Synopsis

In this book, we have described and demonstrated in practice the concepts and implementations behind a robot ping-pong player. The task was a challenging one due to the stringent performance requirements, but especially because of the loosely defined problem and the resulting interactions between the task and robot constraints. We have broken out of the rigid approach of most robot tasks. The program has a different feel, and much more power and flexibility. We have demonstrated that we can efficiently perform loosely defined tasks where there is no "optimal trajectory."

Our most important lesson is that we have to view short-term task planning as an ongoing process, not something that is done once then followed by blind plan-execution. A sense of time pervades our entire system. We have to view every task in the continuous-time domain, because we live in a continuous-time world. Every task contains redundant degrees of freedom which the controller may exploit. We have to identify these degrees of freedom, and invest the controller with the authority to alter them. To ensure an informed decision, the controller must be supplied with a continuous stream of external and internal sensor data. Our low-level controller was designed to predict the robot's own limits, so that it could be operated as close as possible to those limits. The robot controller must evaluate and refine the task plan while the plan is being executed. By doing so, the robot can maximize efficiency, while avoiding exceptions.

The continuous self-perception of the robot's motion and the critical evaluation of that motion's quality seems much closer to the human experience than the blind plan/move cycles of today's robots.

9.2 Future Research Topics

In any project this complex, there are many opportunities for improvement, both large and small. Many have been described earlier in the text, but in this section we will summarize long-term research areas arising from the work.

Computer vision is a major field of research in its own right. Vision work aimed at robotics applications must emphasize the acquisition of useful results in real time. For example, generating depth maps from multiple images is an important skill, but from a robotics standpoint, a depth map alone is of little use since it does not directly specify relevant information. Robot motion planning requires the timely determination of an object's identity, position, orientation, and trajectory. Object representations must emphasize what can be done to the object, not just how it looks or feels. Computer vision algorithms and implementation technologies (i.e. VLSI) continue to advance in ability, so we need to find appropriate combinations useful to the robotics domain.

One limitation of the robot trajectory planning process is that it does not take into account the effects of the changing arm configuration and dynamics, even though the controller compensates for them during arm motion. The dynamics calculations are expensive to execute even once, yet we must assess their effect over an entire trajectory. We need algorithms to automatically generate good estimates of each joint's worst-case instant during a particular motion. We can postulate two opposing approaches: 1) a closed-form algorithm similar to the back-EMF limit calculation, and 2) an expert system approach that tries to identify the most likely limiting points from higher-level information about a trajectory.

A broader long-term topic is to attempt to interface conventional AI systems with the expert controller presented in this work. A baseball player must plan a response to every possible situation before the ball is hit, then rapidly select and execute the right play. The combination of an AI program and an expert controller should be able to attain the same behavioral sophistication. The structure of our approach avails itself to high-level coaching by slower but more symbolically intelligent systems, so that the long-term performance of the system may be improved. We have demonstrated and taken advantage of this capability while constructing the system, though the high-level system was a human. For an AI system to write a real-time system, it must be capable of understanding the system's organization, and able to make modifications to it. A specialized style can greatly simplify these tasks. The model data structure and program structure we have presented are clear steps in the right direction.

We must attempt even more complex tasks to understand what the real long-term issues are. The vision system required accurate models not only of optical characteristics, but, surprisingly, of the sensor's temporal characteristics as well. The exception handling mechanism should be thoroughly explored on even more challenging tasks. Additional problem areas will help resolve the question of whether or when learning is needed for this application domain, and whether general techniques or specialized algorithms are required.

The importance of trying real problems, as well as studying idealized theoretical models, can not be overstated. By building complete systems, we discover where the real issues lie. We must gain more experience before we will fully understand expert controllers. For this reason, this book describes one example of an expert controller, instead of definitively characterizing all possible instances.

A process-oriented task that requires constant attention and switching from mode to mode would be particularly educational, and contrast sharply with the ping-pong task. Assuming we had solved the vision problem, could a machine drive a car in traffic?

9.3 Man versus Machine

Any book on robot ping-pong must address the question of whether or not a machine can ultimately beat the best human players on their own terms, namely, on a full-sized table. The competition represents a simple robotic analog of the Turing Test for conventional artificial intelligence research. Clearly, the existing system would continue to operate if a full-sized table was placed in front of it, and some simple modifications could compensate somewhat for the larger table. However, in the remainder of this section we will consider what it would take to play a very good game.

To begin with, the vision system would need a much larger field of view. Not only should the field of view encompass the table, but the robot's work space as well, since the lack of post-bounce data significantly limits the current system. We could accomplish this by an appropriate choice of camera location and lens, but it would most likely result in inadequate accuracy: certainly less accuracy than the current configuration. Multiple cameras could capture the full scene. Two fast pan and tilt cameras on a wide baseline with a smaller individual field of view could achieve total coverage with high accuracy. By feeding trajectory data forward into the pan and tilt system, the image may be frozen on the camera, reducing motion blur and the interaction of scan rate and camera orientation. The price is additional complexity, as the pan and tilt system is a robot in its own right; its position must be precisely known during the sampling interval to dynamically compute the camera calibration matrix. The pan and tilt system can use the same techniques as the robot manipulator to obtain high accuracy in position, velocity, and time.

The robot ping-pong table's end frames and high net limit the maximum ball speed. In the absence of such speed limits, the robot's available reaction time can be quite short. This implies we need a fast robot, the ability to move away from the table to get more time, and possibly, a way to watch the opponent to estimate his shot before we observe it. Even the small robot ping-pong table strains the range and speed of the PUMA 260. A full-sized table requires a working area a few meters on a side.

Rather than use a mammoth robot, a two-dimensional gross positioner capable of moving the smaller manipulator would be preferable, much as the human player uses a gross positioning system — legs, and a fine positioning system — an arm. A gantry robot or a two-dimensional linear motor system [73] could do the job. The PUMA 260 weighs only 15 pounds, so 100 lb thrust would create 3—4 G acceleration depending on the 2-D actuator mass. A direct drive arm with higher accelerations and no gear backlash or joint flexibility would be helpful.

Once again, accurately planned and synchronized motions would be required, and could be attained with the techniques developed in this work. The expert controller could readily control this system, and in some respects the job would be easier than dealing with the tight constraints of the robot table. Another initial planner and tuner could easily control the additional free variables describing the position of the robot.

The robot player must not only return incoming shots, but cause the human to fail to return the robot's. The robot would clearly need to analyze the opponent's weaknesses. The range of speeds, spins, and return types necessary to win remains to be seen.

Can a robot beat the best human players? There is only one way to find out. Robots keep getting better. Do you? Time will tell.

Appendix 1

Robat — The Official Rules

1. The ball is a standard table-tennis ball, with no special markings.

2. The table is 2 meters long and 0.5 meters wide. It stands 0.75 meters above floor level.

3. The table surface is smooth and matte black without boundary lines. For the first heats the surface may be smooth-side hardboard, painted with black emulsion, supported on a chip-board or block-board base.

4. At each end of the table is a vertical "playing frame," internal size 0.5 meter square. The boundary of these frames will be formed by a wire or thread which carries the edge of a fine net, supported on a rigid outer frame 1 meter wide and 0.75 meter high, thus minimizing optical obstruction.

5. In the center of the table a third vertical frame is mounted, internal measurements 0.5 meter wide and 0.75 meter high, of a material similar to the playing frames. A fine wire is stretched across this frame 0.25 meter above the table, supporting a transparent net (similar to hair-net material). Nets will not obstruct more than ten percent of light passing through them — probably much less. The outer supporting frame will be 1 meter wide, but the top cross member is rigid at a height of 0.75 meter above the table.

6. The top of the net frame supports a serving device. This holds the ball in full view of both robots, with center about 0.625 meter above the center of the table surface. The structure is of wire not more than one millimeter thick, and after serving the ball the mechanism retracts entirely above the level of the top of the net frame. The ball is served towards the "serving" robot, to bounce once before emerging from the playing frame.

7. Lighting is provided by tungsten lights, mounted at a height of 2 meters on poles at the corners of a 4 meter square, square with and centered on the table. The light level is likely to be around a Weston meter reading of 10, corresponding to an exposure of 1/60 second at f5.6 on 100 ASA film.

8. A level space one meter square is provided abutting each end of the table within which each robot must stand. No part of the robot must touch or project forward of the playing frame. The robot should not extend laterally more than one meter to either side of the frame center, i.e. 2 meters overall. A power outlet will be provided at the edge of each standing space. In Europe this will be 220–240 volts at 50 Hz, fused at 5 amps; in the USA it may be 110v, 60 Hz, fused at 10 amps.

9. A movable vertical black sight-screen 1.5 meters wide and 2 meters high will be located behind each robot, 2 meters behind the playing frame.

10. The bat size must be contained within a circle 12.5 centimeters in diameter. The bat must propel the ball by hitting it once with its surface — no catching, blowing, electrostatic repulsion or other variations are allowed. The bat surface can be curved if desired, but double-hitting will lose the point.

11. Those parts of the robot visible to the opponent must be black, including absorption of infra-red in the region of 1 micron wavelength. This is satisfied by black emulsion paint. If the opponent insists, and can show that he has sensors to detect it (unlikely in the first year), the bat must carry a high-brightness red LED at its center and a green LED 5 cm away from it.

12. Apart from such LED's, the robot must not project light towards its opponent. To detect the approach of the ball to the bat, a cross beam can be used. It must then be clear that any light spilled towards the opponent will come only from the ball itself, and unreasonable brightness levels must not be used.

13. Ultrasonic transmissions are only allowed while the ball is approaching the bat, and must cease on contact. When ultrasonic transmission is used, a high-brightness red LED must be driven by a cable long enough to permit mounting beside the net frame, where it can be viewed by the judges and by a cable-mounted photocell from the opponent — an exception to rule 8b. It must be lit while transmitting. This rule is relaxed if the opponent is non-acoustic.

14. The robots will be allowed fifteen seconds to lock their vision systems onto the ball before it is served. It is desirable but not compulsory that they indicate when they are ready (by tone or voice output) so that this time can be shortened. Five serves will be made in each direction. The scoring will be as in table tennis. The competitors may opt to change ends between games, but this must be accomplished within a time of five minutes. Initial setting-up should also be achieved within a time of five minutes. The number of games to determine a result will be at least best-of-three, and will be determined beforehand in response to the number of competitors.

15. A correct return will cause the ball to bounce just once on the table at the opponent's side of the net, before it passes through the opponent's playing frame. The ball may touch the playing frame, the net wire, or the net frame.

16. If the defender returns the ball 20 times in one rally, it wins the point.

17. The judges may disqualify a robot on the grounds of safety, or penalize it for serious breaches of sportsmanship.

18. All dimensions quoted here may be subject to a tolerance of 2 percent up or down.

19. The robot may have two buttons or their equivalent with which the handler can inform the robot that it has won or lost the point. A further button can tell the robot that the ball has gone out of play, or is ready to be served. Excessive controls which give the judges the impression that strategy is being determined by the handler, rather than the robot, will be looked on with disfavor and may lead to penalty points being awarded.

20. It goes without saying that the robots should be easily transportable, and should be entertaining where possible. They should not be excessively noisy.

John Billingsley,
Department of Electrical and Electronic Engineering
Portsmouth Polytechnic,
Anglesea Road,
Portsmouth, England PO1 3DJ

Appendix 2

Vision Performance Plots

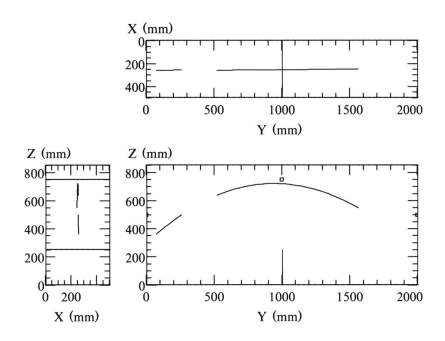

Figure 56. Trajectory of Steel Ball. The gap occurs when the ball is invisible to both camera pairs.

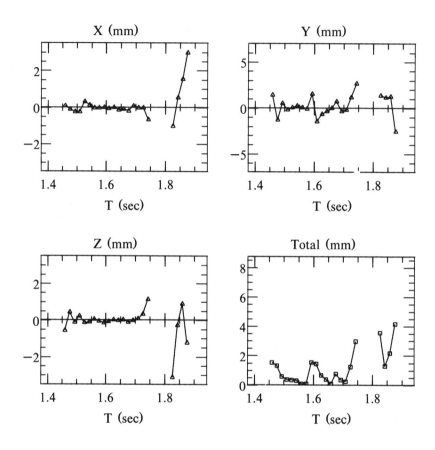

Figure 57. Prediction Errors During Flight

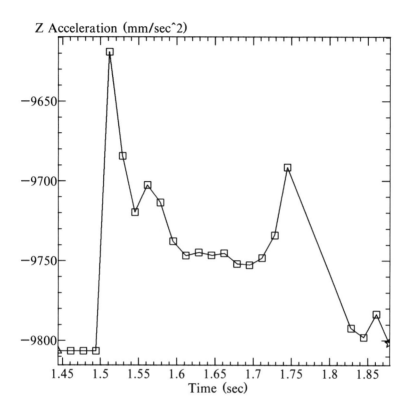

Figure 58. Computed Acceleration of Steel Ball. The first four points are forced to the nominal value.

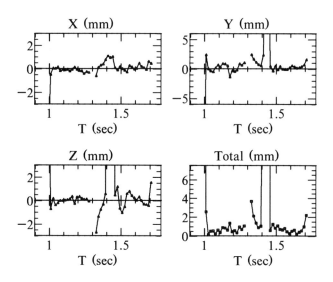

Figure 59. Prediction Errors of Catapulted Ball. The ball changes cameras at 1.3 sec, then bounces at 1.41 sec.

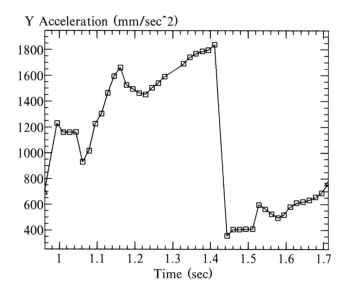

Figure 60. Y Axis Acceleration on Catapulted Ball

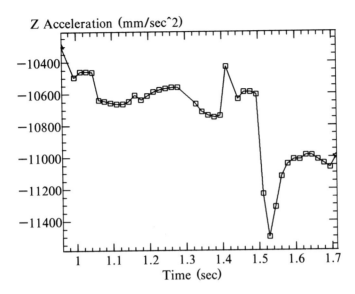

Figure 61. Z Axis Acceleration of Catapulted Ball

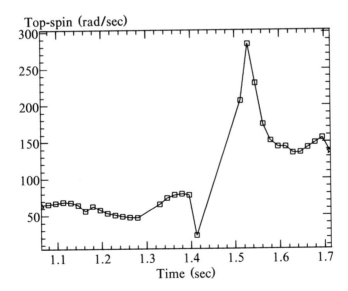

Figure 62. Computed Top-spin of Catapulted Ball

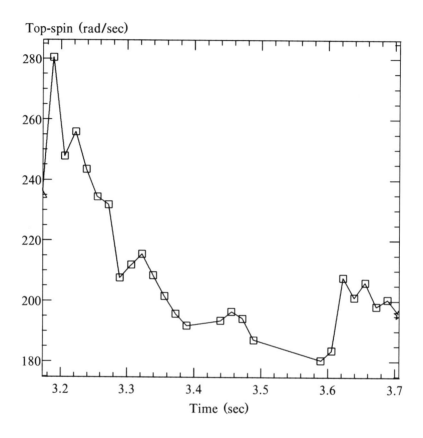

Figure 63. Spin of Ball with Large Top-spin. The ball switches cameras at 3.4 sec, then bounces at 3.5 sec. Several frames elapse before the system begins estimating spin again.

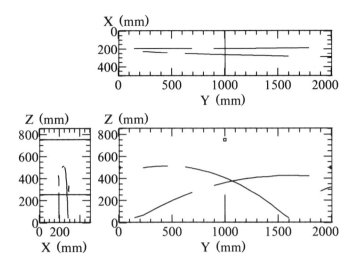

Figure 64. Trajectory of Incoming Volley. The human hits the first shot from right to left.

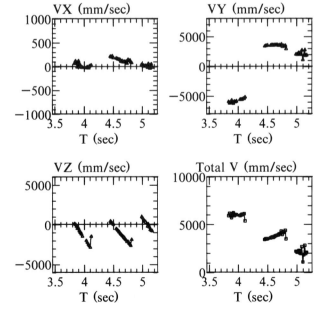

Figure 65. Ball Velocity vs. Time

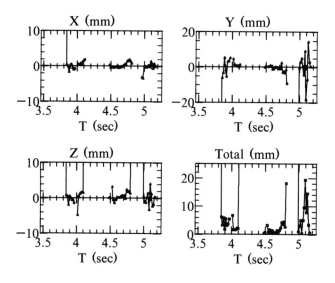

Figure 66. Prediction Errors

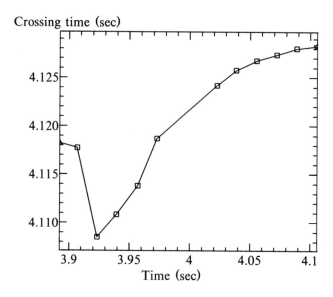

Figure 67. Time of Ball Crossing End Frame

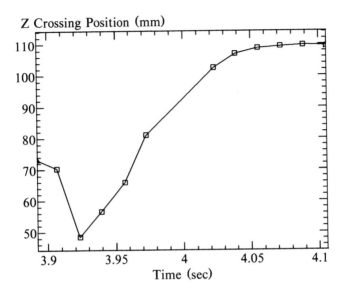

Figure 68. Z Crossing Position

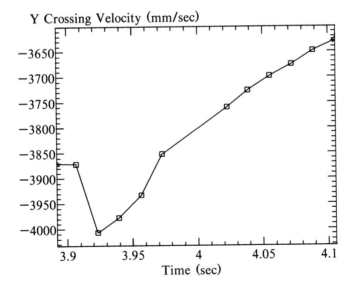

Figure 69. Y Crossing Velocity

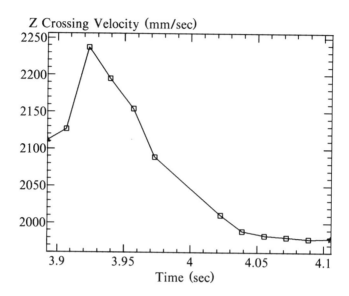

Figure 70. Z Crossing Velocity

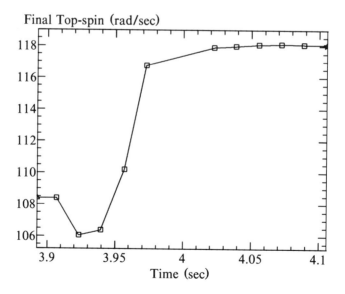

Figure 71. Final Top-spin at Crossing

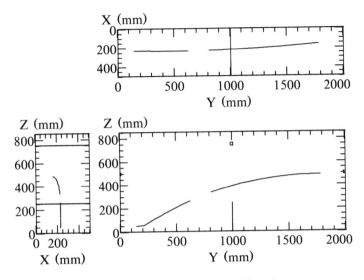

Figure 72. Path of Ball with Side-spin

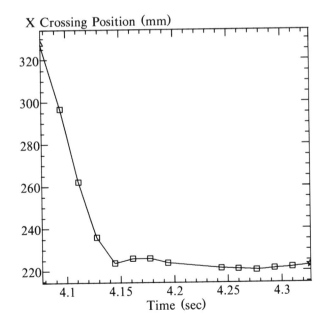

Figure 73. X Crossing Position

Appendix 3

Robot Performance Plots

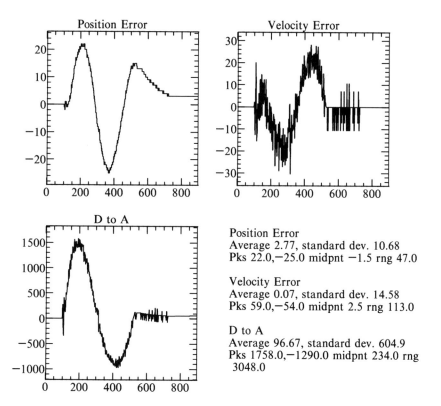

Figure 74. Joint 1 Executing Complex Motion. The units of the position error are encoder ticks, the units of the velocity error are encoder ticks per major cycle (32 servo cycles), and the D to A value ranges from −2048 to +2047. The horizontal scale is servo cycles.

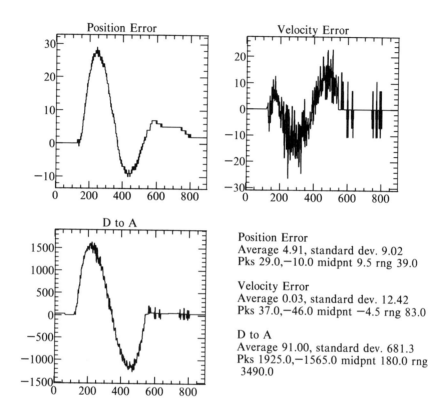

Position Error
Average 4.91, standard dev. 9.02
Pks 29.0,−10.0 midpnt 9.5 rng 39.0

Velocity Error
Average 0.03, standard dev. 12.42
Pks 37.0,−46.0 midpnt −4.5 rng 83.0

D to A
Average 91.00, standard dev. 681.3
Pks 1925.0,−1565.0 midpnt 180.0 rng
3490.0

Figure 75. Joint 1 Alone Moving

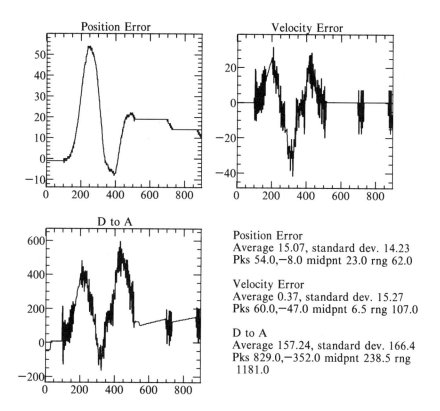

Position Error
Average 15.07, standard dev. 14.23
Pks 54.0,−8.0 midpnt 23.0 rng 62.0

Velocity Error
Average 0.37, standard dev. 15.27
Pks 60.0,−47.0 midpnt 6.5 rng 107.0

D to A
Average 157.24, standard dev. 166.4
Pks 829.0,−352.0 midpnt 238.5 rng
1181.0

Figure 76. Joint 5 Executing Complex Motion

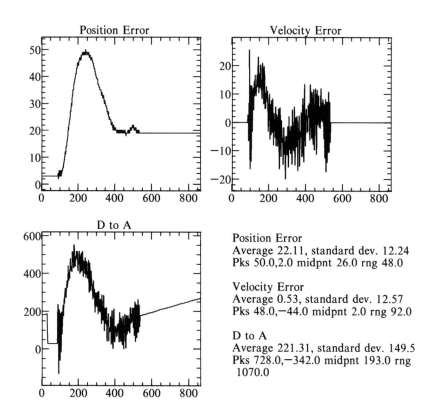

Position Error
Average 22.11, standard dev. 12.24
Pks 50.0,2.0 midpnt 26.0 rng 48.0

Velocity Error
Average 0.53, standard dev. 12.57
Pks 48.0,−44.0 midpnt 2.0 rng 92.0

D to A
Average 221.31, standard dev. 149.5
Pks 728.0,−342.0 midpnt 193.0 rng
1070.0

Figure 77. Joint 5 Alone Moving

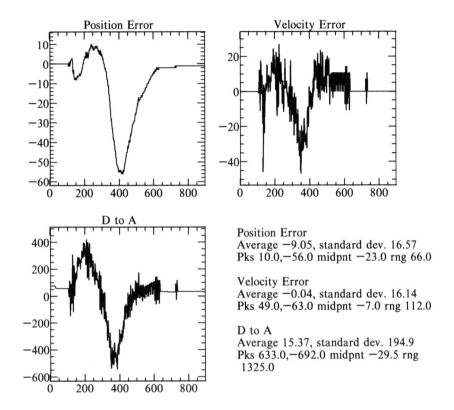

Figure 78. Joint 6 Executing Complex Motion

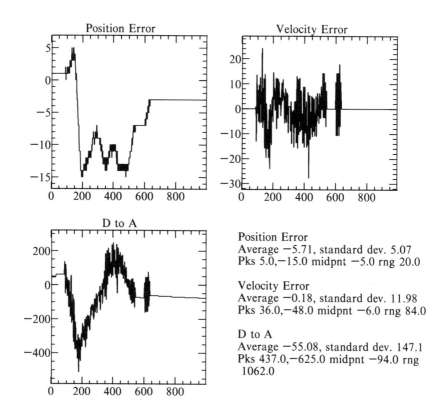

Figure 79. Joint 6 Alone Moving

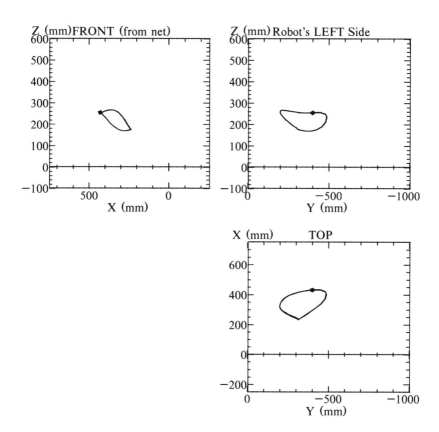

Figure 80. Orthogonal Trace of Paddle Position. The desired and actual paddle positions are superimposed. Markers indicate the position at the expected time of contact with the ball.

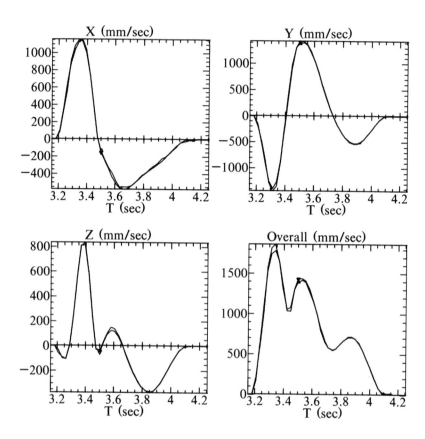

Figure 81. Cartesian Velocities During Motion

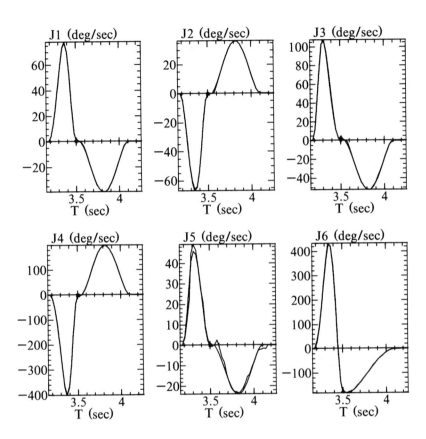

Figure 82. Joint Velocities During Motion

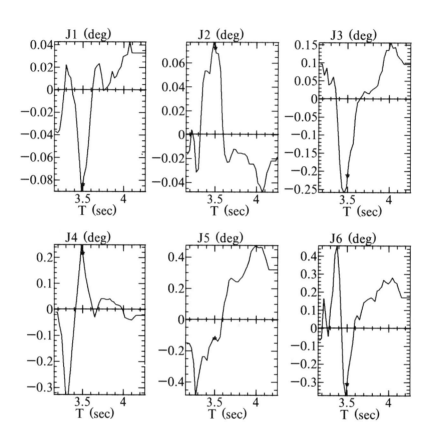

Figure 83. Joint Space Position Errors

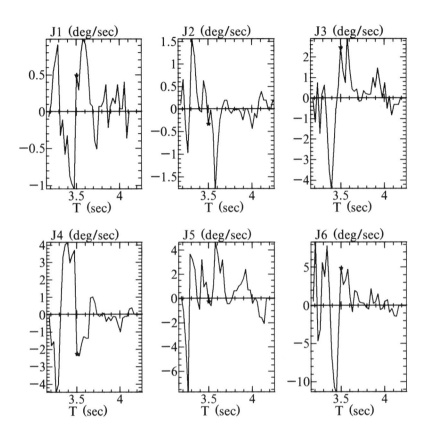

Figure 84. Joint Space Velocity Errors

Appendix 4

Ping-Pong Top Level

```c
#include <stdio.h>
#include "striker.h"
#include "../include/chiefproto.h"

/* Top Level sequencing of how to hit the ball. */
/* Anybody can do a longjmp whenever they want, the assumption */
/*     is that the system will keep running fine: the "Notes" */
/*     control it all. The "if"s are here at the top level to */
/*     eliminate redundant subroutine calls */

extern int VOLLEYREJECT, NOMOTION;

hit_the_ball ()
{
    int hardstop = 0;

/* We always come back to this same spot, we then figure out */
/*     what needs to be done; barely look at setjmp's code */

    if (setjmp (Main_jmp_buf) == 2 || Command == CMD_STOP)
    {
        /* something fairly serious is wrong, */
        /*     don't consider recovery */
        scribble (run_over);
        hardstop = 1;
    };

    if (visible ( run_over ))
    {
        next_stroke = stroke+1;
        printlog (VOLLEYREJECT, -stroke, -next_stroke);
        if (visible ( robot_moving ))
            smooth_stop();
        else
```

```
      {
         if (visible (attempted_stroke))
            printlog (NOMOTION);
         demonize (0xffff0000);   /* Like, forever! */
      };
      if (hardstop)
         return;
      wash_stroke();
   };

   if (invisible (robot_moving))
   {
      if (invisible ( ball_data ))
      {
         wait_for_ball();
         if (stroke > next_stroke)
            next_stroke = stroke;      /* on vision screwups */
         else if (stroke < next_stroke)
         {
            printlog (VOLLEYREJECT, stroke, next_stroke);
            wipe (ball_data);
            Reconsider ();
         };
         scribble (enabprnt);
         scribble (attempted_stroke);
      };
      if (invisible ( delay_complete ))
         valid_delay();
      if (invisible ( valid_hpd ))
         pick_hit_depth();
      if (invisible ( return_trajectory ))
         pick_return();
      if (invisible ( impact_spec ))
         plan_impact();
      if (invisible ( stang_chosen ))
         static_config();
      if (invisible ( paddle_config ))
         real_joint();
      if (invisible ( motion_plan ))
         plan_motion();
      if (invisible ( plan_sent ))
         start_moving();
   };

/* Temporal updating code. save_plan KILLS jnt_traj_desc data */
/*     immediately since it's done with mirrors */
```

```
    if (invisible ( Updating ))
    {
        save_plan (&orig_plan);
        previous_plan = &orig_plan;
        wash_successful ();              /* clean ceo stuff, we're ok now */
        scribble (wash_the_revised_plan);
        scribble (Updating);
    };
```

/* Use of a while is a clarity and efficiency hack. Could simply */
/*   put a longjmp at the end and it would fall through perfectly */

```
    while (1)
    {
        if (visible ( wash_the_revised_plan ))
            wash_revised_plan ();
        if (invisible ( ball_data ))
            wait_for_ball();
        if (invisible ( valid_hpd ))
            redo_hpd();
        if (invisible ( tuned ))
            tuner ();                    /* tune the previous plan */
        if (invisible ( return_trajectory ))
            scribble (return_trajectory); /* subsumed in tuning */
        if (invisible ( impact_spec ))
            plan_impact();               /* SAME AS ORIGINAL */
        if (invisible ( stang_chosen ))
            scribble (stang_chosen);
        if (invisible ( paddle_config ))
            real_joint();
        if (invisible ( motion_plan ))
            revamp_motion();
        if (invisible ( plan_sent ))
            start_moving();              /* SAME AS ORIGINAL */
```

/* Lets do it all again. */

```
        save_plan (&previous_plan_area);
        previous_plan = &previous_plan_area;
        wash_successful ();              /* we're ok now */
        scribble (wash_the_revised_plan);
    };
}
```

Appendix 5

Initial Planning and Updating

910532: mode 2 stroke 1 stamp 864537 cross 1298731 pos 148.7 0.0
139.4 vel −120.23 −2699.09 1855.58 spin 110.8 −4.5 0.0
928407: mode 2 stroke 1 stamp 881277 cross 1298282 pos 150.3 0.0
144.6 vel −118.65 −2713.69 1816.18 spin 110.6 −4.4 0.0
928678: skipped the first 1 valid frames of data, tof 0.370
931645: erif took 2855 usec
933076: robot intrpt at 923715 cycle5 208 avg torque 256 13600 −3776
768 960 2112
933188: feed forward 0 1736 −469 81 55 226
933294: actual: −257536 634400 267424 71072 90176 4512
933452: target: −257480 634392 267440 71132 90288 4576
933671: t 1335310 p 146.0 −100.0 204.4 v −117.4 −2687.8 1421.9 qt
0.804 qx 0.949 qz 0.986 qth 0.359 qcum 0.990 qo0 −0.153
qo1 −0.960
935016: t 1391525 p 139.4 −250.0 267.7 v −115.7 −2648.8 832.1 qt
0.883 qx 0.943 qz 0.873 qth 0.529 qcum 0.967 qo0 0.395 qo1
−0.978
936360: t 1448597 p 132.9 −400.0 298.3 v −114.0 −2609.6 247.6 qt
0.921 qx 0.943 qz 0.758 qth 0.863 qcum 0.934 qo0 −0.265
qo1 −0.998
937029: hpd# 2 factors 3.604468 3.801466 3.859097
938063: safehit thknob 0.246 vsafe 6170 theta 0.235
938219: return vector 115.4 6000.4 1436.8
940152: paddle v 2460.608154 O 0.024 1.000 0.004
940254: jmp −0 −8 1255 wf 52 −2 2 io sens −0.195 0.325
948126: ec 0 t 0.460 zn 359 yb 1956 xzc 176 44 dzdy 0.56 cd 5,25
949034: opt 0.275964 hurry 0.235504 safe 0.872696 L,O,H 0.171806
0.343612 0.343612
949576: crnch xyz 132.854813 −400.000000 298.303864 hit_desc 2
IDopt 2

957617:   joint angle conv. times 4886 jacobian 3573
957733:   jnt 1 dp/dth 100.0 317.1 0.0 dr/dth 0.000 0.000 −1.000
957858:   jnt 2 dp/dth 356.0 −226.0 −321.3 dr/dth −0.536 −0.844 0.000
957984:   jnt 3 dp/dth 456.8 −290.0 −156.9 dr/dth −0.536 −0.844 0.000
958107:   jnt 4 dp/dth −212.6 −367.0 −36.9 dr/dth −0.765 0.486 −0.423
958233:   jnt 5 dp/dth 196.7 70.0 22.4 dr/dth 0.241 −0.394 −0.887
958357:   jnt 6 dp/dth −5.8 −449.9 −20.2 dr/dth −0.962 0.025 −0.272
958487:   jnt 1 dth/dp 0.002 0.002 −0.000 dth/dr −1.102 0.700 −0.078
958611:   jnt 2 dth/dp −0.005 0.001 −0.002 dth/dr −0.486 −2.515 −0.157
958734:   jnt 3 dth/dp 0.010 −0.002 −0.001 dth/dr 1.028 4.517 0.298
958856:   jnt 4 dth/dp 0.007 −0.004 −0.006 dth/dr 1.975 4.652 −0.445
958981:   jnt 5 dth/dp −0.002 −0.002 0.001 dth/dr 1.109 −1.421 −0.846
959103:   jnt 6 dth/dp −0.009 0.003 0.006 dth/dr −2.634 −5.171 0.064
959210:   crunch pose 1..6 −1.005 −3.770 2.636 −1.366 −0.530 1.168
              dposdstang −0.962 0.025 −0.272
959306:   stick angle 0.275964 wrist at 34.8 −418.4 738.3
959617:   robot intrpt at 950257 cycle5 216 avg torque 256 13600 −3776
              768 960 2112
959727:   feed forward 0 1736 −469 81 55 226
959831:   actual: −257536 634400 267424 71072 90176 4512
959943:   target: −257480 634392 267440 71132 90288 4576
960443:   rates eff4 −205 −22 −372 eff5 194 32 75 det 56670.7 v4 0.000
              v5 0.000
962372:   j# 1 Jwc 53.31 limits 198 61 −61 −198 k 21.29
962624:   j# 2 Jwc 61.67 limits 273 96 −63 −240 k 41.28
962870:   j# 3 Jwc 22.27 limits 444 143 −122 −424 k 43.15
963121:   j# 4 Jwc 2.73 limits 794 289 −288 −793 k 30.55
963367:   j# 5 Jwc 2.63 limits 751 276 −272 −747 k 26.04
963616:   j# 6 Jwc 3.10 limits 513 188 −183 −508 k 14.38
963962:   eti_proposed 982598 avail motion time 0.465999
964909:   J1 dp 0.077 tof 0.46449 eta 1446978 setl 0.00151 stress 0.033
              emfmargin 191.0 alh −2.1 2.1 vlh 0.0 0.3 plh −1.082 −1.005
966072:   J2 dp −0.419 tof 0.46449 eta 1446978 setl 0.00151 stress 0.178
              emfmargin 168.4 alh −11.2 11.2 vlh −1.7 0.0 plh −3.770
              −3.351
967184:   J3 dp −0.156 tof 0.46449 eta 1446978 setl 0.00151 stress 0.034
              emfmargin 395.9 alh −4.2 4.2 vlh −0.6 0.0 plh 2.636 2.793
968306:   J4 dp −0.965 tof 0.46449 eta 1446978 setl 0.00151 stress 0.089
              emfmargin 669.1 alh −25.8 25.8 vlh −3.9 0.0 plh −1.366
              −0.401
969451:   J5 dp 0.375 tof 0.46449 eta 1446978 setl 0.00151 stress 0.037

emfmargin 709.4 alh −10.0 10.0 vlh 0.0 1.5 plh −0.563
−0.188

972277:   J6 dp 1.254 dpa 1.262 dv −5.468 tof 0.46449 eta 1446978 setl
0.00151 stress 0.253 emf 393.4 alh −79.9 56.3 vlh 0.0 −5.5
plh −0.035 1.227

972663:   xfer poly jnt 1 from 225 to 365 coefs0..5 −1.082104 0.000000
0.000000 7.672245 −24.776543 21.336721

972968:   xfer poly jnt 2 from 225 to 365 coefs0..5 −3.351032 0.000000
0.000000 −41.778343 134.917862 −116.186707

973278:   xfer poly jnt 3 from 225 to 365 coefs0..5 2.792527 0.000000
0.000000 −15.612906 50.419899 −43.419910

973623:   xfer poly jnt 4 from 225 to 365 coefs0..5 −0.401426 0.000000
0.000000 −96.276802 310.913727 −267.748383

973934:   xfer poly jnt 5 from 225 to 365 coefs0..5 −0.562869 0.000000
0.000000 37.395294 −120.763359 103.997322

974240:   xfer poly jnt 6 from 225 to 365 coefs0..5 −0.035355 0.000000
0.000000 227.357361 −788.786377 702.770752

974503:   polynomials sent, update flg 0, bounced 0

974905:   ok to go on, next completion 1024868, j6 eta 1446978

975231:   mode 2 stroke 1 stamp 914971 cross 1305026 pos 156.9 0.0
177.9 vel −88.08 −2798.48 1646.89 spin 150.7 −4.9 9.1

979295:   t 1450609 bounced 0 p 144.6 −400.0 304.7 v −80.5 −2695.6
113.8 spin 150.72

979696:   hpd factor 1 wei 0.037 val −251.0

979814:   hpd factor 8 wei 1.000 val −400.0

980032:   hpd factor 9 wei 31.996 val −400.0

982844:   tunehpd hitpos 144.6 −399.5 304.7 vel −80.5 −2695.7 115.6

983519:   tunecontact m,nfact 2,2 contact at 13.0 −2.9 will be at 6.5 −1.5

983880:   tune 2 rules alpha 0.021 wv 1.00 0.000 1.00 0.004 0.00 0.000

984436:   rad stang fix rad −17.653 −0.334 −9.539, dpds −0.962 0.025
−0.272 dot prod 19.570, xz rad stang −98.0 440.0 crit 20.07

984701:   tune 2 rules stang 0.302 wv 1.00 0.000 1.49 0.043 0.00 0.000

984846:   vyz factor ec 3 Z wv 1.000 8.2

984955:   vyz factor ec 9 Y wv 1.000 −308.6

985264:   tune vyz 1 y and 1 z rules, new 5691.9 1445.0

985472:   return vector 119.6 5691.9 1445.0

987548:   paddle v 2200.717041 O 0.030 0.998 −0.046

987652:   jmp −49 70 1709 wf 60 −2 4 io sens −0.182 0.304

988830:   robot intrpt at 976799 cycle5 224 avg torque 256 13600 −3776
768 960 2112

988940:   feed forward −98 1645 −335 −322 322 745

989044:   actual: −257536 634400 267424 71072 90176 4512

989156:   target: −257480 634392 267440 71132 90288 4576
996122:   ec 0 t 0.490 zn 355 yb 1870 xzc 190 95 dzdy 0.53 cd 5,76
996643:   crnch xyz 144.614380 −399.508667 304.655762 hit_desc 2
          IDopt 2
1004686: joint angle conv. times 4271 jacobian 4167
1004803: jnt 1 dp/dth 100.5 305.4 0.0 dr/dth 0.000 0.000 −1.000
1004927: jnt 2 dp/dth 339.8 −238.8 −307.6 dr/dth −0.575 −0.818 0.000
1005053: jnt 3 dp/dth 429.1 −301.5 −136.2 dr/dth −0.575 −0.818 0.000
1005176: jnt 4 dp/dth −242.9 −366.5 −30.7 dr/dth −0.763 0.536
          −0.362
1005302: jnt 5 dp/dth 95.7 71.6 12.7 dr/dth 0.288 −0.220 −0.932
1005467: jnt 6 dp/dth −7.8 −448.9 2.6 dr/dth −0.954 0.015 −0.298
1005596: jnt 1 dth/dp 0.002 0.002 −0.000 dth/dr −1.022 0.718 −0.147
1005720: jnt 2 dth/dp −0.006 0.002 −0.002 dth/dr −0.749 −2.754
          −0.081
1005844: jnt 3 dth/dp 0.011 −0.003 −0.001 dth/dr 1.408 4.918 0.155
1005967: jnt 4 dth/dp 0.008 −0.003 −0.005 dth/dr 1.576 4.946 −0.211
1006091: jnt 5 dth/dp −0.002 −0.002 0.000 dth/dr 1.231 −0.920 −0.796
1006214: jnt 6 dth/dp −0.010 0.003 0.006 dth/dr −2.332 −5.534 −0.116
1006322: crunch pose 1..6 −0.958 −3.708 2.508 −1.556 −0.566 1.402
          dposdstang −0.954 0.015 −0.298
1006418: stick angle 0.301967 wrist at 29.3 −395.0 738.9
1006908: rates eff4 −236 −24 −372 eff5 94 13 74 det 17578.9 v4 0.000
          v5 0.000
1008045: j# 1 Jwc 55.65 limits 190 59 −59 −190 k 20.40
1008296: j# 2 Jwc 63.32 limits 266 94 −61 −233 k 40.21
1008543: j# 3 Jwc 22.27 limits 444 143 −122 −423 k 43.15
1008793: j# 4 Jwc 2.87 limits 757 276 −275 −756 k 29.15
1009041: j# 5 Jwc 2.63 limits 750 275 −272 −747 k 26.03
1009291: j# 6 Jwc 3.10 limits 512 187 −183 −508 k 14.38
1009544: eti_proposed 1029049 avail motion time 0.421378
1012676: J1 d(pf) 0.047 d(vf) 0.000 d(tf) −0.04645 pf −0.958 tof
          0.41804 eta 1446991 setl 0.00334 emf 1.0 alh −3.6 3.5 vlh
          0.0 0.0 plh −1.081 −0.958
1014155: J2 d(pf) 0.062 d(vf) 0.000 d(tf) −0.04645 pf −3.708 tof
          0.41804 eta 1446991 setl 0.00334 emf 1.0 alh −9.6 9.2 vlh
          −0.2 0.0 plh −3.355 −3.708
1014580: robot intrpt at 1003342 cycle5 232 avg torque 544 15981
          −3962 1691 818 −149
1014689: feed forward −136 1612 −282 −474 428 950
1014794: actual: −257504 634464 267424 71232 90144 4192
1014905: target: −257468 634532 267448 71288 90276 4360

1016233: J3 d(pf) −0.128 d(vf) 0.000 d(tf) −0.04645 pf 2.508 tof
0.41804 eta 1446991 setl 0.00334 emf 1.0 alh −8.2 8.4 vlh
−0.1 0.0 plh 2.791 2.508

1017716: J4 d(pf) −0.190 d(vf) 0.000 d(tf) −0.04645 pf −1.556 tof
0.41804 eta 1446991 setl 0.00334 emf 1.0 alh −31.4 32.1 vlh
−0.5 0.0 plh −0.410 −1.556

1019149: J5 d(pf) 0.011 d(vf) 0.000 d(tf) −0.04645 pf −0.177 tof
0.41804 eta 1446991 setl 0.00334 emf 1.0 alh −10.4 10.3 vlh
0.2 0.0 plh −0.560 −0.177

1020609: J6 d(pf) 0.242 d(vf) 0.562 d(tf) −0.04645 pf 1.469 tof 0.41804
eta 1446991 setl 0.00334 emf 1.0 alh −82.4 60.4 vlh 1.2
−4.9 plh −0.016 1.469

1021027: xfer poly jnt 1 from 239 to 365 coefs0..5 −1.081446 0.040227
0.769774 9.946828 −42.849064 43.371021

1021339: xfer poly jnt 2 from 239 to 365 coefs0..5 −3.354617 −0.219050
−4.191718 −10.776868 77.647186 −87.206947

1021696: xfer poly jnt 3 from 239 to 365 coefs0..5 2.791187 −0.081861
−1.566479 −24.745335 103.357315 −103.722206

1022008: xfer poly jnt 4 from 239 to 365 coefs0..5 −0.409686 −0.504793
−9.659675 −70.322311 342.152832 −357.140381

1022322: xfer poly jnt 5 from 239 to 365 coefs0..5 −0.559660 0.196069
3.751957 18.703598 −102.000595 109.155113

1022634: xfer poly jnt 6 from 239 to 365 coefs0..5 −0.016088 1.171832
22.175533 116.230034 −690.599121 761.316040

1022904: polynomials sent, update flg 1, bounced 0

(several more updating cycles)

1261475: ok to go on, next completion 1311439, j6 eta 1430462

1261803: mode 2 stroke 1 stamp 1220946 cross 1309437 pos 137.3 0.0
187.5 vel −142.98 −3130.77 1501.57 spin 169.3 −7.4 −11.8

1264445: t 1439417 bounced 0 p 118.7 −399.5 291.0 v −145.0 −3015.0
109.2 spin 169.26

1264845: hpd factor 1 wei 0.076 val −407.4

1264964: hpd factor 8 wei 1.000 val −400.0

1265182: hpd factor 9 wei 31.996 val −399.5

1268002: tunehpd hitpos 118.7 −399.5 291.0 vel −145.0 −3015.0 109.2

1268671: tunecontact m,nfact 2,2 contact at −3.4 11.1 will be at −1.6
5.3

1269677: tune 2 rules alpha 0.018 wv 1.00 0.000 1.00 0.001 0.00 0.000

1270231: rad stang fix rad −2.970 0.373 15.728, dpds −0.970 −0.001
−0.243 dot prod −0.940, xz rad stang −80.4 444.5 crit 16.01

1270496:   tune 2 rules stang 0.245 wv 1.00 0.000 0.00 −0.002 0.00 0.000
1270641:   vyz factor ec 3 Z wv 1.000 13.0
1270750:   vyz factor ec 9 Y wv 1.000 −7.1
1271051:   tune vyz 1 y and 1 z rules, new 5424.6 1518.4
1271216:   return vector 97.0 5424.6 1518.4
1273300:   paddle v 1893.815674 O 0.016 0.998 −0.065
1273443:   jmp 72 107 1918 wf 65 −3 −2 io sens −0.159 0.265
1280075:   robot intrpt at 1268765 cycle5 312 avg torque 1804 16190
            −4546 6954 −4781 5987
1280185:   feed forward 252 1832 −966 1244 −66 −1616
1280289:   actual: −230688 732608 224288 217888 51904 −190208
1280401:   target: −230584 732320 224292 217984 51244 −189576
1280920:   ec 0 t 0.519 zn 346 yb 1800 xzc 163 135 dzdy 0.49 cd 3,77
1281483:   crnch xyz 118.674248 −399.508667 291.037964 hit_desc 2
            IDopt 2
1288890:   joint angle conv. times 4276 jacobian 3567
1289006:   jnt 1 dp/dth 100.5 331.3 0.0 dr/dth 0.000 0.000 −1.000
1289129:   jnt 2 dp/dth 343.8 −256.5 −325.7 dr/dth −0.598 −0.802 0.000
1289255:   jnt 3 dp/dth 433.6 −323.5 −156.1 dr/dth −0.598 −0.802 0.000
1289422:   jnt 4 dp/dth −259.1 −353.0 −8.0 dr/dth −0.739 0.551 −0.388
1289549:   jnt 5 dp/dth 145.0 78.2 7.5 dr/dth 0.229 −0.337 −0.913
1289673:   jnt 6 dp/dth −2.6 −455.6 11.3 dr/dth −0.970 −0.001 −0.243
1289804:   jnt 1 dth/dp 0.002 0.002 0.000 dth/dr −1.038 0.774 −0.087
1289927:   jnt 2 dth/dp −0.006 0.002 −0.002 dth/dr −0.819 −2.621 0.013
1290050:   jnt 3 dth/dp 0.011 −0.003 −0.001 dth/dr 1.497 4.833 −0.024
1290172:   jnt 4 dth/dp 0.006 −0.003 −0.004 dth/dr 1.649 4.209 −0.525
1290296:   jnt 5 dth/dp −0.002 −0.002 0.000 dth/dr 1.087 −1.339 −0.832
1290418:   jnt 6 dth/dp −0.008 0.003 0.006 dth/dr −2.449 −4.884 0.211
1290525:   crunch pose 1..6 −0.930 −3.726 2.554 −1.437 −0.626 1.294
            dposdstang −0.970 −0.001 −0.243
1290621:   stick angle 0.244829 wrist at 34.8 −387.9 739.7
1291112:   rates eff4 −254 −31 −356 eff5 143 23 80 det 30464.7 v4 0.000
            v5 0.000
1292248:   j# 1 Jwc 55.83 limits 187 57 −59 −189 k 20.33
1292500:   j# 2 Jwc 62.75 limits 268 95 −61 −235 k 40.58
1292750:   j# 3 Jwc 21.17 limits 473 156 −126 −442 k 45.40
1292998:   j# 4 Jwc 2.86 limits 757 275 −236 −718 k 29.21
1293246:   j# 5 Jwc 0.84 limits 2334 850 −851 −2335 k 81.38
1293534:   j# 6 Jwc 3.10 limits 476 151 −189 −514 k 14.38
1293747:   eti_proposed 1314374 avail motion time 0.125043
1296762:   J1 d(pf) −0.003 d(vf) 0.000 d(tf) −0.04977 pf −0.930 tof
            0.11280 eta 1427152 setl 0.01224 emf 1.0 alh −8.3 0.7 vlh

0.4 0.0 plh −0.942 −0.930

1298245: J2 d(pf) 0.013 d(vf) 0.000 d(tf) −0.04977 pf −3.726 tof 0.11280 eta 1427152 setl 0.01224 emf 1.0 alh −0.5 17.9 vlh −1.1 0.0 plh −3.686 −3.726

1299683: J3 d(pf) 0.007 d(vf) 0.000 d(tf) −0.04977 pf 2.554 tof 0.11280 eta 1427152 setl 0.01224 emf 1.0 alh −3.1 12.4 vlh −0.5 0.0 plh 2.560 2.554

1301136: J4 d(pf) 0.029 d(vf) 0.000 d(tf) −0.04977 pf −1.437 tof 0.11280 eta 1427152 setl 0.01224 emf 1.0 alh −8.4 50.2 vlh −2.4 0.0 plh −1.383 −1.437

1302598: J5 d(pf) −0.007 d(vf) 0.000 d(tf) −0.04977 pf −0.266 tof 0.11280 eta 1427152 setl 0.01224 emf 1.0 alh −10.8 1.0 vlh 0.6 0.0 plh −0.283 −0.266

1304048: J6 d(pf) −0.028 d(vf) 0.049 d(tf) −0.04977 pf 1.410 tof 0.11280 eta 1427152 setl 0.01224 emf 1.0 alh −102.8 1.0 vlh 2.2 −4.2 plh 1.658 1.410

1304467: xfer poly jnt 1 from 325 to 359 coefs0..5 −0.941594 0.425455 −3.831432 −17.103813 382.686432 −1365.328979

1304779: xfer poly jnt 2 from 325 to 359 coefs0..5 −3.686135 −1.096120 5.235638 103.243813 −1226.422241 3724.453369

1305097: xfer poly jnt 3 from 325 to 359 coefs0..5 2.560465 −0.489679 5.481816 36.802238 −794.430542 2975.991211

1305451: xfer poly jnt 4 from 325 to 359 coefs0..5 −1.382986 −2.363015 20.736330 184.862656 −3256.367188 11517.514648

1305768: xfer poly jnt 5 from 325 to 359 coefs0..5 −0.283048 0.577582 −4.318587 −41.746021 661.808472 −2235.062256

1306081: xfer poly jnt 6 from 325 to 359 coefs0..5 1.657932 2.199325 −43.902195 −288.198486 4577.635254 −14495.129883

1306350: polynomials sent, update flg 1, bounced 0

1306638: robot intrpt at 1295307 cycle5 320 avg torque −2511 12481 −3471 6366 −4197 7395

1306748: feed forward 249 1811 −969 1160 −82 −1456

1306851: actual: −226432 745696 219168 235200 48064 −206720

1306962: target: −226420 745376 219288 235372 47540 −206700

1333143: robot intrpt at 1321849 cycle5 328 avg torque −4620 9376 −2001 4297 −3820 7671

1333253: feed forward 234 1795 −968 1003 −84 −1229

1333397: actual: −223456 756672 215712 247584 45280 −215712

1333510: target: −223416 756344 216008 247784 44836 −216232

1359707: robot intrpt at 1348391 cycle5 336 avg torque −3646 2812 −489 4366 −4707 12666

1359817: feed forward 133 1739 −846 253 −29 −323

1359921:   actual: −221920 764160 214080 253888 43776 −215968
1360032:   target: −221744 763884 214540 254448 43236 −217072
1377173:   better stop now, instead of processing additional inputs
1377290:   got data for stroke −1, waiting for −2 data
1377425:   final hit time 1439417
1377566:   coast for 0.026402 sec at v −4.159323
1377995:   xfer poly jnt 6 from 359 to 370 coefs0..5 1.410152 −4.159323
           0.000000 0.000000 0.000000 0.000000
1378528:   stopping times 0.026402 0.548042 from v −4.159323
1381989:   xfer poly jnt 1 from 370 to 535 coefs0..5 −0.929879 0.000000
           0.000000 −9.278956 25.425032 −18.577726
1385493:   xfer poly jnt 2 from 370 to 535 coefs0..5 −3.725517 0.000000
           0.000000 22.826927 −62.547478 45.702599
1385939:   robot intrpt at 1374933 cycle5 344 avg torque 42 4075 −1146
           5259 −4709 14598
1386051:   feed forward 29 1703 −763 −186 48 17
1386155:   actual: −221504 767328 213888 255168 43264 −208512
1386269:   target: −221208 767232 214544 255892 42704 −209504
1389706:   xfer poly jnt 3 from 370 to 535 coefs0..5 2.553531 0.000000
           0.000000 14.568106 −39.917694 29.167320
1393237:   xfer poly jnt 4 from 370 to 535 coefs0..5 −1.437226 0.000000
           0.000000 63.137791 −173.002243 126.410400
1396872:   xfer poly jnt 5 from 370 to 535 coefs0..5 −0.266434 0.000000
           0.000000 −18.069313 49.511265 −36.177212
1401265:   xfer poly jnt 6 from 370 to 535 coefs0..5 1.258356 −4.159323
           0.000000 4.416433 13.252028 −18.945766
1402185:   Demons awake! Supposed to stop by 2008388
1403524:   Actual ETI delay 10541, expected 18636, initial(1)/update(0)
           0
1404934:   Actual ETI delay 13360, expected 19505, initial(1)/update(0)
           1
1406385:   Actual ETI delay 13377, expected 20861, initial(1)/update(0)
           1
1407715:   Actual ETI delay 13176, expected 19489, initial(1)/update(0)
           1
1409126:   Actual ETI delay 13226, expected 19418, initial(1)/update(0)
           1
1410579:   Actual ETI delay 13169, expected 21726, initial(1)/update(0)
           1
1410914:   robot intrpt at 1401476 cycle5 352 avg torque 2071 12186
           −3261 2542 −2466 11870
1411027:   feed forward 0 1712 −776 −155 76 −146

1411131:   actual: −221536 767680 214368 254560 43200 −196128
1411245:   target: −221220 767900 215004 255132 42712 −196776
1412646:   Actual ETI delay 13248, expected 20142, initial(1)/update(0)
           1
1414018:   Actual ETI delay 12603, expected 2062⁷, initial(1)/update(0)
           1
1414984:   Demons sleeping, processed 9308 ints, rbno 0 wbno 0

Appendix 6

Flight Path Correction

1059522: polynomials sent, update flg 0, bounced 0
1059922: ok to go on, next completion 1109886, j6 eta 1423714
1060292: mode 2 stroke 1 stamp 1018769 cross 1282725 pos 76.8 0.0
170.7 vel −514.56 −3112.83 1276.07 spin −94.8 −6.0
−190.0
1062954: t 1414873 bounced 0 p 3.5 −400.0 254.4 v −597.0 −2952.2
−0.0 spin −94.78
1063358: hpd factor 1 wei 0.228 val −399.9
1063475: hpd factor 8 wei 1.000 val −400.0
1063692: hpd factor 9 wei 31.996 val −400.0
1066529: tunehpd hitpos 3.6 −399.5 254.4 vel −596.9 −2952.4 1.5
1067199: tunecontact m,nfact 2,2 contact at −103.0 0.9 will be at −54.7
0.5
1067593: robot intrpt at 1056365 cycle5 272 avg torque 0 13888 −4096
640 788 1952
1067706: feed forward −115 1647 −343 −330 300 635
1067810: actual: −257504 634368 267488 71104 90208 4544
1067924: target: −257480 634392 267440 71132 90288 4576
1068241: tune 2 rules alpha 0.004 wv 1.00 0.000 1.00 −0.035 0.00 0.000
1068798: rad stang fix rad 155.488 −1.127 26.376, dpds −0.987 0.011
−0.159 dot prod −157.707, xz rad stang −45.5 442.4 crit
157.71
1069059: tune 2 rules stang −0.054 wv 1.00 0.000 1.50 −0.355 0.00
0.000
1069202: vyz factor ec 3 Z wv 1.000 3.6
1069311: vyz factor ec 9 Y wv 1.000 −267.8
1069619: tune vyz 1 y and 1 z rules, new 5487.5 1645.1
1069788: return vector 19.8 5487.5 1645.1
1071875: paddle v 2244.018066 O −0.088 0.925 0.370
1071979: jmp 976 486 −1004 wf −3 −9 −50 io sens −0.172 0.313

1073725:   ec 11 t 0.484 zn 363 yb 1924 xzc 175 69 dzdy 0.62 cd 11,134
1073918:   worth fun 110e00 critp 12c494 critv n 39.557 o 0.000 pass 1 rv
          1 nw 1
1074390:   tune 3 rules alpha 0.183 wv 1.00 0.000 1.00 0.000 39.56 0.189
1074604:   return vector 1018.0 5487.5 1645.1
1077548:   paddle v 2245.160156 O 0.050 0.930 0.363
1077653:   jmp 984 332 −1002 wf −4 −9 −63 io sens −0.169 0.308
1085142:   ec 12 t 0.530 zn 318 yb 1724 xzc 524 176 dzdy 0.42 cd 12,49
1085330:   worth fun 110e00 critp 12be90 critv n −83.768 o 0.000 pass 1
          rv 1 nw 2
1085750:   tune 3 rules alpha 0.149 wv 1.00 0.000 1.00 0.004 83.77
          −0.035
1085963:   return vector 825.9 5487.5 1645.1
1088050:   paddle v 2235.774170 O 0.024 0.931 0.365
1088195:   jmp 983 362 −1004 wf −4 −9 −61 io sens −0.170 0.308
1094103:   robot intrpt at 1082905 cycle5 280 avg torque 72 15662 −3664
          1228 682 684
1094216:   feed forward −160 1617 −298 −487 406 795
1094320:   actual: −257504 634464 267552 71136 90240 4384
1094434:   target: −257484 634512 267488 71196 90312 4492
1096500:   ec 0 t 0.528 zn 318 yb 1728 xzc 436 174 dzdy 0.42 cd 12,45
1097023:   crnch xyz 3.635778 −399.508667 254.414230 hit_desc 2 IDopt
          2

Appendix 7

Acceleration Limit Correction

5081944: ok to go on, next completion 5131907, j6 eta 5398675

5082272: mode 2 stroke 3 stamp 5037491 cross 5276418 pos 359.7 0.0 207.4 vel −53.96 −3421.96 1598.56 spin 185.4 −1.5 −44.9

5084954: t 5395424 bounced 0 p 351.8 −400.0 318.7 v −80.3 −3298.3 290.7 spin 185.37

5085356: hpd factor 1 wei 0.022 val −338.5

5085474: hpd factor 8 wei 1.000 val −400.0

5085693: hpd factor 9 wei 31.991 val −400.0

5088508: tunehpd hitpos 351.9 −399.5 318.7 vel −80.3 −3298.5 292.3

5089184: tunecontact m,nfact 2,2 contact at −13.9 −20.2 will be at −7.2 −10.5

5089549: tune 2 rules alpha −0.034 wv 1.00 0.000 1.00 −0.010 0.00 0.000

5090106: rad stang fix rad 36.336 −0.288 −8.201, dpds −0.735 −0.067 −0.675 dot prod −21.132, xz rad stang −285.4 349.4 crit 37.25

5090431: jnt 16 critical by −0.094 jacob −3.438 dstang −0.027

5090680: tune 3 rules stang 0.736 wv 1.00 0.000 0.02 −0.047 0.49 −0.027

5090825: vyz factor ec 3 Z wv 1.000 39.0

5090934: vyz factor ec 9 Y wv 1.000 −23.1

5091880: vyz factor ec 206 Y wv 0.539 29.2 Z wv 0.539 451.4

5092178: tune vyz 2 y and 2 z rules, new 5670.4 1541.3

5092347: return vector −191.3 5670.4 1541.3

5095275: paddle v 1886.130493 O −0.053 0.994 −0.097

5095379: jmp 255 196 2091 wf 73 0 −10 io sens −0.151 0.252

5102231: robot intrpt at 5091029 cycle5 1472 avg torque 1376 13216 −4952 928 4640 1275

5102343: feed forward −203 1507 −112 −1110 354 2143

5102447: actual: −257632 634496 267808 71136 89664 4768

5102603:   target: −257480 634424 267472 71164 90320 4576
5103072:   ec 0 t 0.486 zn 396 yb 1975 xzc 284 35 dzdy 0.65 cd 5,16
5103596:   crnch xyz 351.850739 −399.508667 318.678314 hit_desc 2
           IDopt 2
5111064:   joint angle conv. times 4289 jacobian 3574
5111181:   jnt 1 dp/dth 100.5 98.1 0.0 dr/dth 0.000 0.000 −1.000
5111306:   jnt 2 dp/dth 308.7 −256.5 −139.7 dr/dth −0.639 −0.769 0.000
5111430:   jnt 3 dp/dth 399.5 −331.9 25.7 dr/dth −0.639 −0.769 0.000
5111555:   jnt 4 dp/dth −191.1 −374.0 −106.5 dr/dth −0.582 0.484
           −0.654
5111680:   jnt 5 dp/dth 60.4 94.9 34.1 dr/dth 0.671 −0.168 −0.722
5111806:   jnt 6 dp/dth 36.0 −437.5 28.5 dr/dth −0.740 −0.104 −0.664
5111934:   jnt 1 dth/dp 0.002 0.002 0.000 dth/dr −0.931 0.774 −0.562
5112060:   jnt 2 dth/dp −0.004 0.001 −0.003 dth/dr −0.517 −2.268
           −0.268
5112183:   jnt 3 dth/dp 0.008 −0.003 0.000 dth/dr 1.032 3.226 0.555
5112306:   jnt 4 dth/dp 0.005 −0.003 −0.004 dth/dr 1.066 2.714 0.239
5112428:   jnt 5 dth/dp −0.000 −0.002 −0.001 dth/dr 1.498 −0.440
           −0.230
5112552:   jnt 6 dth/dp −0.008 0.001 0.005 dth/dr −1.275 −3.359 −0.645
5112658:   crunch pose 1..6 −0.877 −3.762 2.903 −1.875 −0.619 1.437
           dposdstang −0.740 −0.104 −0.664
5112756:   stick angle 0.735750 wrist at 82.9 −398.9 668.4
5113246:   rates eff4 −251 −36 −351 eff5 77 12 88 det 5079.7 v4 0.000
           v5 0.000
5114387:   j# 1 Jwc 53.00 limits 199 62 −60 −198 k 21.42
5114680:   j# 2 Jwc 59.48 limits 281 98 −67 −250 k 42.80
5114924:   j# 3 Jwc 22.25 limits 439 137 −126 −427 k 43.18
5115177:   j# 4 Jwc 2.88 limits 717 239 −275 −753 k 28.98
5115420:   j# 5 Jwc 2.63 limits 750 275 −262 −738 k 26.05
5115670:   j# 6 Jwc 3.10 limits 512 186 −139 −464 k 14.38
5115881:   eti_proposed 5136638 avail motion time 0.258637
5118892:   J1 d(pf) 0.006 d(vf) 0.000 d(tf) −0.05308 pf −0.877 tof
           0.25547 eta 5392047 setl 0.00317 emf 1.0 alh −13.4 12.9 vlh
           0.3 0.0 plh −1.077 −0.877
5120341:   J2 d(pf) 0.021 d(vf) 0.000 d(tf) −0.05308 pf −3.762 tof
           0.25547 eta 5392047 setl 0.00317 emf 1.0 alh −26.0 26.1 vlh
           −0.7 0.0 plh −3.363 −3.762
5121734:   J3 d(pf) −0.077 d(vf) 0.000 d(tf) −0.05308 pf 2.903 tof
           0.25547 eta 5392047 setl 0.00317 emf 1.0 alh −5.8 10.6 vlh
           0.3 0.0 plh 2.798 2.903
5123220:   J4 d(pf) −0.077 d(vf) 0.000 d(tf) −0.05308 pf −1.875 tof

0.25547 eta 5392047 setl 0.00317 emf 1.0 alh −92.8 96.9 vlh −2.2 0.0 plh −0.439 −1.875

5124653: J5 d(pf) −0.039 d(vf) 0.000 d(tf) −0.05308 pf −0.150 tof 0.25547 eta 5392047 setl 0.00317 emf 1.0 alh −25.8 26.5 vlh 0.7 0.0 plh −0.551 −0.150

5126117: J6 d(pf) 0.118 d(vf) 0.123 d(tf) −0.05308 pf 1.501 tof 0.25547 eta 5392047 setl 0.00317 emf 1.0 alh −157.1 122.4 vlh 3.1 −4.3 plh 0.017 1.501

5126452: too much acc J6 got −157 122 clip at 139 tof 0.255 avail 0.259 nsetl −0.053 osetl 0.003 emf 1

5127138: worth fun 11111c critp 12b8d4 critv n −0.353 o 0.000 pass 1 rv 1 nw 1

5127496: jnt 16 critical by −0.353 jacob −3.359 dstang −0.105

5127696: tune 2 rules stang 0.701 wv 1.00 0.000 0.49 −0.105 0.00 0.000

5128265: crnch xyz 351.850739 −399.508667 318.678314 hit_desc 2 IDopt 2

5128785: robot intrpt at 5117571 cycle5 1480 avg torque 5383 22278 −2917 3579 −317 −5435

5128898: feed forward −202 1478 −45 −1175 283 2355

5129003: actual: −257376 635200 268032 72736 89408 2464

5129117: target: −257216 635280 267700 72544 89916 3168

5136379: joint angle conv. times 4943 jacobian 3566

5136497: jnt 1 dp/dth 100.5 98.1 0.0 dr/dth 0.000 0.000 −1.000

5136623: jnt 2 dp/dth 300.4 −266.1 −140.1 dr/dth −0.663 −0.749 0.000

5136747: jnt 3 dp/dth 397.8 −352.3 16.0 dr/dth −0.663 −0.749 0.000

5136873: jnt 4 dp/dth −197.9 −362.4 −100.5 dr/dth −0.552 0.489 −0.676

5136998: jnt 5 dp/dth 102.1 97.3 53.7 dr/dth 0.639 −0.273 −0.719

5137123: jnt 6 dp/dth 35.5 −437.6 28.0 dr/dth −0.763 −0.103 −0.638

5137250: jnt 1 dth/dp 0.002 0.002 −0.000 dth/dr −0.964 0.854 −0.542

5137376: jnt 2 dth/dp −0.004 0.001 −0.003 dth/dr −0.537 −2.195 −0.249

5137499: jnt 3 dth/dp 0.008 −0.003 0.000 dth/dr 1.045 3.050 0.508

5137623: jnt 4 dth/dp 0.004 −0.003 −0.004 dth/dr 1.276 2.329 0.129

5137746: jnt 5 dth/dp −0.001 −0.002 −0.001 dth/dr 1.443 −0.701 −0.273

5137871: jnt 6 dth/dp −0.007 0.002 0.005 dth/dr −1.467 −3.014 −0.547

5137976: crunch pose 1..6 −0.846 −3.836 3.007 −1.791 −0.640 1.332 dposdstang −0.763 −0.103 −0.638

5138075: stick angle 0.701227 wrist at 95.0 −397.4 677.4

5138605: rates eff4 −252 −36 −340 eff5 122 21 86 det 19807.9 v4 0.000 v5 0.000

5139747:   j# 1 Jwc 53.00 limits 199 62 −60 −198 k 21.42
5139997:   j# 2 Jwc 59.47 limits 281 97 −67 −251 k 42.81
5140241:   j# 3 Jwc 22.28 limits 437 136 −126 −427 k 43.13
5140493:   j# 4 Jwc 2.82 limits 731 242 −281 −770 k 29.62
5140736:   j# 5 Jwc 2.64 limits 747 273 −264 −737 k 25.96
5140985:   j# 6 Jwc 3.10 limits 512 186 −134 −459 k 14.38
5141196:   eti_proposed 5159863 avail motion time 0.235412
5144974:   J1 d(pf) 0.038 d(vf) 0.000 d(tf) −0.07963 pf −0.846 tof
           0.22893 eta 5388736 setl 0.00649 emf 1.0 alh −17.4 14.4 vlh
           0.6 0.0 plh −1.066 −0.846
5146424:   J2 d(pf) −0.054 d(vf) 0.000 d(tf) −0.07963 pf −3.836 tof
           0.22893 eta 5388736 setl 0.00649 emf 1.0 alh −29.2 34.9 vlh
           −1.3 0.0 plh −3.385 −3.836
5147894:   J3 d(pf) 0.027 d(vf) 0.000 d(tf) −0.07963 pf 3.007 tof 0.22893
           eta 5388736 setl 0.00649 emf 1.0 alh −15.6 13.0 vlh 0.6 0.0
           plh 2.807 3.007
5149336:   J4 d(pf) 0.007 d(vf) 0.000 d(tf) −0.07963 pf −1.791 tof
           0.22893 eta 5388736 setl 0.00649 emf 1.0 alh −85.0 93.7 vlh
           −4.2 0.0 plh −0.513 −1.791
5150766:   J5 d(pf) −0.082 d(vf) 0.000 d(tf) −0.07963 pf −0.192 tof
           0.22893 eta 5388736 setl 0.00649 emf 1.0 alh −22.3 27.3 vlh
           1.3 0.0 plh −0.527 −0.192
5152232:   J6 d(pf) 0.033 d(vf) 0.123 d(tf) −0.07963 pf 1.417 tof 0.22893
           eta 5388736 setl 0.00649 emf 1.0 alh −155.3 112.1 vlh 5.7
           −4.3 plh 0.118 1.417
5152576:   re-settling time, aclip 133.8 awc 155.3 a_m_t 0.235412 setl
           0.006487 new setl 0.000000 adj 0.812 emf 1.0
5153698:   J6 d(pf) 0.019 d(vf) 0.123 d(tf) −0.07631 pf 1.402 tof 0.23224
           eta 5392053 setl 0.00317 emf 1.0 alh −149.6 111.8 vlh 5.7
           −4.3 plh 0.118 1.402
5154036:   too much acc J6 got −150 112 clip at 134 tof 0.232 avail 0.235
           nsetl −0.046 osetl 0.003 emf 1
5154731:   worth fun 11111c critp 12b8d4 critv n −0.210 o −0.210 pass 2
           rv 1 nw 1
5155087:   jnt 16 critical by −0.210 jacob −3.014 dstang −0.070
5155319:   robot intrpt at 5144114 cycle5 1488 avg torque 11518 35305
           −1565 1810 −4856 −15821
5155431:   feed forward −133 1517 −88 −893 85 2019
5155535:   actual: −255808 640032 269888 80992 87360 −5696
5155649:   target: −255652 640364 269064 80744 87512 −5120
5155941:   tune 2 rules stang 0.678 wv 1.00 0.000 0.49 −0.070 0.00 0.000
5156512:   crnch xyz 351.850739 −399.508667 318.678314 hit_desc 2

IDopt 2

5164730: joint angle conv. times 5043 jacobian 3569

5164847: jnt 1 dp/dth 100.5 98.1 0.0 dr/dth 0.000 0.000 −1.000

5164971: jnt 2 dp/dth 294.4 −272.8 −140.3 dr/dth −0.680 −0.734 0.000

5165097: jnt 3 dp/dth 395.2 −366.2 9.4 dr/dth −0.680 −0.734 0.000

5165221: jnt 4 dp/dth −202.6 −353.7 −96.6 dr/dth −0.532 0.493 −0.689

5165347: jnt 5 dp/dth 127.4 98.1 63.5 dr/dth 0.614 −0.335 −0.714

5165471: jnt 6 dp/dth 35.2 −437.6 27.8 dr/dth −0.778 −0.102 −0.621

5165600: jnt 1 dth/dp 0.002 0.002 −0.000 dth/dr −0.985 0.913 −0.528

5165724: jnt 2 dth/dp −0.004 0.001 −0.003 dth/dr −0.555 −2.157 −0.238

5165849: jnt 3 dth/dp 0.007 −0.003 0.000 dth/dr 1.059 2.953 0.480

5165971: jnt 4 dth/dp 0.004 −0.003 −0.004 dth/dr 1.382 2.061 0.059

5166096: jnt 5 dth/dp −0.001 −0.002 −0.001 dth/dr 1.404 −0.851 −0.296

5166218: jnt 6 dth/dp −0.006 0.002 0.005 dth/dr −1.563 −2.777 −0.486

5166326: crunch pose 1..6 −0.824 −3.884 3.073 −1.743 −0.659 1.270 dposdstang −0.778 −0.102 −0.621

5166422: stick angle 0.678359 wrist at 103.3 −396.4 683.1

5166949: rates eff4 −254 −37 −331 eff5 148 26 85 det 27755.6 v4 0.000 v5 0.000

5168085: j# 1 Jwc 52.94 limits 200 62 −61 −199 k 21.44

5168333: j# 2 Jwc 59.35 limits 281 97 −67 −251 k 42.90

5168579: j# 3 Jwc 22.33 limits 437 136 −126 −426 k 43.04

5168830: j# 4 Jwc 2.77 limits 753 256 −286 −783 k 30.12

5169077: j# 5 Jwc 2.66 limits 740 271 −268 −738 k 25.74

5169325: j# 6 Jwc 3.10 limits 512 186 −141 −467 k 14.38

5169538: eti_proposed 5189723 avail motion time 0.205552

5172557: J1 d(pf) 0.060 d(vf) 0.000 d(tf) −0.11280 pf −0.824 tof 0.19575 eta 5385426 setl 0.00980 emf 1.0 alh −22.8 14.9 vlh 0.9 0.0 plh −1.044 −0.824

5174001: J2 d(pf) −0.102 d(vf) 0.000 d(tf) −0.11280 pf −3.884 tof 0.19575 eta 5385426 setl 0.00980 emf 1.0 alh −28.9 45.5 vlh −2.0 0.0 plh −3.435 −3.884

5175475: J3 d(pf) 0.093 d(vf) 0.000 d(tf) −0 11280 pf 3.073 tof 0.19575 eta 5385426 setl 0.00980 emf 1.0 alh −26.9 19.0 vlh 0.9 0.0 plh 2.829 3.073

5177624: J4 d(pf) 0.055 d(vf) 0.000 d(tf) −0.11280 pf −1.743 tof 0.19575 eta 5385426 setl 0.00980 emf 1.0 alh −68.3 92.9 vlh −6.5 0.0 plh −0.673 −1.743

5179063: J5 d(pf) −0.113 d(vf) 0.000 d(tf) −0.11280 pf −0.223 tof

0.19575 eta 5385426 setl 0.00980 emf 1.0 alh −21.6 22.1 vlh 2.1 0.0 plh −0.475 −0.223

5180488: J6 d(pf) −0.025 d(vf) 0.123 d(tf) −0.10949 pf 1.359 tof 0.19907 eta 5388743 setl 0.00649 emf 1.0 alh −149.9 83.9 vlh 8.7 −4.3 plh 0.334 1.359

5180835: re-settling time, aclip 141.5 awc 149.9 a_m_t 0.205552 setl 0.006486 new setl 0.000000 adj 0.842 emf 1.0

5181862: robot intrpt at 5170656 cycle5 1496 avg torque 12411 39050 −1963 1996 −7407 −20825

5181972: feed forward −33 1614 −262 −403 −65 1269

5182076: actual: −252256 651392 273344 99584 82144 −23936

5182188: target: −252176 651660 272084 98948 82172 −23280

5182641: J6 d(pf) −0.039 d(vf) 0.123 d(tf) −0.10617 pf 1.344 tof 0.20238 eta 5392060 setl 0.00317 emf 1.0 alh −143.9 83.9 vlh 8.7 −4.3 plh 0.334 1.344

5182974: too much acc J6 got −144 84 clip at 141 tof 0.202 avail 0.206 nsetl −0.033 osetl 0.003 emf 1

5183630: worth fun 11111c critp 12b8d4 critv n −0.078 o −0.078 pass 3 rv 1 nw 1

5183986: jnt 16 critical by −0.078 jacob −2.777 dstang −0.028

5184185: tune 2 rules stang 0.669 wv 1.00 0.000 0.49 −0.028 0.00 0.000

5184753: crnch xyz 351.850739 −399.508667 318.678314 hit_desc 2 IDopt 2

5192973: joint angle conv. times 4286 jacobian 4329

5193091: jnt 1 dp/dth 100.5 98.1 0.0 dr/dth 0.000 0.000 −1.000

5193216: jnt 2 dp/dth 291.8 −275.5 −140.4 dr/dth −0.687 −0.727 0.000

5193341: jnt 3 dp/dth 393.8 −371.8 6.6 dr/dth −0.687 −0.727 0.000

5193467: jnt 4 dp/dth −204.6 −349.9 −95.1 dr/dth −0.524 0.495 −0.693

5193590: jnt 5 dp/dth 137.0 98.3 66.8 dr/dth 0.604 −0.358 −0.712

5193715: jnt 6 dp/dth 35.0 −437.7 27.7 dr/dth −0.783 −0.101 −0.613

5193842: jnt 1 dth/dp 0.002 0.002 −0.000 dth/dr −0.993 0.938 −0.522

5193968: jnt 2 dth/dp −0.004 0.001 −0.003 dth/dr −0.563 −2.144 −0.234

5194091: jnt 3 dth/dp 0.007 −0.003 0.000 dth/dr 1.065 2.917 0.470

5194216: jnt 4 dth/dp 0.003 −0.003 −0.004 dth/dr 1.417 1.952 0.031

5194339: jnt 5 dth/dp −0.001 −0.002 −0.001 dth/dr 1.388 −0.907 −0.304

5194463: jnt 6 dth/dp −0.006 0.002 0.005 dth/dr −1.594 −2.682 −0.462

5194610: crunch pose 1..6 −0.814 −3.904 3.099 −1.726 −0.667 1.246 dposdstang −0.783 −0.101 −0.613

5194709: stick angle 0.669158 wrist at 106.6 −396.0 685.4

5195200:   rates eff4 −254 −37 −328 eff5 158 28 84 det 30540.6 v4 0.000
            v5 0.000
5196338:   j# 1 Jwc 52.85 limits 200 62 −62 −200 k 21.48
5196588:   j# 2 Jwc 59.12 limits 282 97 −67 −251 k 43.07
5196832:   j# 3 Jwc 22.38 limits 439 139 −125 −425 k 42.93
5197083:   j# 4 Jwc 2.75 limits 776 275 −288 −789 k 30.33
5197930:   j# 5 Jwc 2.65 limits 741 270 −272 −743 k 25.82
5198181:   j# 6 Jwc 3.10 limits 512 186 −159 −484 k 14.38
5198391:   eti_proposed 5219588 avail motion time 0.175687
5200802:   J1 d(pf) 0.069 d(vf) 0.000 d(tf) −0.14598 pf −0.814 tof
            0.16257 eta 5382121 setl 0.01312 emf 1.0 alh −29.5 16.0 vlh
            1.1 0.0 plh −1.012 −0.814
5202253:   J2 d(pf) −0.122 d(vf) 0.000 d(tf) −0.14598 pf −3.904 tof
            0.16257 eta 5382121 setl 0.01312 emf 1.0 alh −28.9 57.9 vlh
            −2.5 0.0 plh −3.502 −3.904
5203842:   J3 d(pf) 0.119 d(vf) 0.000 d(tf) −0.14598 pf 3.099 tof 0.16257
            eta 5382121 setl 0.01312 emf 1.0 alh −39.4 26.4 vlh 1.1 0.0
            plh 2.859 3.099
5205239:   J4 d(pf) 0.073 d(vf) 0.000 d(tf) −0.14598 pf −1.726 tof
            0.16257 eta 5382121 setl 0.01312 emf 1.0 alh −34.6 95.0 vlh
            −8.1 0.0 plh −0.892 −1.726
5206705:   J5 d(pf) −0.126 d(vf) 0.000 d(tf) −0.14598 pf −0.236 tof
            0.16257 eta 5382121 setl 0.01312 emf 1.0 alh −33.0 11.2 vlh
            2.6 0.0 plh −0.404 −0.236
5208131:   J6 d(pf) −0.046 d(vf) 0.123 d(tf) −0.13935 pf 1.337 tof
            0.16921 eta 5388755 setl 0.00648 emf 1.0 alh −147.4 31.1
            vlh 10.4 −4.3 plh 0.623 1.337
5208421:   robot intrpt at 5197198 cycle5 1504 avg torque 11257 35852
            −229 3149 −12155 −15708
5208533:   feed forward 57 1730 −526 208 −60 259
5208638:   actual: −246784 669152 278016 128128 74304 −52064
5208752:   target: −246796 669148 276768 127140 73908 −50916
5210174:   xfer poly jnt 1 from 1510 to 1559 coefs0..5 −1.012298
            1.145181 2.458313 155.930450 −1844.792358 4981.395508
5210489:   xfer poly jnt 2 from 1510 to 1559 coefs0..5 −3.502499
            −2.484828   −5.334077   −271.034851   3381.844971
            −9280.717773
5210844:   xfer poly jnt 3 from 1510 to 1559 coefs0..5 2.858539 1.082937
            2.324697 270.983246 −2884.288818 7515.008301
5211158:   xfer poly jnt 4 from 1510 to 1559 coefs0..5 −0.892245
            −8.051942   −17.284775   207.517029   940.328857
            −5423.745117

5211472:   xfer poly jnt 5 from 1510 to 1559 coefs0..5 −0.403869
           2.608399 5.599343 −304.680176 1886.335938 −3633.779297
5211786:   xfer poly jnt 6 from 1510 to 1561 coefs0..5 0.623049 10.425766
           15.532269 −387.286560 −418.387543 5221.079590
5212051:   polynomials sent, update flg 1, bounced 0

References

[1]   A.V. Aho, J.E. Hopcroft, J.D. Ullman, "The Design and Analysis of Computer Algorithms," Addison-Wesley, 1974.

[2]   S.R. Ahuja, "S/Net: A High Speed Interconnect for Multiple Computers," IEEE Journal of Selected Areas in Communication, Vol. SAC-1, No. 5, p. 751−756, November 1983.

[3]   C.H. An, C.G. Atkeson, J.M. Hollerbach, "Experimental Determination of the Effect of Feedforward Control on Trajectory Tracking Errors," Proceedings of the IEEE International Conference on Robotics and Automation, Vol. 1, p. 55−60, April 1986.

[4]   R.L. Andersson, "Real-Time Gray-Scale Video Processing Using a Moment-Generating Chip," IEEE Journal of Robotics and Automation, Vol. RA-1, No. 2, p. 79−85, June 1985.

[5]   R.L. Andersson, "Real-time video moment generator chip," in N.H.E. Weste, K. Eshraghian, "Principles of CMOS VLSI Design: A Systems Perspective," Addison-Wesley, p. 407−424, 1985.

[6]   R.L. Andersson, "Living in a Dynamic World," Proceedings of the ACM-IEEE Fall Joint Computer Conference, p. 97−104, November 1986.

[7]   L. Berton, "In Pingpong Match, Our Reporter Loses To Green Opponent," Wall Street Journal, January 15, 1985.

[8]   J. Billingsley, "Machineroe joins new title fight," Practical Robotics, p. 14−16, May/June 1984.

[9]   A.D. Birrell, B.J. Nelson, "Implementing Remote Procedure Calls," ACM Transactions on Computer Systems, Vol. 2, No. 1, p. 39−59, February 1984.

[10]   J.A. Bixby, "High-speed television camera and video tape recording system for motion analysis," Proceedings of SPIE − The International Society for Optical Engineering, Vol. 301, August 1981.

[11]   R.C. Bolles, H.H. Baker, "Epipolar-Plane Image Analysis: Technique for Analyzing Motion Sequences," Third International Symposium on Robotics Research, p. 41–48, 1986.

[12]   M.E. Brandan, M. Gutierrez, *et al*, "Measurement of the terminal velocity in air of a Ping-Pong ball using a time-to-amplitude converter in the millisecond range," American Journal of Physics, Vol. 52, No. 10, p. 890–893, October 1984.

[13]   L.J. Briggs, "Effect of Spin and Speed on the Lateral Deflection (Curve) of a Baseball; and the Magnus Effect for Smooth Spheres," American Journal of Physics, Vol. 27, p. 589–596, 1959.

[14]   H. Brody, "That's how the ball bounces," The Physics Teacher, p. 494–497, November 1984.

[15]   B.G. Buchanan, E.H. Shortliffe, "Rule-Based Expert Systems," Addison-Wesley, 1984.

[16]   J.W. Burdick, "An Algorithm for Generation of Efficient Manipulator Dynamic Equations," IEEE International Conference on Robotics and Automation, Vol. 1, p. 212–218, April 1986.

[17]   D. Casasent, D. Psaltis, "Hybrid Processor to Compute Invariant Moments for Pattern Recognition," Optics Letters, Vol. 5, No. 9, p. 395–397, September 1980.

[18]   A.M. Chande, R.W. Newcomb, "A Decision Tree for Inflight Data Processing for Robot Spacecraft Trajectory Guidance," IEEE International Conference on Robotics and Automation, p. 215–220, March 1985.

[19]   J.J. Craig, "Introduction to Robotics: Mechanics and Control," Addison-Wesley, 1986.

[20]   J. Denavit, R.S. Hartenberg, "A Kinematic Notation for Lower-Pair Mechanisms Based on Matrices," Journal of Applied Mechanics, p. 215–221, June 1955.

[21]   H.F. Durrant-Whyte, "Integration, Coordination and Control of Multi-Sensor Robot Systems," Ph.D. dissertation, Department of Computer and Information Science, University of Pennsylvania, Philadelphia, PA, August 1985.

[22]   C.L. Forgy, "Rete: A Fast Algorithm for the Many Pattern/Many Object Pattern Match Problem," Artificial Intelligence, Vol. 19, No. 1, p. 17—38, September 1982.

[23]   L. Foulloy, D. Kechemair, B. Burg, E. LaMotte, B. Zavidovique, "A Rule-Based Decision System for the Robotization of Metal Laser Cutting," IEEE International Conference on Robotics and Automation, p. 192—197, March 1985.

[24]   C.A. Fowler, M.T. Turvey, "Skill Acquisition: An Event Approach with Special Reference to Searching for the Optimum of a Function of Several Variables," in "Information Processing in Motor Control and Learning," George E. Stelmach, Ed., Academic Press, 1978.

[25]   C. Frohlich, "Aerodynamic drag crisis and its possible effect on the flight of baseballs," American Journal of Physics, Vol. 52, No. 4, p. 325—334, April 1984.

[26]   T. Fukushima, et al, "ISP: A Dedicated LSI For Gray Image Local Operations," Proceedings of the Seventh International Conference on Pattern Recognition, Vol. 1, p. 581—584, July 1984.

[27]   R.D. Gaglianello, H.P. Katseff, "Meglos: An Operating System for a Multiprocessor Environment," Proceedings of the Fifth International Conference on Distributed Computing Systems, May 1985.

[28]   S.K. Ganapathy, "Decomposition of Transformation Matrices for Robot Vision," IEEE International Conference on Robotics, p. 130—139, March 1984.

[29]   G.J. Gleason, G.J. Agin, "A Modular Vision System For Sensor-Controlled Manipulation and Inspection," Proceedings of the Ninth International Symposium on Industrial Robots, SME/RIA, p. 57—70, March 1979.

[30]   W.E.L. Grimson, "From Images to Surfaces: A Computational Study of the Human Early Visual System," The MIT Press, 1981.

[31]   V.K. Gupta, G. Shanker, N.K. Sharma, "Experiment on fluid drag and viscosity with an oscillating sphere," American Journal of Physics, Vol. 54, No. 7, p. 619—622, July 1986.

[32]   F. Hayes-Roth, D.A. Waterman, D.B. Lenat, "Building Expert Systems," Addison-Wesley, 1983.

[33]   B.K.P. Horn, B.G. Schunck, "Determining Optical Flow," Artificial Intelligence, Vol. 17, p. 185–203, 1981.

[34]   M. Hu, "Visual Pattern Recognition by Moment Invariants," IRE Transactions on Information Theory, IT-8, p. 179–187, February 1962.

[35]   International Table Tennis Federation, "Technical File," East Sussex, England.

[36]   A. Izaguirre, R.P. Paul, "Automatic Generation of the Dynamic Equations of the Robot Manipulators Using a LISP Program," IEEE International Conference on Robotics and Automation, Vol. 1, p. 220–226, April 1986.

[37]   R.N. Kackar, A.C. Shoemaker, "Robust Design: A Cost-Effective Method for Improving Manufacturing Processes," AT&T Technical Journal, Vol. 65, No. 2, p. 39–50, March 1986.

[38]   A. Kaufman, M.M. Gupta, "Introduction to Fuzzy Arithmetic," Van Nostrand Reinhold, New York, 1985.

[39]   J. Knight, D. Lowery, "Pingpong-playing robot controlled by a microcomputer," Microprocessors and Microsystems, Vol. 10, No. 6, p. 332–335, July 1986.

[40]   B.W. Kernighan, D.M. Ritchie, "The C Programming Language," Prentice-Hall, 1978.

[41]   C.S.G. Lee, "Robot Arm Kinematics, Dynamics, and Control," IEEE Computer, p. 62–80, December 1982.

[42]   E.H. Mamdani, J.J. Ostergaard, E. Lembessis, "Use of Fuzzy Logic for Implementing Rule-Based Control of Industrial Processes," in H.J. Zimmermann, L.A. Zadeh, B.R. Gaines, Eds., "Fuzzy Sets and Decision Analysis," Vol. 20 of Studies in the Management Sciences, North-Holland, New York, p. 429–445, 1984.

[43]   J. McDermott, "R1: A Rule-Based Configurer of Computer Systems," Artificial Intelligence, Vol. 19, No. 1, p. 39–88, September 1982.

[44]   D.E. Meyer, J.E.K. Smith, C.E. Wright, "Models for the Speed and Accuracy of Aimed Movements," Psychological Review, Vol. 89, No. 5, p. 449—482, September 1982.

[45]   A. Mukerjee, D.H. Ballard, "Self-Calibration in Robot Manipulators," Proceedings of the IEEE Conference on Robotics and Automation, p. 1050—1057, March 1985.

[46]   S.-Y. Oh, "Control of Redundant Manipulators by Inverse Kinematics," Proceedings of the IEEE Workshop on Intelligent Control, p. 53—57, August 1985.

[47]   H.B. Olsen, G.A. Bekey, "Identification of Parameters in Models of Robots with Rotary Joints," Proceedings of the IEEE Conference on Robotics and Automation, p. 1045—1049, March 1985.

[48]   C.D. Ortiz, "A Cinematographic Analysis of the Forehand Counterdrive, Forehand Loop, and Forehand Topspin Serve in Table-Tennis," Master's thesis, Texas Woman's University, Denton, Texas, May 1972.

[49]   R.P. Paul, "Robot Manipulators: Mathematics, Programming, and Control," The MIT Press, 1981.

[50]   R.P. Paul, H. Zhang, "Computationally Efficient Kinematics for Manipulators with Spherical Wrists Based on the Homogeneous Transformation Representation," International Journal of Robotics Research, Vol. 5, No. 2, p. 32—44, Summer 1986.

[51]   B.T. Phong, "Illumination for Computer Generated Pictures," Communications of the ACM, Vol. 18, No. 6, p. 311—317, June 1975.

[52]   K. Prazdny, "Egomotion and Relative Depth Map from Optical Flow," Biology and Cybernetics, Vol. 36, p. 87—102, 1980.

[53]   Lord Rayleigh, "On the irregular flight of a tennis ball," Scientific Papers 1, p. 344, 1869—1881.

[54]   A.P. Reeves, A. Rostampour, "Shape Analysis of Segmental Objects Using Moments," Proceedings of the IEEE Computer Society Conference on Pattern Recognition and Image Processing, p. 171—176, August 1981.

[55]   A.F. Rex, "The effect of spin on the flight of batted baseballs," American Journal of Physics, Vol. 53, No. 11, p. 1073−1075, November 1985.

[56]   D. Robbins, Robbins Sports, Warren, Michigan, private correspondence.

[57]   Robbins Sport, "Robbins Sport Guide to Advanced Equipment," Warren, Michigan.

[58]   S.M. Selby, Ed., "Standard Mathematical Tables," CRC Press, 23rd edition, 1974.

[59]   H. Shariat, "The Motion Problem: How to Use More Than Two Frames," Ph.D. dissertation, Institute for Robotics and Intelligent Systems, University of Southern California (Los Angeles), October 1986.

[60]   A.C. Shaw, "The Logical Design of Operating Systems," Prentice-Hall, 1974.

[61]   M.L.G. Shaw, B.R. Gaines, "Constructs underlying decision," in H.J. Zimmermann, L.A. Zadeh, B.R. Gaines, Eds., "Fuzzy Sets and Decision Analysis," Vol. 20 of Studies in the Management Sciences, North-Holland, New York, p. 353, 1984.

[62]   B.F. Skinner, "Two Synthetic Social Relations," Journal of the Experimental Analysis of Behavior, Vol. 5, No. 4, p. 531−533, October 1962.

[63]   M.M. Stanisic, G.R. Pennock, "A Non-Degenerate Orientation Solution of a Four-Jointed Wrist," IEEE International Conference on Robotics and Automation, p. 998−1003, March 1985.

[64]   G. Strang, "Linear Algebra and Its Applications," Academic Press, 1976.

[65]   R.Y. Tsai, "An Efficient and Accurate Camera Calibration Technique for 3-D Machine Vision," Proceedings of the IEEE Computer Society Conference on Computer Vision and Pattern Recognition, p. 364−374, May 1986.

[66]   J.V. Uspensky, "Theory of Equations," McGraw-Hill, 1948.

[67]   R.G. Watts, R. Ferrer, "The lateral force on a spinning sphere: Aerodynamics of a curveball," American Journal of Physics, Vol. 55, No. 1, p. 40−44, January 1987.

[68] N.H.E. Weste, "Virtual Grid Symbolic Layout," Proceedings of the 18th Design Automation Conference, p. 225−233, June 1981.

[69] R. Yager, "Knowledge Representation for Intelligence Controllers," Proceedings of the IEEE Workshop on Intelligent Control, p. 139−144, August 1985.

[70] J.M. Zayas, "Experimental determination of the coefficient of drag of a tennis ball," American Journal of Physics, Vol. 54, No. 7, p. 622−625, July 1986.

[71] H. Zhang, "Design and Implementation of a Robot Force and Motion Server," Ph.D. dissertation, Purdue University, West Lafayette, Indiana, May 1986.

[72] "DC Motors, Speed Controls, Servo Systems," Electro-Craft Co., 1980.

[73] "Robotworld: A Self-contained Work Environment for Assembly," Robotics Today, p. 26, October 1986.

[74] "Macsyma Reference Manual," Symbolics, Inc., 1985.

Index

The MIT Press, with Peter Denning, general consulting editor, and Brian Randell, European consulting editor, publishes computer science books in the following series:

ACM Doctoral Dissertation Award and Distinguished Dissertation Series

Artificial Intelligence, Patrick Winston and Michael Brady, editors

Charles Babbage Institute Reprint Series for the History of Computing, Martin Campbell-Kelly, editor

Computer Systems, Herb Schwetman, editor

Exploring with Logo, E. Paul Goldenberg, editor

Foundations of Computing, Michael Garey and Albert Meyer, editors

History of Computing, I. Bernard Cohen and William Aspray, editors

Information Systems, Michael Lesk, editor

Logic Programming, Ehud Shapiro, editor; Fernando Pereira, Koichi Furukawa, and D. H. D. Warren, associate editors

The MIT Electrical Engineering and Computer Science Series

Scientific Computation, Dennis Gannon, editor